2 SAMUEL

Brazos Theological Commentary on the Bible

2 SAMUEL

ROBERT BARRON

BrazosPress
a division of Baker Publishing Group
Grand Rapids, Michigan

Published by Brazos Press
a division of Baker Publishing Group
P.O. Box 6287, Grand Rapids, MI 49516-6287
www.brazospress.com

Printed in the United States of America

Library of Congress Cataloging-in-Publication Data
Barron, Robert E., 1959–
2 Samuel / Robert Barron.
pages cm. — (Brazos theological commentary on the Bible)
Includes bibliographical references and index.
ISBN 978-1-58743-291-0 (cloth)
1. Bible. Samuel, 2nd—Commentaries. I. Title.
BS1325.53.B38 2015
222′.4407—dc23 2014041611

15 16 17 18 19 21 22 7 6 5 4 3 2 1

To Jim and Molly Perry,

Heroes of the New Evangelization

CONTENTS

ACKNOWLEDGMENTS

Writing this book was a joy. Though I have long been a student of the Bible, most of my published work has been in the fields of philosophy, theology, and spirituality. To delve deeply, therefore, into the text of 2 Samuel itself, as well as to explore the rich and fascinating tradition of commentary upon it, both ancient and modern, was thrilling and illuminating.

For giving me the opportunity to roam through at least this small corner of the biblical world, I am very grateful to Rusty Reno, the general editor of the Brazos series. I am also deeply indebted to Jack Thornton, who helped enormously with the research required to finish this project. Jack's patience, diligence, and concentration throughout the lengthy process were impressive indeed. I want to thank as well Brandon Vogt, who read the text with great care and who was an indispensable help in getting it into publishable shape. A word of gratitude also to Prof. Robert Louis Wilken, Fr. Robert Schoenstene, and Dr. Matthew Levering, all of whom read the manuscript and made extremely helpful suggestions for its improvement. I want, finally, to express my thanks to my good friend Fr. Stephen Grunow, who thought through this project with me from beginning to end and made the book far better than it would have been without his wise guidance.

SERIES PREFACE

Near the beginning of his treatise against Gnostic interpretations of the Bible, *Against Heresies*, Irenaeus observes that scripture is like a great mosaic depicting a handsome king. It is as if we were owners of a villa in Gaul who had ordered a mosaic from Rome. It arrives, and the beautifully colored tiles need to be taken out of their packaging and put into proper order according to the plan of the artist. The difficulty, of course, is that scripture provides us with the individual pieces, but the order and sequence of various elements are not obvious. The Bible does not come with instructions that would allow interpreters to simply place verses, episodes, images, and parables in order as a worker might follow a schematic drawing in assembling the pieces to depict the handsome king. The mosaic must be puzzled out. This is precisely the work of scriptural interpretation.

Origen has his own image to express the difficulty of working out the proper approach to reading the Bible. When preparing to offer a commentary on the Psalms he tells of a tradition handed down to him by his Hebrew teacher:

> The Hebrew said that the whole divinely inspired scripture may be likened, because of its obscurity, to many locked rooms in our house. By each room is placed a key, but not the one that corresponds to it, so that the keys are scattered about beside the rooms, none of them matching the room by which it is placed. It is a difficult task to find the keys and match them to the rooms that they can open. We therefore know the scriptures that are obscure only by taking the points of departure for understanding them from another place because they have their interpretive principle scattered among them.[1]

1. Fragment from the preface to *Commentary on Psalms 1–25*, preserved in the *Philokalia*, trans. Joseph W. Trigg (London: Routledge, 1998), 70–71.

As is the case for Irenaeus, scriptural interpretation is not purely local. The key in Genesis may best fit the door of Isaiah, which in turn opens up the meaning of Matthew. The mosaic must be put together with an eye toward the overall plan.

Irenaeus, Origen, and the great cloud of premodern biblical interpreters assumed that puzzling out the mosaic of scripture must be a communal project. The Bible is vast, heterogeneous, full of confusing passages and obscure words, and difficult to understand. Only a fool would imagine that he or she could work out solutions alone. The way forward must rely upon a tradition of reading that Irenaeus reports has been passed on as the rule or canon of truth that functions as a confession of faith. "Anyone," he says, "who keeps unchangeable in himself the rule of truth received through baptism will recognize the names and sayings and parables of the scriptures."[2] Modern scholars debate the content of the rule on which Irenaeus relies and commends, not the least because the terms and formulations Irenaeus himself uses shift and slide. Nonetheless, Irenaeus assumes that there is a body of apostolic doctrine sustained by a tradition of teaching in the church. This doctrine provides the clarifying principles that guide exegetical judgment toward a coherent overall reading of scripture as a unified witness. Doctrine, then, is the schematic drawing that will allow the reader to organize the vast heterogeneity of the words, images, and stories of the Bible into a readable, coherent whole. It is the rule that guides us toward the proper matching of keys to doors.

If self-consciousness about the role of history in shaping human consciousness makes modern historical-critical study critical, then what makes modern study of the Bible modern is the consensus that classical Christian doctrine distorts interpretive understanding. Benjamin Jowett, the influential nineteenth-century English classical scholar, is representative. In his programmatic essay "On the Interpretation of Scripture," he exhorts the biblical reader to disengage from doctrine and break its hold over the interpretive imagination. "The simple words of that book," writes Jowett of the modern reader, "he tries to preserve absolutely pure from the refinements or distinctions of later times." The modern interpreter wishes to "clear away the remains of dogmas, systems, controversies, which are encrusted upon" the words of scripture. The disciplines of close philological analysis "would enable us to separate the elements of doctrine and tradition with which the meaning of scripture is encumbered in our own day."[3] The lens of understanding must be wiped clear of the hazy and distorting film of doctrine.

2. *Against Heresies* 9.4.

3. Benjamin Jowett, "On the Interpretation of Scripture," in *Essays and Reviews* (London: Parker, 1860), 338–39.

Postmodernity, in turn, has encouraged us to criticize the critics. Jowett imagined that when he wiped away doctrine he would encounter the biblical text in its purity and uncover what he called "the original spirit and intention of the authors."[4] We are not now so sanguine, and the postmodern mind thinks interpretive frameworks inevitable. Nonetheless, we tend to remain modern in at least one sense. We read Athanasius and think him stage-managing the diversity of scripture to support his positions against the Arians. We read Bernard of Clairvaux and assume that his monastic ideals structure his reading of the Song of Songs. In the wake of the Reformation, we can see how the doctrinal divisions of the time shaped biblical interpretation. Luther famously described the Epistle of James as a "strawy letter," for, as he said, "it has nothing of the nature of the Gospel about it."[5] In these and many other instances, often written in the heat of ecclesiastical controversy or out of the passion of ascetic commitment, we tend to think Jowett correct: doctrine is a distorting film on the lens of understanding.

However, is what we commonly think actually the case? Are readers naturally perceptive? Do we have an unblemished, reliable aptitude for the divine? Have we no need for disciplines of vision? Do our attention and judgment need to be trained, especially as we seek to read scripture as the living word of God? According to Augustine, we all struggle to journey toward God, who is our rest and peace. Yet our vision is darkened and the fetters of worldly habit corrupt our judgment. We need training and instruction in order to cleanse our minds so that we might find our way toward God.[6] To this end, "the whole temporal dispensation was made by divine Providence for our salvation."[7] The covenant with Israel, the coming of Christ, the gathering of the nations into the church—all these things are gathered up into the rule of faith, and they guide the vision and form of the soul toward the end of fellowship with God. In Augustine's view, the reading of scripture both contributes to and benefits from this divine pedagogy. With countless variations in both exegetical conclusions and theological frameworks, the same pedagogy of a doctrinally ruled reading of scripture characterizes the broad sweep of the Christian tradition from Gregory the Great through Bernard and Bonaventure, continuing across Reformation differences in both John Calvin and Cornelius Lapide, Patrick Henry and Bishop Bossuet, and on to more recent figures such as Karl Barth and Hans Urs von Balthasar.

4. Ibid., 340.
5. *Luther's Works*, vol. 35, ed. E. Theodore Bachmann (Philadelphia: Fortress, 1959), 362.
6. *On Christian Doctrine* 1.10.
7. *On Christian Doctrine* 1.35.

Is doctrine, then, not a moldering scrim of antique prejudice obscuring the Bible, but instead a clarifying agent, an enduring tradition of theological judgments that amplifies the living voice of scripture? And what of the scholarly dispassion advocated by Jowett? Is a noncommitted reading, an interpretation unprejudiced, the way toward objectivity, or does it simply invite the languid intellectual apathy that stands aside to make room for the false truism and easy answers of the age?

This series of biblical commentaries was born out of the conviction that dogma clarifies rather than obscures. The Brazos Theological Commentary on the Bible advances upon the assumption that the Nicene tradition, in all its diversity and controversy, provides the proper basis for the interpretation of the Bible as Christian scripture. God the Father Almighty, who sends his only begotten Son to die for us and for our salvation and who raises the crucified Son in the power of the Holy Spirit so that the baptized may be joined in one body—faith in *this* God with *this* vocation of love for the world is the lens through which to view the heterogeneity and particularity of the biblical texts. Doctrine, then, is not a moldering scrim of antique prejudice obscuring the meaning of the Bible. It is a crucial aspect of the divine pedagogy, a clarifying agent for our minds fogged by self-deceptions, a challenge to our languid intellectual apathy that will too often rest in false truisms and the easy spiritual nostrums of the present age rather than search more deeply and widely for the dispersed keys to the many doors of scripture.

For this reason, the commentators in this series have not been chosen because of their historical or philological expertise. In the main, they are not biblical scholars in the conventional, modern sense of the term. Instead, the commentators were chosen because of their knowledge of and expertise in using the Christian doctrinal tradition. They are qualified by virtue of the doctrinal formation of their mental habits, for it is the conceit of this series of biblical commentaries that theological training in the Nicene tradition prepares one for biblical interpretation, and thus it is to theologians and not biblical scholars that we have turned. "War is too important," it has been said, "to leave to the generals."

We do hope, however, that readers do not draw the wrong impression. The Nicene tradition does not provide a set formula for the solution of exegetical problems. The great tradition of Christian doctrine was not transcribed, bound in folio, and issued in an official, critical edition. We have the Niceno-Constantinopolitan Creed, used for centuries in many traditions of Christian worship. We have ancient baptismal affirmations of faith. The Chalcedonian definition and the creeds and canons of other church councils have their places in official church documents. Yet the rule of faith cannot be limited to a specific set of words, sentences, and creeds. It is instead a pervasive habit of thought, the animating culture of the church in its intellectual aspect. As Augustine observed, commenting on Jer. 31:33, "The creed is learned by listening; it is written, not on stone tablets nor on any material, but on the heart."[8] This is why Irenaeus is able to appeal to the rule of faith more than a century before the first ecumenical council, and this is why we need not itemize the contents of the Nicene tradition in order to appeal to its potency and role in the work of interpretation.

Because doctrine is intrinsically fluid on the margins and most powerful as a habit of mind rather than a list of propositions, this commentary series cannot settle difficult questions of method and content at the outset. The editors of the series impose no particular method of doctrinal interpretation. We cannot say in advance how doctrine helps the Christian reader assemble the mosaic of scripture. We have no clear answer to the question of whether exegesis guided by doctrine is antithetical to or compatible with the now-old modern methods of historical-critical inquiry. Truth—historical, mathematical, or doctrinal—knows no contradiction. But method is a discipline of vision and judgment, and we cannot know in advance what aspects of historical-critical inquiry are functions of modernism that shape the soul to be at odds with Christian discipline. Still further, the editors do not hold the commentators to any particular hermeneutical theory that specifies how to define the plain sense of scripture—or the role this plain sense should play in interpretation. Here the commentary series is tentative and exploratory.

Can we proceed in any other way? European and North American intellectual culture has been de-Christianized. The effect has not been a cessation of Christian activity. Theological work continues. Sermons are preached. Biblical scholars turn out monographs. Church leaders have meetings. But each dimension of a formerly unified Christian practice now tends to function independently. It is as if a weakened army had been fragmented, and various corps had retreated to isolated fortresses in order to survive. Theology has lost its competence in exegesis. Scripture scholars function with minimal theological training. Each decade finds new theories of preaching to cover the nakedness of seminary training that provides theology without exegesis and exegesis without theology.

Not the least of the causes of the fragmentation of Christian intellectual practice has been the divisions of the church. Since the Reformation, the role of the rule of faith in interpretation has been obscured by polemics and counterpolemics about

8. *Sermon* 212.2.

sola scriptura and the necessity of a magisterial teaching authority. The Brazos Theological Commentary on the Bible series is deliberately ecumenical in scope, because the editors are convinced that early church fathers were correct: church doctrine does not compete with scripture in a limited economy of epistemic authority. We wish to encourage unashamedly dogmatic interpretation of scripture, confident that the concrete consequences of such a reading will cast far more light on the great divisive questions of the Reformation than either reengaging in old theological polemics or chasing the fantasy of a pure exegesis that will somehow adjudicate between competing theological positions. You shall know the truth of doctrine by its interpretive fruits, and therefore in hopes of contributing to the unity of the church, we have deliberately chosen a wide range of theologians whose commitment to doctrine will allow readers to see real interpretive consequences rather than the shadow boxing of theological concepts.

The Brazos Theological Commentary on the Bible has no dog in the current translation fights, and we endorse a textual ecumenism that parallels our diversity of ecclesial backgrounds. We do not impose the thankfully modest inclusive-language agenda of the New Revised Standard Version, nor do we insist upon the glories of the Authorized Version, nor do we require our commentators to create a new translation. In our communal worship, in our private devotions, in our theological scholarship, we use a range of scriptural translations. Precisely as scripture—a living, functioning text in the present life of faith—the Bible is not semantically fixed. Only a modernist, literalist hermeneutic could imagine that this modest fluidity is a liability. Philological precision and stability is a consequence of, not a basis for, exegesis. Judgments about the meaning of a text fix its literal sense, not the other way around. As a result, readers should expect an eclectic use of biblical translations, both across the different volumes of the series and within individual commentaries.

We cannot speak for contemporary biblical scholars, but as theologians we know that we have long been trained to defend our fortresses of theological concepts and formulations. And we have forgotten the skills of interpretation. Like stroke victims, we must rehabilitate our exegetical imaginations, and there are likely to be different strategies of recovery. Readers should expect this reconstructive—not reactionary—series to provide them with experiments in postcritical doctrinal interpretation, not commentaries written according to the settled principles of a well-functioning tradition. Some commentators will follow classical typological and allegorical readings from the premodern tradition; others will draw on contemporary historical study. Some will comment verse by verse; others will highlight passages, even single words that trigger theological analysis of scripture. No reading strategies are proscribed, no interpretive methods foresworn. The central premise in this commentary series is that doctrine provides structure and cogency to scriptural interpretation. We trust in this premise with the hope that the Nicene tradition can guide us, however imperfectly, diversely, and haltingly, toward a reading of scripture in which the right keys open the right doors.

R. R. Reno

INTRODUCTION

The figure of King David has beguiled painters, poets, musicians, artists, and spiritual writers up and down the centuries. To appreciate the hold of this character on the imagination, one has only to think of the sculptures of David by Donatello, Michelangelo, and Bernini, paintings of David by Rembrandt and Chagall, literary portraits of the Israelite king by figures as diverse as John Dryden, Joseph Heller, and Robert Pinsky, and musical celebrations of David from Handel to Leonard Cohen. What accounts for this fascination? With the possible exception of Jesus himself, David is the most fully developed character in the Bible. The author of the "Samuel literature" (a term I will use throughout this commentary to designate the books of 1 and 2 Samuel construed as one text) allows us to see almost the entire arc of David's life, from his boyhood preoccupations with the flock of his father, Jesse, through his adventure with Goliath, his struggle with Saul, his ascention to power as king, his establishment of empire, his terrible moral failing, his humiliation by his son Absalom, and his painful and conflicted old age. No other figure in the Old Testament—neither Abraham nor Jacob nor Moses nor Isaiah nor Jeremiah—is characterized with such thoroughness and psychological perceptiveness. I find myself in agreement with Robert Pinsky's rejoinder to those who would suggest that David is but a literary invention. The former poet laureate of the United States argues that a story as textured and psychologically credible as David's can only be grounded in a very real person vividly remembered.[9]

Moreover, King David is one of the most pivotal persons in the entire corpus of scripture. He is the terminus of a trajectory that runs from Adam through Noah,

9. Robert Pinsky, *The Life of David* (New York: Schocken Books, 2005), 4.

Abraham, Jacob, Moses, Joshua, and Samuel. Many of God's promises to those patriarchal and prophetic figures seem to come to fulfillment in David's rule over a united Israel. At the same time, David looks beyond himself to a new David, one who would definitively fulfill what he himself left incomplete and unfinished. In a word, he is perhaps *the* cardinal point on which the biblical revelation turns both backward and forward.

One of the themes that emerges most clearly in 2 Samuel is that of kingship. On the biblical reading, the bad rule of Adam in the garden led to the disaster of the fall, and ever since that calamity, humanity has been in search of right rule. At the heart of the Old Testament sensibility is the conviction that God chose a people, Israel, whom he would shape according to his own mind and heart so that they might draw all of humanity into right relationship with God. Hence, they would be a kingly people. But this holy nation would endure only in the measure that they themselves were rightly ruled, and therefore the search for a righteous and godly king of Israel—an Adam who would properly govern a reconstituted Eden—became a preoccupation for biblical Israel. Abraham, Isaac, Jacob, Joseph, Judah, Moses, Joshua, Gideon, Samson, and Samuel were all, after a manner of speaking, kings of Israel, but they ruled to varying degrees of adequacy. Having united the northern and southern tribes, established his fortified capital at Jerusalem, and subdued the enemies of Israel, David emerged as the most stirring and successful king of Israel.

Adam was not only a king; he was also a priest, which is to say, someone who affects a mystical union between divinity and humanity. After him, Noah, Abraham, Jacob, Moses, Aaron, and Samuel were also, to varying degrees of intensity, priests. Wearing the sacred vestment of the priesthood and dancing before the ark of the covenant, King David emerged as David the high priest and hence recapitulated and brought to full expression the priesthood of the work of his predecessors. Samuel's anointing of David the shepherd boy could thus be seen as both a kingly and priestly designation. When the first followers of Jesus referred to him as *Christos* (anointed), they were appreciating him as David in full. The Christian reader will thus see in David the most compelling anticipation of Jesus, the definitive priest-king. Though this sort of move is always hermeneutically dangerous, one could make a good case that the most important interpretive key for the New Testament is found in the seventh chapter of 2 Samuel: Nathan's prophecy that the line of David would never fail and that a descendant of David would reign forever. Not only did this prophecy haunt the biblical tradition that followed it—look especially here at the prophets and the Psalms—but it also decidedly influenced the manner in which the Gospel writers came to understand the significance of Jesus.

Still another central motif of 2 Samuel is that of bad fathering and bad kingship. David is presented as Israel's greatest, indeed archetypal, king, and at the same time his flaws are on clear, often disturbing, display. As many point out, ancient authors tend to apotheosize political rulers, but the writer/editor of 2 Samuel, even as he extols David as a uniquely privileged agent of the divine purpose, ruthlessly exposes the king's moral and political failures. David is indeed a new Adam ruling a restored Eden, but he is also, ethically and spiritually, a descendant of the Adam who allowed the garden to be compromised by the serpent. In this, he stands in the tradition of Eli and sets the tone for the long line of his decadent and wicked successors as king of Israel, bad governors who would preside over the splintering of the people and the weakening of the nation. This is another way of signaling that Israel, even as it celebrates David, has to await another king.

The theme in 2 Samuel that I take to be most basic theologically is that of the noncompetitive transcendence of God. One of the distinctive marks of this text is that Yahweh rarely acts in a direct and interruptive way, involving himself as one competitive cause among many. Instead God is consistently portrayed as acting noninvasively through a bevy of ordinary and secondary agents. The events described in 2 Samuel could, almost without exception, be explained easily enough through recourse to psychological or political categories, and yet the author clearly supposes that God is, through it all, definitively working his purposes out. This noncompetitive co-agency of God and human beings represents a major breakthrough in the religious consciousness of Israel and thus makes 2 Samuel a milestone in the evolution of that consciousness. What grounds it, at least implicitly, is a keen sense of God as the Creator of the universe and not an agent or element within the universe. Were God simply one being, however supreme, among many, then he would stand over and against other worldly things, jockeying with them on the same metaphysical plane. But as the Creator of all finite things, God can relate to particular agents in a nonintrusive manner, acting through them but not violating their own causal integrity. God is certainly other, but he is, if I may borrow the language of Kathryn Tanner, "otherly-other"; this very strangeness is what allows him to operate in and with human agents.[10] We will see this dynamic over and over in the course of 2 Samuel.

10. Kathryn Tanner, *Jesus, Humanity, and the Trinity* (Minneapolis: Fortress, 2001), 12.

When was this text written and by whom? The answers to both questions, unfortunately, are elusive. Most contemporary scholars more or less follow the suggestion made by Martin Noth in the 1940s that 1–2 Samuel comprise, along with the books of Deuteronomy, Joshua, Judges, and 1–2 Kings, a coherent historical and theological narrative. This suggests, of course, that they were written, or at least edited, essentially by one author. To be sure, every one of the texts in question includes elements from a variety of sources, but the Noth hypothesis proposes that a fundamental thematic, literary, and theological unity obtains across these books. But who this author was no one knows to any degree of certainty. The numerous allusions that he makes to other texts within the Hebrew biblical tradition imply that he was trained in the context of a fairly sophisticated theological and literary culture. This in turn indicates that he was probably writing at a time of relative peace and after the Hebrew religious worldview had reached a high degree of maturity and complexity. Both of these conditions suggest that he was operating in the early Second Temple period following the return of the exiles from Babylon. Of course, the vividly detailed descriptions of the Davidic court in 2 Samuel have led others to speculate that the author is a much earlier figure, someone far closer to David's own time. Since my purpose here is properly theological commentary, I will leave these historical and literary speculations to the specialists.

What we call 1 and 2 Samuel were originally one text, and they appear as such in most Jewish Bibles to the present day. The division into two—largely a result of the length of scroll available to scribes—took place at the time of the Septuagint translation into Greek and was later adopted by most Latin translators of the sacred scriptures. In his Vulgate translation, Jerome refers to 1 Samuel as the *Primum Regum* (the First of the Kings) and 2 Samuel as *Secundum Regum* (the Second of the Kings). For the purpose of literary and theological commentary, therefore, it would be artificial in the extreme to treat 1 and 2 Samuel as two discrete texts. Common themes, literary devices, allusive patterns, and so forth abound.

When one considers the extraordinary number of memorable passages in 2 Samuel—David's elegy to Saul and Jonathan, the king's dance before the ark, the jealousy of Michal, the seduction of Bathsheba and its dreadful aftermath, Nathan's "Thou art the man!," the rape of Tamar, the rebellion of Absalom, David's lament over his fallen son—and when one takes in the literary complexity, theological depth, and psychological insight contained in its pages, it is difficult not to agree with Robert Alter's contention that 2 Samuel is one of the most impressive texts to come down to us from the ancient world.

SERIES ONE

DAVID COMES TO POWER

2 SAMUEL 1

Although the division of the original text into two books at this point is, as I indicated above, a consequence of the length of scrolls available to the scribe, it is nevertheless significant that this major portion of the story commences with a mention of the death of Saul: "After the death of Saul, when David had returned from defeating the Amalekites, David remained two days in Ziklag" (2 Sam. 1:1). First, this brings the text into line with both the book of Joshua and the book of Judges, which similarly commence with a reference to the death of famous figures, Moses and Joshua respectively. If, as seems likely, the Samuel literature is an ingredient in the work of the editor known as the Deuteronomistic Historian, then this device indicates a sort of trajectory leading from the conquest of the promised land conducted by Joshua through the era of the judges to the establishment of David as king of a united Israel (Polzin 1993: 1). Second, the reference to the death of Saul draws attention to what is perhaps the dominant theme of 2 Samuel: contrast between the kingly path taken by Saul and that taken by David. The particularly ignominious death of Saul—by his own hand, surrounded by his enemies, and abandoned by Yahweh—is presented as the consequence of certain disastrous moves and decisions he made. It therefore sets the stage for the sharply contrasting picture of David's kingship that will emerge in the course of 2 Samuel. Does Israel require a king? What makes a king good or bad? How does the kingship of Yahweh relate to human kingship? These are among the questions that principally preoccupy the author of the text under consideration (Beale 2011: 65–66).

Even a relatively adequate treatment of this issue requires a return to the very beginning of the Bible, to the accounts of creation and the garden of Eden. The stately liturgical language that marks the opening of the book of Genesis is meant to demonstrate the lordship of God over all things and, consequently, the dethronement of any false claimants to such absolute authority. God creates the sun, moon, stars, all the animals that walk upon the earth, and all the fish that swim in the sea. In many of the cultures that surrounded ancient Israel, all of those things were, at various times and to varying degrees, worshiped. By relegating them to the level of creatures, the author of Genesis is suggesting, none too subtly, that authentic cosmic kingship belongs to the Creator God alone. Finally, as the crown of his creation, God brings forth human beings: "Then God said, 'Let us make humankind in our image, according to our likeness; and let them have dominion over the fish of the sea, and over the birds of the air, and over the cattle, and over all the wild animals of the earth, and over every creeping thing that creeps upon the earth'" (Gen. 1:26). To be sure, human beings had become, in some cultures, objects of worship; one needs only to think of the variety of deified kings on offer in the ancient world. Therefore, portraying the human being as a creature of the one God certainly undermines all attempts to turn humans into gods (Beale 2011: 30–32).

But there is more here than a mere cautioning against ego inflation, for the first humans are presented not simply as servants but as viceroys of the supreme king, God. Their purpose is precisely to have dominion over the various other things that God has made, ruling, as it were, as kings in the name of the supreme king. In fact, this stewardship of creation is a function of the first humans having been made "in the image of God." Just as God cares for and delights in the things he has fashioned, so his vice-regents are given the task of "tilling" and "keeping" the garden in which God placed them. The use of those terms of cultivation should preclude any temptation to interpret "dominion" as domination or oppression. In these very first verses of the scripture, an affirmation of the kingship of the Creator can be found, as well as a concomitant affirmation that it pleases God to involve his human creatures in a kind of kingly fellowship, granting to them the privilege and responsibility of tending the garden in line with God's purposes. According to a standard rabbinic reading of this passage, the point of Adam's kingship was to expand the boundaries of the garden of Eden until it contained the whole world. His good stewardship was meant to turn all of creation, both human and nonhuman, into a place of order and harmony. Part of this task was epistemological and philosophical, an act of "cataloging" creation, naming it *kata logon* after the intelligibility placed in it by the Creator. Thus, the early interpreters saw Adam as the first scientist, the first philosopher, exercising a sort of intellectual kingship. Tilling the soil, naming the animals, and walking in easy fellowship with God, Adam functioned as a good king, mimicking the moves and instantiating the purposes of the Creator King. From these earliest verses of the Bible, a theme runs like a golden thread through the whole of the scripture: dynamic incarnationalism. God is the Lord of creation, but he delights in allowing humanity to participate in his lordship and thereby brings the created order to its proper fulfillment.

But all does not go swimmingly with the Adamic kingship, and the fall of the first king (and his consort) from grace establishes the tension between good and bad rule that marks almost the entirety of the biblical narrative (Beale 2011: 46). Part of the task of a king is to cultivate the realm under his jurisdiction, but another dimension of his leadership is the protection of his kingdom from deleterious outside influence. The third chapter of the book of Genesis commences with a reference to "the serpent" who was "more crafty than any other wild animal that the LORD God had made" (Gen. 3:1). Adam and Eve not only allow this dangerous figure into the garden; they also listened to him and obeyed him, taking his suggestion and ignoring the command of God (Beale 2011: 35). In this they demonstrate the opposite of dominion, allowing a negative power to have lordship over them. The result of their failed leadership is a compromising of the order and harmony that obtained within them and within the garden. The first indication that all is not well is that they hide from God: "They heard the sound of the LORD God walking in the garden at the time of the evening breeze, and the man and his wife hid themselves from the presence of the LORD God among the trees of the garden" (Gen. 3:8). Since the human king is meant to operate in concord with the dictates of the divine king, the clearest sign of dysfunctional human kingship is a rupture with God, a refusal by the earthly king to allow the divine to become incarnate in his concrete moves and decisions. In the immediate wake of their sin, Adam and Eve become aware of their nakedness, and this causes them shame, signaling a disconnect between their spiritual and physical natures. This interior disintegration is followed by a falling apart at the communal and interpersonal levels: "The man said, 'The woman whom you have to be with me, she gave me fruit from the tree, and I ate.' . . . The woman said, 'The serpent tricked me, and I ate'" (Gen. 3:12–13). God's expulsion of the failed king and queen from the garden ought to be interpreted not as capricious divine punishment but rather as an expression of a kind of karmic law, the inevitable consequence of bad leadership. The expulsion from the garden might best be read as the dissolution of the kingdom around them once they sought to rule without reference to God.

In the chapters of Genesis that immediately follow the story of the fall, ample evidence can be found of bad kingly leadership. Cain allows sin to have dominion over him and consequently slays his brother. Then this paradigmatically wicked king becomes the founder of cities: "Cain knew his wife, and she conceived and bore Enoch; and he built a city, and named it Enoch after his son Enoch" (Gen. 4:17). The rather clear implication is that the dysfunction of virtually every human community represents a falling away from the order and harmony of a properly governed Eden. The builders of the tower of Babel are, similarly, derelict in their kingship. Instead of abiding by the will and purpose of God, they seek to make names for themselves and to challenge the supremacy of God. The inevitable result of this bad leadership is a division—precisely the opposite of the coming together that God desires for his creation: "So the LORD scattered them abroad from there over the face of all the earth, and they left off building the city" (Gen. 11:8). The great exception to this tendency is Noah, who is correctly identified as a second Adam, a renewer of humanity. Following the prompts of God, Noah gathers together a remnant of Yahweh's good creation and governs it effectively during a time of moral and spiritual chaos. He then allows the life that he had preserved to flood the world, thereby universalizing the harmony and integrity that obtained on the ark. Interestingly, even Noah is a compromised king. Instead of maintaining a consistent dominion over his family and over the earth, Noah drinks excessively of the fruit of the vine and allows himself to be displayed shamefully before his sons. Thus this new Adam shares in the ambiguity of the first Adam.

The definitive rescue operation that God launches is described in the twelfth chapter of Genesis.[1] God summons Abram from Ur of the Chaldeans, calls him to go in quest of a promised land, and then makes an extravagant promise: "I will make of you a great nation, and I will bless you, and make your name great . . . and in you all the families of the earth shall be blessed" (Gen. 12:2–3). Abram will be a new Adam, cultivating a new Eden and expanding the boundaries of that ordered garden to include all the peoples of the world (Beale 2011: 46–48). The people who will spring from his loins and who will be shaped by his consciousness and practices will become the vehicle by which salvation is born to the rest of creation. This promise is reiterated later in Genesis, just after the halted sacrifice of Isaac: "I will indeed bless you, and I will make your offspring as numerous as the stars of heaven and as the sand that is on the seashore. And your offspring shall possess the gate of their enemies, and by your offspring shall all the nations of the earth

1. Michael Dauphinais and Matthew Levering, *Holy People, Holy Land: A Theological Introduction to the Bible* (Grand Rapids: Brazos, 2005), 46.

gain blessing for themselves" (Gen. 22:17–18). The emphasis on Abram's numerous descendants calls to mind the command given to the first king to "be fruitful and multiply" (Gen. 1:28). The royal promise is extended to Abram's grandson. After his nightlong wrestling match with an angel, Jacob hears God: "No longer shall you be called Jacob, but Israel shall be your name. . . . I am God Almighty: be fruitful and multiply; a nation and a company of nations shall come from you, and kings shall spring from you" (Gen. 35:10–11). This royal and fruitful nation, this people set apart to operate according to God's heart, is perhaps best characterized as a "corporate Adam" endowed with the privileges and bearing the responsibilities of the first tender of the garden. At the conclusion of the book of Genesis is Jacob's last will and testament, the patriarch's solemn blessing for his twelve sons. To his son Judah, Jacob says, "The scepter shall not depart from Judah, nor the ruler's staff from between his feet, until tribute comes to him; and the obedience of the peoples is his" (Gen. 49:10). In other words, the kingly task will be passed on to and through Judah and his tribe. We will see the crucial significance of this promise in the rise of David from the tribe of Judah to supreme kingship in Israel.

The kingship motif continues throughout the Old Testament narrative. Moses, Joshua, Samson, Gideon, Jephthah, and Samuel are kingly, new Adam figures in the measure that they order the people Israel. But even the most cursory reading of the relevant stories discloses that none of these figures is a flawless king; indeed, all share in the spiritual ambiguity of the first Adam, which means that the quest for definitive leadership in Israel is ongoing and open-ended. When the book of Judges concludes with the line "in those days there was no king in Israel; all the people did what was right in their own eyes" (Judg. 21:25), a certain sense of despair can be detected, signaling that the Adamic role, essential to the flourishing of the garden of Israel, is not being exercised. Throughout these opening books of the Bible, Yahweh has not yet found the king in whom his own divine purposes can become utterly incarnate. Hence Israel's identity remains compromised and its mission unfulfilled.

It is against this rich and complex background that the emergence of Saul and David in the first book of Samuel has to be interpreted. When the people ask for a king who will unite and protect them, they are not asking for something out of step with God's purposes. On the contrary, their request is utterly congruent with the mission of the Adamic ruler. What is deeply problematic, however, is their insistence that this king should rule in the manner of the kings of "other nations" (1 Sam. 8:5). This is why God reacts negatively ("They have not rejected you, but they have rejected me from being king over them" [1 Sam. 8:7]) and also why

Samuel the prophet utters his devastating prediction of what this worldly king would do ("He will take your male and female slaves and the best of your cattle and donkeys and put them to his work. He will take one-tenth of your flocks, and you shall be his slaves. And in that day you will cry out because of your king, whom you have chosen for yourselves" [1 Sam. 8:16–18]). Samuel is implying that a king like those of the surrounding nations will not properly cultivate Israel, governing it according to the mind of God, but instead will order the people through oppression and violence and therefore undermine rather than sustain the mission of Israel. When the people press Samuel for a king, God says to Samuel, "Listen to their voice and set a king over them" (1 Sam. 8:22). The standard reading of this odd back and forth, this rejection and acceptance of a king, is that two sources—one anti-monarchical and the other pro-monarchical—exist in tension throughout the Samuel literature (Murphy 2010: 56–64). Be that as it may, I do not think that the interpreter ought to feel left in a lurch, caught on the horns of a desperate dilemma. A reasonable hermeneutical solution can be discerned along the lines that I have been suggesting: from Adam on, Israel is marked by both good and bad kingship. God (and Samuel) stand opposed to those forms of kingship that mimic the style and substance of the kings of the surrounding nations, but they ardently desire a form of kingship in accord with God's designs. A king that they "have chosen for themselves" will indeed be, as Samuel sees with such clarity, a disaster, but a king "after the LORD's heart" will be indispensible for the flourishing of the nation. The playing out of this difference—between Saul and David and also within David's own interiority—will be the dominant motif of the Samuel literature.

Why, precisely, is Saul rejected as king? What paves the way for his shameful demise on Mount Gilboa? Two major offenses typically are brought forward as an explanation. First, prior to the battle of Gilgal, Saul proceeded with the performance of a sacrifice though Samuel had instructed the king to wait for the prophet himself to do it. When, after seven days, some of his troops began to drift away, Saul impatiently seized the moment and sacrificed, only to find Samuel arriving just as the ceremony was completed. Enraged, the prophet says, "You have done foolishly; you have not kept the commandment of the LORD your God. . . . The LORD would have established your kingdom over Israel forever, but now your kingdom will not continue" (1 Sam. 13:13–14). Though it might seem a relatively minor infraction, this disobedience on the part of Saul is at the heart of the matter, spiritually speaking. Adam seized at godliness, making himself the criterion of good and evil, arrogating to himself the prerogative that belongs to

God alone. In this primal act of refusing to abide by a higher will, he fell into bad kingship. Saul's impatience, his refusal to wait on God and Samuel, participates in that original dysfunction. Saul's sin is not unlike that of Moses at the waters of Meribah, when the great lawgiver did not listen precisely to God's instructions (Num. 20:2–13), and it is very much like Jacob's aggressive and canny seizure of Esau's blessing from Isaac (Gen. 27:1–29). Whenever the will of the leader does not correspond to the divine will, God's desire to incarnate his grace in the world is frustrated (Murphy 2010: 111).

The second great offense committed by Saul is connected to his conquest of the Amalekites described in the fifteenth chapter of 1 Samuel. God instructs Saul through Samuel that he "will punish the Amalekites for what they did in opposing the Israelites when they came up out of Egypt" (1 Sam. 15:2), and so he commands Saul to attack and utterly destroy Amalek: "Kill both man and woman, child and infant, ox and sheep, camel and donkey" (1 Sam. 15:3). After defeating Amalek, Saul did not carry out God's command in its fullness, instead preserving the lives of the best of the sheep, cattle, and lambs as well as that of Agag, the Amalekite king. When he discovers this state of affairs, Samuel upbraids Saul, strips him of his kingship, and "hew[s] Agag to pieces before the LORD at Gilgal" (1 Sam. 15:33). A key to interpreting this startling passage is God's mention of the offense of the Amalekites when the Israelites were coming out of Egypt. The reference is to the battle described in the book of Exodus, during which Moses, in a pose both priestly and kingly, stretches his arms out in prayer, invoking the aid of Yahweh. When the battle is successfully completed, God speaks to Moses: "Write this as a reminder in a book and recite it in the hearing of Joshua: I will utterly blot out the remembrance of Amalek from under heaven" (Exod. 17:14). The author concludes his description of this scene with "The LORD will have war with Amalek from generation to generation" (Exod. 17:16).

If this story is simply and straightforwardly about a battle with an obscure ancient Middle Eastern tribe, it makes little sense. Why in the world would God decree that this beleaguered little people should be ruthlessly and relentlessly attacked? The allegorizing approach taken by Origen of Alexandria proves helpful in this case. Origen argues that, throughout the Bible, Israel stands for the ways and purposes of God, and the enemies of Israel stand for those powers that are opposed to God.[2] Thus, Egypt, Philistia, Assyria, Babylon, Greece, and Rome, among many others, evoke what Karl Barth calls *das Nichtige*, the nothingness,

2. Origen, *Homilies on Genesis and Exodus*, trans. Ronald E. Heine (Washington, DC: Catholic University of America Press, 1982), 232–38.

the nonbeing, which pits itself against Yahweh's creative intentions.[3] These various peoples are symbolically akin both to the *tōhû wābōhû* (Gen. 1:2) from which God brought the ordered world and to the serpent that Adam rather unsuccessfully managed in the garden.[4] Though it is not entirely clear why this should be the case, the biblical authors seem to isolate Amalek as particularly expressive of this "nothing" that militates against Israel. When the story is read from this symbolic perspective, one can perhaps begin to comprehend the ferocity of God's command to Saul. Certain forms of evil have to be utterly destroyed. Certain moves, ideas, perspectives, actions, and convictions are so radically opposed to the purposes of God that no compromise with them can be struck, no halfway measures can be adopted. One might argue, for example, that abortion, slavery, the sexual abuse of children, racial discrimination, and the direct killing of the innocent are so morally repugnant, so intrinsically evil, that they can never be justified under any circumstances or through appeal to any further end. Might Saul's unwillingness to slaughter the herds of the Amalekites and to put to death their king symbolically represent the sort of confusion in regard to intrinsically evil acts that undermines God's purposes? And therefore might one come to sympathize with Samuel's conviction that Saul has, by this act, effectively forfeited his kingship? If one stays within the Origenistic hermeneutic, Saul's unwillingness to "hack Agag to pieces" could be paired with Adam's inability to prevent the serpent from invading the garden as two decisive failures in kingly ordering (Beale 2011: 34–35). Saul's failure to listen and obey means that the incarnational coinherence that God desires to achieve through an earthly king is once more blocked.

As Samuel leaves the presence of Saul, the king desperately clings to the robe of the prophet and tears away a piece of cloth. With devastating laconism, Samuel says, "The LORD has torn the kingdom of Israel from you this very day, and has given it to a neighbor of yours, who is better than you" (1 Sam. 15:28). The one who is better than Saul is none other than the "man after [God's] own heart" (1 Sam. 13:14), to whom God promised the kingdom following Saul's first poor exercise of kingship. This is the son of Jesse whom Samuel anoints at the prompting of God. The remainder of 1 Samuel is the long and rather desperate tale of Saul's ever-weakening grasp on kingship and David's waxing skill and authority. The final and devastating indication that Saul is grossly incapable of leadership is his recourse

3. Karl Barth, *The Doctrine of Creation*, vol. 3.3 of *Church Dogmatics*, trans. G. W. Bromiley and R. J. Ehrlich, ed. G. W. Bromiley and T. F. Torrance (Edinburgh: T&T Clark, 1960), 289.

4. R. R. Reno, *Genesis*, Brazos Theological Commentary on the Bible (Grand Rapids: Brazos, 2010), 39–46.

to a medium at Endor in violation of his own prohibition against consulting such figures. Incapable of listening to God, Saul listens to a representative of the dark powers that, in a scene both comic and tragic, conjures up for him the shade of Samuel, who promptly reminds the hapless Saul that God has indeed torn the kingdom from him and given it to David (Murphy 2010: 257). God was able to commence the formation of his people Israel when he found someone who was willing to listen to his word. The leaders of this people were successful precisely in the measure that they were capable of hearing the word of a power that stretched beyond them and their own purposes. Saul proved remarkably inept at listening, which proved to be his undoing. His last act of "dominion," pathetically enough, is the taking of his own life, the exact opposite of the command to "be fruitful and multiply," to be the bearer of life.[5]

At this point, we are ready to return to the beginning of 2 Samuel. After the death of Saul, we hear, "David had returned from defeating the Amalekites" and "remained two days in Ziklag" (2 Sam. 1:1). As I have been arguing, the act of defeating the Amalekites must be interpreted as far more than a conquest in a petty tribal struggle; in fact, it is a foreshadowing of David's successful kingly warfare against the enemies of the God of Israel. But why had David been warring with Amalek in Ziklag, a town on the border between Philistine lands and Judah? Thereupon hangs a tale with important theological and spiritual overtones. Harassed relentlessly by Saul, David finally reaches a point of desperation and exclaims, "I shall now perish one day by the hand of Saul; there is nothing better for me than to escape to the land of the Philistines" (1 Sam. 27:1). In the manner typical of biblical narrative, the matter is stated so simply that it is easy enough to pass over the sheer strangeness of this move. David, who made his name as the killer of Goliath, was celebrated as the slayer of tens of thousands of Philistines, and famously collected the foreskins of two hundred dead Philistine warriors, now goes over to the enemy, even proposing himself as a sort of bodyguard to the warlord Achish of Gath. Achish, perhaps wary of David, suggests that the Israelite defector take up headquarters not in Gath but at Ziklag. Robert Alter wryly comments that this would be akin to Winston Churchill, at the height of World War II, becoming an advisor to a Nazi general and taking up residence in Berlin (Alter 1999: 168). This curious defection of David to the enemy is one of the clearest indications of how morally devastating Saul's jealousy was. An Israel united under a God-fearing king would be able to fulfill its mission to bring

5. Reno, *Genesis*, 56–58.

Edenic order to the wider world. But divided against itself, Israel cannot serve as the vehicle for the coming together of the nations; in fact, it becomes prey to the aggression of its enemies, and this is what Saul's uncontrolled resentment against David made possible. But Saul should not have to shoulder all of the blame. David's willingness to fight side by side with Israel's chief opponent—going so far as to accompany Achish at the battle of Mount Gilboa before being turned away by understandably suspicious Philistine officers—is certainly a sign of the weakness and moral ambiguity that will dog him throughout his reign as king. The struggle of Adam runs through the heart of David.

While he is at Ziklag, David receives a visitor, a man with torn clothes and dirt upon his head, who had come from "the camp of Israel," from the disaster at Mount Gilboa. Prostrating himself at David's feet, the man conveys the news that the Israelite army has been defeated and that Jonathan and Saul are among the dead. A parallel can be seen with the story of the messenger who brought the news of the deaths of Eli's sons and the loss of the ark, an earlier catastrophe that prompted a shift in Israelite leadership. When David presses the man for details, we begin to see that the visitor is a most unreliable narrator (Polzin 1993: 3). First, he says that he "happened to be on Mount Gilboa" (2 Sam. 1:6) during the terrible battle between Israel and the Philistines. It certainly strains credulity to believe that a person just happened to be wandering around the site of a pitched military conflict (Alter 1999: 196). It seems far more likely that he was scavenging the ground in the wake of the fight. Further, at the close of 1 Samuel, we heard that Saul had fallen on his own sword, but this man reports to David that he himself put the gravely wounded king out of his misery and then taken Saul's crown and armlet and brought them directly to David. Both the boast that he had killed Saul and the carrying of the symbols of kingship to David are rather obvious attempts to curry favor with the one who will presumably be the next ruler of Israel, but things backfire on the man in dramatic fashion. After mourning intensely until evening, David calls the messenger and inquires as to his origins. The young man blithely responds that he is an Amalekite, which first helps to explain why he felt no particular hesitation at doing violence to the king of Israel but also makes clear the wider theological context for understanding his act. A member of that tribe of archetypal enemies of Israel, the messenger is evocative of those forces that would divide and conquer the people of God. Though he correctly intuits that David will be the next king, and though he signals, by the delivery of the crown and armlet, the fulfillment of Samuel's prophecy, he reveals himself as a divider, a fomentor of civil strife, and a killer of Yahweh's anointed one. He is a serpent in the garden. Therefore, David, acting here as a righteous king, does to him what Samuel did to Agag the Amalekite and what Adam should have done to the snake: "David called one of the young men and said, 'Come here and strike him down.' So he struck him down and he died" (2 Sam. 1:15; Beale 2011: 34).

At this point, I must address an issue that preoccupies the author of the Samuel literature from the beginning to the end of his work: David's consistent refusal to do violence to Saul or his house despite Saul's deep and abiding hostility toward David. To be sure, almost every contemporary commentator is skeptical on this score, seeing the presentation of David's gentleness toward Saul as either hagiographical whitewashing or a none-too-subtle attempt to exonerate David for what was, doubtless, his aggressive usurpation of his predecessor.[6] Obviously, it is next to impossible to adjudicate the historical truth in this regard with anything approaching exactitude. What is more available, and far more interesting theologically, is the presentation of David that the author gives in the text—the picture of a prince relentlessly respectful of Yahweh's anointed one.

In 1 Samuel we find two remarkable stories of David consciously refusing to kill Saul when the opportunity to do so arises. In both cases, advisors urge him to perform the act and hence put an end to the desperate civil war that is bedeviling Israel, but David demurs. Though it would benefit him personally and prove advantageous to the nation politically, David will not do violence to one that Yahweh himself anointed as king. To understand the attitude of David, one must come to terms with a biblical sense of divine providence and human freedom, both of which are starkly at odds with a modern understanding of the same two realities. On the modern reading, freedom is best characterized as sovereign choice. The free subject stands indifferently above a variety of options and, on the basis of no internal or external constraint, determines which to choose. Given this interpretation, two of the principal foes of freedom are a circumscribing law and the fussy intervention of a rival divine freedom. This is why, having elevated this "liberty of indifference," much of modern philosophy and religion is compelled to construe divine providence along vaguely deist lines, whereby God sets the context in which human freedom operates but does not function as a real actor in cooperation with that freedom.[7] But all of this is alien to the biblical consciousness. For the biblical writers (as for most classical philosophers as well), freedom

6. Walter Brueggemann, *David's Truth in Israel's Imagination and Memory* (Minneapolis: Fortress, 2002), 31–32.

7. Servais Pinckaers, *Morality: The Catholic View*, trans. Michael Sherwin (South Bend, IN: St. Augustine's Press, 2001), 72–75.

is not so much sovereign, uncompelled choice as the disciplining of desire so as to make the achievement of the good first possible and then effortless. Think of the process by which a person learns to play the piano or to swing a golf club with easy confidence. Given this construal of freedom, one is becoming free—able to play any piece one wishes or make any shot the round is calling for—precisely in the measure that one internalizes a whole set of laws, regulations, and disciplines and submits to the tutelage of a skilled teacher able to communicate this freedom to the learner. The lawgiving instructor is therefore not the enemy of the student's freedom but rather the condition for its possibility. On this interpretation, God, the supreme lawgiver, does not have to be transformed into an abstraction or relegated to the sidelines of free human activity. On the contrary, God can and should be viewed as an enabling partner to free human actors involved in the drama of history.

Operating with this notion of freedom and providence, David knew that God chooses and moves within Israelite history and that God's acts, having a legitimate sovereignty, must become the matrix for properly functioning human moral activity. Hence God's decision to anoint Saul as king could not be taken lightly, and whatever David might become through his own volition should not countermand the prior decision that God made. The apostle Paul states that there is a "power at work within us" that is able "to accomplish abundantly far more than all we can ask or imagine" (Eph. 3:20). That statement, intelligible only on the reading of biblical freedom that I have presented here, expresses well what David must have had in mind when he played his complex and emotionally wrenching cat-and-mouse game with Saul. God's choice of Saul—perhaps incomprehensible to David and most right-thinking people in Israel—was the brute fact with which David had to contend, and it was simply not his place to freely move against it. God was, inscrutably enough, working out his purposes precisely through allowing Saul's wickedness, as king, to express itself. In light of Samuel's anointing, David must have suspected strongly that he would become king, but at the same time he knew that this royal accession could never take place through his own violent action against Saul.

All of this raises the even deeper theological question regarding God's permission of evil. David seems to have intuited (correctly enough, at least in the mind of the author of 2 Samuel) that Saul's very wickedness was an ingredient in God's providential design, especially in regard to David himself. While I could certainly speak of God's general allowance of the twisted exercise of human freedom, there seems to be more at stake in these stories, something denser and more puzzling:

God is accomplishing what he wants through the moral depravity of Saul. We can see this odd relationship in a number of other stories of biblical heroes. Joseph is presented initially as a supremely annoying young man, the coddled favorite of his father and a taunting nemesis to his understandably jealous brothers. He was in absolutely no position, at that stage of his moral development, to assume leadership. But God used the wickedness of Joseph's own brothers, the slave traders who purchased him, and the wife of Potiphar, who had him imprisoned, in order to discipline Joseph in the direction of mature leadership. Similarly Moses, who is introduced to us as a headstrong, violent, and morally irresponsible prince of Egypt, is forced into exile by an overreacting Pharaoh and hence compelled to commence the process by which he would be prepared for his role as liberator. It appears as though God, who is sovereign over both history and nature, can work into his providential design even the sinful behavior of bad people. Therefore (and this seems to be a principal point throughout the David stories) one should be wary of preempting this providence or presuming to improve upon it through one's moral acts, even those acts that seem, on the surface of it, altogether praiseworthy. David's stubborn unwillingness to do violence to Saul is another sign of his kingly worthiness, for it indicates that his actions were predicated not primarily on self-interest but rather on an attentive listening to the voice of God. Saul would be the anointed king until God saw fit to remove him, and it was not David's place to question God's wisdom or meddle interruptively in God's designs.

But there is even more at stake theologically in David's gentleness toward Saul, and here we will look for the first time toward Christ Jesus, the definitive Son of David. Just after hearing the taunting song of the women, "Saul has slain his thousands, but David his ten thousands" (1 Sam. 18:7), Saul is consumed with jealousy toward his protégé. Twice he hurls a spear at David, and then, over the course of many months, he doggedly pursues the younger man. Through all of it, David never responds with violence. Instead, he gets out of Saul's way—running, avoiding, and evading but never directly confronting his persecutor. Indeed, after refraining from killing the king when Saul wandered unescorted into a cave where David and his men were hiding, David bows to the ground before Saul, does "obeisance" (1 Sam. 24:8), and says, "I have not sinned against you, though you are hunting me to take my life. . . . May the LORD avenge me on you; but my hand shall not be against you" (1 Sam. 24:11–12). David's gesture and speech so impress the king that Saul says, with tears, "You are more righteous than I; for you have repaid me good, whereas I have repaid you evil" (1 Sam. 24:17). What we see here is something fairly rare in the Old Testament: the employment of active and provocative nonviolence as a moral strategy. David does not engage Saul directly, using the conventional weapons of war; rather, he strategically retreats and feints, using the stronger man's energy against him. Moreover, as the speech just rehearsed suggests, he "killed Saul with kindness," stubbornly returning good for the king's evil, thereby shaming his pursuer and compelling him to look at things from David's perspective. Aikido, a particularly effective form of martial art, involves precisely this sort of subtlety and indirection. The practitioner of aikido does not directly engage the enemy punch for punch; instead, the practitioner redirects the opponent's force by deftly getting out of the way and giving in to the aggression, but doing so in such a way that the aggression itself doubles back against the aggressor.[8] We see something of this in young David's battle with Goliath. Putting aside the armor of Saul, which prohibited him from maneuvering, David meets the giant armed only with a slingshot and uses Goliath's arrogance and heavy-handedness against him.

Jesus, born in David's hometown of Bethlehem, certainly came as a warrior King. C. S. Lewis remarks that Jesus arrived so quietly, born in a cave in a little outpost of the Roman Empire, precisely because he had to slip clandestinely behind enemy lines.[9] The new David's manner of fighting was unconventional to say the least, though it was anticipated by David's aikido-like engagement of Saul. In the Sermon on the Mount Jesus recommends that, when confronted with violence or aggression—"if anyone strikes you on the right cheek" (Matt. 5:39)—one should respond not with answering violence but rather with a turning of the other cheek.[10] It is tempting indeed to read this simply as a recommendation toward passivity, but that temptation should be strenuously resisted. The two classic responses to aggression, evident both in the animal kingdom and among human beings, are fight or flight. Either one answers violence with counterviolence or one acquiesces to it. Though in our conflicted and sinful world one or the other of these responses is sometimes all that is reasonably possible, most people realize that neither fight nor flight truly solves the problem of violence. The former tends to increase it, and the latter tends to condone it. What Jesus is proposing is a third way. In the society of his time and place, people would never use the left hand for any form of social interaction. Therefore, anyone who struck someone on the right cheek would be hitting that person with the back of the hand, a gesture indicative of contempt and aggressive superiority. To

8. Walter Wink, *Jesus and Nonviolence: A Third Way* (Minneapolis: Fortress, 2003), 43.
9. C. S. Lewis, *Mere Christianity* (New York: Simon & Schuster, 1943), 51.
10. Wink, *Jesus and Nonviolence*, 14–16.

turn the other cheek, therefore, is certainly not to fight back, but neither is it to acquiesce. It is to stand one's ground and signal, in a provocative manner, that the aggressor will not be allowed to strike in the same way again. Mirroring back the aggression of the aggressor, turning the other cheek is an aikido-like move.[11] Or, to use a metaphor employed by Paul, it is "to pour burning coals upon the head" (Prov. 25:22) of the violent person, answering evil with good and thereby intensifying the wicked person's cognizance of his or her own wickedness. John Cassian finds an anticipation of New Testament nonviolence in David's moves in regard to Saul: "We know that David went beyond the precepts of the law when, despite Moses's command to pay back one's enemies in kind, he not only did not do this but even embraced his persecutors in love, prayed devoutly to the Lord on their behalf, and even wept mournfully for them."[12]

Cassian's reference to David's weeping provides a nice segue into a consideration of David's famous elegy to the slain Saul and Jonathan, the "Song of the Bow" (2 Sam. 1:19–27), one of the most hauntingly beautiful songs of its type anywhere in the literature of the world. That David is a singer of songs is one of the first things we learn about him; we are told that he was summoned from the tending of Jesse's sheep in order to sing and play for the troubled Saul (1 Sam. 16:18). At the end of 2 Samuel we find David described, in the King James Version's lovely rendering of the Hebrew, as the "sweet psalmist of Israel" (2 Sam. 23:1). And of course David is associated, either as author or inspiration, with the majority of the songs that comprise the book of Psalms. He is a warrior, to be sure, indeed the consummate warrior of Israel; he is a king, to be sure, indeed the archetypal king; but he is also a singer, a poet, someone capable of leading the people through the beautiful articulation of their anxieties and aspirations. In this regard, David is a forerunner of Lincoln or Churchill. How many Americans today can remember the particular political and military decisions that Lincoln made during the Civil War? But is there an American who does not know the words, rhythms, and cadences of the Gettysburg Address? Lincoln led as much through poetic speech as through canny administration. How many Britons can recall the details of Churchill's practical direction of the war against Hitler? But is there a Briton who has forgotten about the prime minister who promised "blood, toil, tears, and sweat"? Leadership is a complex, multifaceted skill involving management and vision but also the capacity to engage the imaginations of those to be led.

11. Ibid., 9–28.

12. John Cassian, "Conference 21.4.2," in *Joshua, Judges, Ruth, 1–2 Samuel*, ed. John R. Franke, Ancient Christian Commentary on Scripture: Old Testament 4 (Downers Grove, IL: InterVarsity, 2005), 331.

Therefore, if this association of David with singing and playing has any historical validity, there seems no ground for doubting David's authorship of the lament.

We are told that David himself instructed, presumably when he was king in Hebron, that the Song of the Bow be taught to the people of Judah (2 Sam. 1:18; Alter 1999: 198). A somewhat cynical reading would suggest that David wanted to advertise as far as possible his warm feelings toward the house of Saul so as to hold off the suspicion that he had been actively involved in causing the death of the king. Though attractive to postmodern interpreters, such a reading, in my view, does not shed the most light.[13] Yes, Saul relentlessly pursued David, but nothing in a straightforward reading of 1 Samuel would justify the claim that David was harboring a hidden grudge against the king. Rather the younger man is consistently presented as respectful toward Saul and bewildered at the king's behavior. Therefore I see no need to read the praise offered in the elegy nor the command to publish it as cynical political maneuvering on David's part. Perhaps it is best interpreted as David's attempt not only to express his own feelings but also to make some sense of God's providence as it played itself out in the tragedy of Saul.

David begins, "Your glory, O Israel, lies slain upon your high places! How the mighty have fallen!" (2 Sam. 1:19). There is a wonderful ambiguity in the Hebrew here: *haṣṣĕbî* can mean either "glory" or "gazelle" (Baldwin 1988: 191–92). Thus the author may be using a beautiful trope suggesting that the warriors of Israel are like skilled and graceful animals killed in their last redoubt after having been relentlessly pursued by their enemies. The reference to the heights also evokes Israel's typical hiding place from the Philistines, who preferred to do battle on the plains, where their chariots were more efficiently utilized. The sense is that even there, in their usual place of safety, the flower of Israel's youth has been tragically cut down. But "high places" carries a further overtone and brings out the distinctively spiritual or religious dimension of the disaster. Throughout the Torah and the Deuteronomistic History, the "high places" designates the locales where false gods are worshiped (Polzin 1993: 24–25). Again and again Israel is counseled by its leaders and prophets to tear down the Asherah poles on those heights, which had been erected to the gods of the surrounding peoples. Thus, "I will destroy your high places and cut down your incense altars; I will heap your carcasses on the carcasses of your idols" (Lev. 26:30); and "You shall drive out all the inhabitants of the land from before you, destroy all their figured stones, destroy all their cast images, and demolish all their high places" (Num. 33:52).

13. Brueggemann, *David's Truth*, 9–10.

God issues this utterly representative warning through the prophet Ezekiel: "I will destroy your high places. . . . Your towns shall be waste and your high places ruined. . . . The slain shall fall in your midst" (Ezek. 6:3, 6–7). In short, there is a causal connection between the worship of idols on the high places and the piling up of the corpses of Israelites. In the subtle insinuation of David's verse, is there the sense that the reason for the downfall of Saul was none other than his bad worship, his refusal to obey and honor God? We ought not forget that just before the disaster on Mount Gilboa, Saul had sought out the ministrations of the medium at Endor—precisely the sort of debased religiosity that the law of Israel precluded.

The lament continues with David exhorting, "Tell it not in Gath, proclaim it not on the streets of Ashkelon"—two of the principal cities of the Philistines—"or the daughters of the Philistines will rejoice, the daughters of the uncircumcised will exult" (2 Sam. 1:20). There are ironic overtones here. First, when David was a vassal of the king of Gath and engaged in raids on the border towns of Judah, he slaughtered all of his enemies, lest word of his activities get back to Gath (1 Sam. 27:11). Second, David cannot bear to hear the rejoicing songs of the Philistine women, echoing the songs of the Israelite women who had sung of David slaying "his ten thousands." The sweet singer of Israel certainly understands the political power of songs and myths. The loss of Israel's reputation among its enemies could cost it more dearly than the loss of troops and king in the field.

Next, David utters a sort of curse on the territory where the terrible battle took place: "You mountains of Gilboa, let there be no dew or rain upon you, nor bounteous fields!" (2 Sam. 1:21). One of Yahweh's principal promises to Israel was to give them a land flowing with milk and honey. This earth was meant as a recapitulation of the garden of Eden, which Adam and Eve, prior to the fall, cultivated and made fruitful. Therefore the place where the Philistines triumphed over Israel and its king should, by rights, become barren ground. David chooses a vivid and heartbreaking image to evoke the defeat of Saul: "For there the shield of the mighty was defiled, the shield of Saul, anointed with oil no more" (2 Sam. 1:21). In ancient times warriors anointed their shields to make them both more beautiful and more resistant to blows, and thus there is great sadness in envisioning the dented shield of the king lying unadorned and useless against his enemies (Alter 1999: 199). But there is a more theological valence to the image as well, for Saul was the *māšîaḥ*, the anointed of Yahweh (indeed, this is the term that David often uses for him), and so his unanointed shield is evocative of the loss of his kingship, which came because of his refusal to attend to God (Baldwin 1988:

193). Many scholars comment that this elegy by David represents the moment of transition, the passing of the torch from Saul to the new king, and one might see the grimy, battered, and unanointed shield of Saul as clear indication that it was time for another *māšîaḥ*.

After the mention of the defensive implement of the shield, David turns to a retrospective look at the offensive weapons wielded by Saul and his son: "From the blood of the slain, from the fat of the mighty, the bow of Jonathan did not turn back, nor the sword of Saul return empty" (2 Sam. 1:22). This trope of the victors' weapons feasting on the flesh of the conquered is fairly common in the ancient world, but it is intended here to highlight the warlike quality of the anointed king of Israel. At their best, Saul and Jonathan did the hard work of protecting the garden and did not shrink from using lethal violence to do it. But now that the bow and sword are lying in the dust, Israel needs a new defender. Of course, the poet refrains from mentioning that the spear of Saul was, at least two times, directed at David himself! He also makes the curious observation that Saul and his son Jonathan were "in life and death . . . not divided" (2 Sam. 1:23). Though Jonathan certainly fought at Saul's side, the son showed his clear preference for David. Sensing this shift in loyalty, Saul even hurled a spear in the direction of Jonathan. Does one sense here a touch of propaganda, a bit of the elegist's understandable tendency toward idealization (Alter 1999: 200)? Or is this another example of David's consistent resolution to answer the violence of Saul with nonviolence, this time at the level of speech? Obviously, destroying a cruel enemy's reputation is one of the best ways to inflict harm, especially after the enemy is dead and thus unable to defend it. This, however, David nobly refuses to do.

The peroration to the "daughters of Israel" to weep over Saul neatly balances the earlier command that the daughters of the Philistines should not rejoice over the defeat at Gilboa, but it is also an evocation of the songs of the Israelite women that initially prompted Saul to hate his protégé. The elegist seems to suggest that the mourning of the Israelite women for the fallen king might in some sense make up for their cries of joy that provoked such calamity for the nation. What follows is the achingly poignant address to the poet's fallen friend: "Jonathan lies slain upon your high places. I am distressed for you, my brother Jonathan; greatly beloved were you to me; your love to me was wonderful, passing the love of women" (2 Sam. 1:25–26). Though Jonathan had several times declared his love for David, only after Jonathan's death does David reciprocate, calling his companion "brother" and speaking frankly of his love for him. Though some have suggested, especially in recent years, that the characterization of this love as "passing the love of women" is an indication of a homoerotic element in David's affection for his friend, this is unconvincing. Robert Alter argues convincingly that in the warrior culture of this time, "the bond between men could easily be stronger than the bond between men and women" (Alter 1999: 200–201). In the cultural context of ancient Greece, Aristotle comments that a man can cultivate a real friendship only with another male since friendship has to take place between equals.[14] Aristotle's remark insinuates homosexuality as little as David's does.

However, one should not overlook the importance of David's intense friendship with the son of Saul. From Jonathan's side, it signals the orientation of true love, which is directed toward the other. Jonathan willingly surrendered his status and position in favor of David, easily, even gratefully, acknowledging that David and not he would one day succeed Saul. And despite the enormous danger to himself, Jonathan consistently defended and protected David.[15] John Chrysostom comments that Jonathan ought to have been jealous of the upstart shepherd who was rivaling him for the throne, "but he [Jonathan] favored David obtaining the sovereignty; and he didn't spare his father for the sake of his friend. . . . Instead of envying, Jonathan joined in obtaining the kingdom for him."[16] This lovely surrender to the other is what led Aelred of Rievaulx and many others to see in Jonathan's relationship to David the model of true friendship.[17] From David's side, the relationship shows once more his intense tie with the house of Saul despite Saul's murderous opposition. A number of times in the course of 2 Samuel David will endeavor to show kindness to members of Saul's house "for the sake of Jonathan and Saul," answering violence with favor. Chrysostom goes so far as to hint that David's behavior is a model to all those who would show favor to both the living and the dead.[18] Certainly one of the most powerful ways that David demonstrated his love for his friend slain on the slopes of Mount Gilboa was the composition of an elegy read and admired three thousand years after its composition.

14. Aristotle, *The Nichomachean Ethics of Aristotle*, trans. F. H. Peters (London: C. Kegan Paul, 1881), 265–66.

15. Robert Pinsky, *The Life of David* (New York: Schocken, 2005), 31–32.

16. John Chrysostom, "Homilies on 2 Timothy 7," in Franke, *Joshua, Judges, Ruth, 1–2 Samuel*, 334.

17. Aelred of Rievaulx, *The Way of Friendship: Selected Spiritual Writings*, ed. M. Basil Pennington (Hyde Park, NY: New City Press, 2001), 71–73.

18. John Chrysostom, "Homilies on 2 Timothy 7," 334.

2 SAMUEL 2

The second chapter of 2 Samuel is of central importance because it shows the quick moves that David made in order to consolidate his power, but more significantly, it discloses the manner in which David acted, which was steadily under the aegis of God. The chapter commences with the simple declaration that David "inquired of the LORD, 'Shall I go up into any of the cities of Judah?'" (2 Sam. 2:1). David was perhaps consulting an oracle of God, or more likely he was, with a priest's help, casting lots known as the Urim and Thummim, which would yield a yes or no answer to a direct question (Baldwin 1988: 196). Hence God says to David, "Go up," and when pressed for more information, responds "to Hebron" (2 Sam. 2:1). The particular means that David used to discern the divine purpose are less important than the humility and obedience that he showed in submitting his will to God's. In this, he showed himself a worthy new Adam whose kingship consisted in governing Eden according to God's word. As long as David remains in the attitude of attentive listening to the voice of a higher power, he will prosper as king and produce the effects promised to Adam and Abraham: land, life, fruitfulness, and right praise. In many ways, the burden of the second half of 2 Samuel is to show that David's compromised kingship produces just the opposite: the disorder reminiscent of the human condition following the fall.

Politically speaking, David is resolving to leave Ziklag and its Philistine associations and move into leadership of the chosen people. By moving into "the cities of Judah," he is, of course, claiming his own ancestral territory, since he is a member of the tribe of Judah. But a merely political or sociological reading of this text is not sufficient. In theological terms, David is assuming the mantle of his distant ancestor Judah, the son of Jacob, to whom the burden and privilege of leadership, as we saw, had been promised. Only with David's explicit kingship does the prophecy made to Judah concerning the scepter and the ruler's staff come to fulfillment. Why specifically would David have been directed to take up residence at Hebron? Certainly it was one of the leading cities of Judah and a gathering point for the other southern tribes, but it also had very strong patriarchal associations, especially with Abraham, to whom a promise of universal fecundity had been made. In moving confidently there, David shows himself to be a successor to Abraham and an agent of unification. Once again, though David's decision can be read in purely political or tactical terms, the fact that he inquired of Yahweh before making it proves that it is an ingredient in a much larger and more mysterious narrative.

Therefore David comes to Hebron with two of his wives, "Ahinoam of Jezreel, and Abigail the widow of Nabal of Carmel" (2 Sam. 2:2), as well as a number of the men who had been fighting and traveling with him. For the past many years, ever since he was forced to flee from the jealous wrath of Saul, David had been on the move as a nomad and outlaw, and he surrounded himself with desperadoes and guerrilla fighters. He was cagey and resourceful and certainly inspired the loyalty of his little band, but he could hardly be called a "king." What commences in Hebron is the establishment of David—his settling down—so that the process of gathering in and around him might get under way (McCarter 1984: 43). Within the context of the Deuteronomistic History, the culmination of a thematic trajectory is apparent, beginning with Joshua and the invasion of the promised land and continuing through the era of the judges with Israel finding its footing on the land.[1] An Israel that was for several centuries unfocused, harrassed, and unsettled emerges through David as a firmly planted nation capable of fulfilling its mission to gather the rest of the world.[2] Inspired by the presence of the son-in-law of Saul and the conquerer of Goliath, the "people of Judah came, and there they anointed David king over the house of Judah" (2 Sam. 2:4). This anointing, which echoes that of Samuel, makes David doubly messianic, confirming him as leader, and it shows the initial knitting together of the tribes through the person of the king.

In shifting one's focus from the grandly theological to the more particularly political, one might inquire as to the Philistines' reaction to this move of David. Keep in mind that, as far as they knew, David was still a vassal of King Achish of

1. Matthew Levering, *Ezra and Nehemiah*, Brazos Theological Commentary on the Bible (Grand Rapids: Brazos, 2007), 47–49.

2. N. T. Wright, *Jesus and the Victory of God*, Christian Origins and the Question of God 2 (Minneapolis: Fortress, 1996), 245–46.

Gath, and thus they might have assumed that David's assumption of the "crown" of Judah actually represented an encroachment of Philistia into the heart of Israel, indeed as a Philistine challenge to the house of Saul, which was centered in the north. This helps to explain why the Philistines, who certainly enjoyed a military advantage after the battle of Mount Gilboa, did not perceive David's coronation as a *casus belli*. As evidenced throughout the Samuel books, David was a very shrewd operator, especially in regard to the enemies of Israel. He was willing to feint, attack, taunt (think of Goliath), or even form alliances according to the shifting circumstances. Did this wily warrior know that he could safely consolidate his power in the south, precisely because of his ambiguous associations with Achish? Is this a particularly deft strategy of simultaneously building up power, preparing to face the remnants of the house of Saul, and holding off a dangerous enemy? At this stage of the story, David is indeed a cagey and capable new Adam, both tending and defending the new Eden.

The new king of Judah is informed that the people of Jabesh-gilead had done the kindness of burying Saul. Leaving a dead body unburied was the height of scandal in the ancient world, as can be seen clearly enough in both the Bible and in much of classical Greek literature.[3] Permitting the bodies of Saul and Jonathan to decay on the mountain and be picked over by wild animals was so repugnant to the people of Jabesh-gilead, close allies of Saul, that they took action. One might have assumed that this gesture of charity would be perceived by an enemy of Saul as offensive, even a provocation, and therefore it is, once again, surprising and enlightening that David appreciates the kindness shown to his relentless persecutor: "May you be blessed by the LORD, because you showed this loyalty to Saul your lord, and buried him!" (2 Sam. 2:5). Is this wily politics from someone who has ambitions to become king of both Judah and Israel and who therefore would need all the support he can get from the Saulides? Perhaps. But the author wants us to see that this wise political move is also a gesture of love on the part of the anointed one, an answering of evil with good. That David's kindness is related to his ambition to bring the tribes together is clear from his blunt reminder: "Therefore let your hands be strong and be valiant; for Saul your lord is dead, and the house of Judah has anointed me king over them" (2 Sam. 2:7).

At this point, our attention is directed north to Abner, the son of Ner, the capable commander of Saul's army, who "had taken Ishbaal son of Saul, and brought him to Mahanaim" and made him king over the tribes of Israel (2 Sam. 2:8–9).

3. Sophocles, *Antigone*, in *The Complete Greek Tragedies: Sophocles I*, trans. Elizabeth Wyckoff, ed. David Grene and Richard Lattimore (New York: Washington Square, 1967), 164–66.

In the deft and laconic prose so typical of biblical narrators, these few words relay most of what needs to be known about these two figures. Ishbaal is a feckless, propped-up man, and the real power in the north belongs to Abner, who is politically astute enough to realize that he needs to operate behind the façade of a member of Saul's family. There are some who are preoccupied with power but not necessarily with honor, and Abner seems to be such. He does not need to be king in name, but he does crave control. In any event, his machinations have led to a military and political division within the chosen people: "Ishbaal, Saul's son, was forty years old when he began to reign over Israel, and he reigned two years. But the house of Judah followed David" (2 Sam. 2:10). As I pointed out earlier, the immediate result of sin in the garden was division and a frenzy of blaming, and its longer-term consequences were a variety of separations and animosities. Abraham's family was summoned in order to counterbalance this fissiparousness and to draw the rest of humanity into unity. The central tragedy of Israelite history is the division into factions of the very community meant to be the sign and instrument of unity. Abner and Ishbaal, setting themselves against David and fomenting a civil war, operate in the tradition of Cain, the builders of the tower of Babel, Esau, and the worshipers of the golden calf. The civil war that commences here is a tragic foreshadowing of the split between Israel and Judah that bedeviled the chosen people in the period following the reign of Solomon and led finally to conquest and exile for all twelve tribes.

The time of Ishbaal's consolidation of power over the northern regions, David's settling in as king in Hebron, and the civil war itself probably stretched over many years. We hear of Ishbaal reigning for two years and David in Hebron for seven years and six months, and it might be plausible to suggest that the five-year difference corresponds to the period during which Ishbaal and Abner were establishing themselves. Most likely, the two sides waxed and waned, pushed at one another, skirmished, and fought over a long period, and the text presents a few vignettes and scenes that suggest the messy, drawn-out affair of the civil conflict. So we are told of a provocative act whereby "Abner son of Ner, and the servants of Ishbaal son of Saul, went out from Mahanaim to Gibeon" and were met by Joab, David's commander, beside a pool in Gibeon (2 Sam. 2:12–13). Mahanaim is on the eastern side of the Jordan and hence outside of Philistine control and also beyond the reach of David; but Gibeon, just northwest of Jerusalem, is far closer to both Philistine and Davidic spheres of influence. This is why Abner's sallying forth in this way is rightly interpreted by Joab as a provocation and a deliberate show of force that had to be met.

What is fascinating is how the two battle groups meet. Everything at first seems harmless enough, something like a competitive but finally playful encounter between rival teams. As the two groups arrange themselves on opposite sides of the pool, Abner calls out to Joab in the manner of one coach addressing his counterpart: "Let the young men come forward and have a contest before us" (2 Sam. 2:14). Perhaps this scene is something like Goliath's proposal of a representative combat that would, in one fell swoop, determine the outcome of the war. At any rate, the two teams pair off, twelve on each side, which is certainly suggestive of the divided tribes of Israel. Each young man then grabs his opponent by the head (probably the hair is meant) and simultaneously drives his weapon into his counterpart's side, resulting in the death of all of the contestants. There is pictorial evidence that this sort of contest was played out in the ancient world; however, here it seems clear that the author is presenting a beautifully stylized depiction of civil war, a battle between friends and brothers (hence the element of playful contest) that ends in mutual destruction, one act of violence simply giving rise to another, and on and on in a dreadful cycle. This particular civil war continued with brief interruptions for several centuries after David and Solomon's united kingdom split into warring Israel and Judah. And as I have argued already, an Israel turned, like these young gladiators, inward against itself in destructive warfare exercised no compelling influence on the surrounding nations. Instead, it became prey to its enemies. The tragic-comic circle of fallen young men functions, therefore, as a harbinger of the future of Israel (McCarter 1984: 97–99).

In the wake of the bizarre "game," a fierce battle breaks out between Abner and the servants of David, and David's men are victorious. We then hear of a particular skirmish involving three of David's nephews, the sons of his sister Zeruiah: Joab, Abishai, and Asahel. The first mention of Joab and Abishai is in 1 Samuel, the story of the nighttime invasion of the sleeping camp of Saul during the Saul-David war. It was Abishai who asked permission to drive a spear through the head of the slumbering king only to be met with resistance from David. That little scene establishes the pattern that plays out through the rest of the Samuel literature: the hotheaded and impulsive sons of Zeruiah serving David but also existing in somewhat uneasy tension with the milder, more moderate king. In fact, the back and forth between David and Joab provides much of the dramatic tension of 2 Samuel.

If David at this point in the narrative is around thirty years old, these sons of his sister probably are quite young, perhaps teenagers. Asahel, who is described as exceedingly fleet of foot ("as a wild gazelle" [2 Sam. 2:18]), sets off after the retreating Abner, who is doubtless eager to leave the battlefield and who certainly does not savor the prospect of killing a close relative of David. Twice the older man warns his pursuer: "Turn to your right or to your left, and seize one of the young men, and take his spoil. . . . Turn away from following me; why should I strike you to the ground? How then could I show my face to your brother Joab?" (2 Sam. 2:21–22). The cooly confident warrior is actually showing mercy to the relentless and foolhardy youth, giving him an honorable way out, but Asahel keeps coming. So Abner uses an old soldier's trick, suddenly stopping in his tracks and jutting out the butt of his spear, onto which the young man, propelled by his momentum, is impaled. In this awful play of youth against maturity, of son against father, one sees something of the tragedy of Israelite civil war, the tearing apart of what was meant to be a family.

The theme of familial dissolution is, of course, on display throughout the biblical narrative, from Cain and Abel, through Jacob and Esau, to David and his sons. All of this warfare represents the unraveling of what God intended for his human family from the beginning. Abner gives voice to this peculiar agony of Israel when, in the wake of killing Asahel, he turns to Joab and shouts, "Is the sword to keep devouring forever? Do you not know that the end will be bitter?" (2 Sam. 2:26). Violence begets violence; killing gives rise to killing; vendetta produces vendetta. The supreme irony is that Joab will, in short order, provide justification for Abner's lament precisely by killing Abner. The only way out is the path that David walked in regard to Saul, and that Jesus, the Son of David, would walk definitively and unconditionally. The true family of Israel would be gathered around the nonviolent Jesus, the lamb standing as though slain.

SERIES TWO

PRIEST AND KING

2 SAMUEL 3

The third chapter of 2 Samuel tells the tale of the waning of Saul's house and the waxing of David's. The narrative is informed at every turn by the conviction that the dissolution of Saul's family follows as a consequence of his abandonment of the ways of Yahweh. Though it cuts against our more individualistic sensibilities, the biblical authors stubbornly see sin diachronically—actions, reactions, and consequences crisscrossing and echoing one another across time. In the Deuteronomistic reading, there is finally no escaping the bad karma that flows from sin, and so "David grew stronger and stronger, while the house of Saul became weaker and weaker" (2 Sam. 3:1; Polzin 1993: 32–35).

We are told that several sons are born to David at Hebron: "His firstborn was Amnon . . . his second, Chileab . . . the third, Absalom . . . the fourth, Adonijah . . . the fifth, Shephatiah . . . and the sixth, Ithream" (2 Sam. 3:2–5). The author is painting a vivid portrait of David the patriarch, the potent paterfamilias, who is fulfilling the great command made to Adam in the garden: "Be frutiful and multiply." For the biblical tradition, fecundity in the production of children is a sign not only of physical prowess and economic advantage but also of spiritual favor.[1] Rootedness in the living God produces life at all levels. David is presented here as a new Adam but also as a new Abraham (whose descendants would be more numerous than the stars in the sky), a new Jacob (whose twelve sons gave rise to the twelve tribes), and a new Gideon (who was said to have seventy sons) (Hahn 2012: 30). Furthermore, to the two wives already mentioned, Michal

1. R. R. Reno, *Genesis*, Brazos Theological Commentary on the Bible (Grand Rapids: Brazos, 2010), 56–58.

and Abigail, David adds Ahinoam of Jezreel, Maacah daughter of King Talmai of Geshur, Haggith, Abital, and Eglah—a proper royal harem with some strong political ties, linking David (and hence Israel) to the wider world. The implication seems to be that David's family, taking root in Hebron, will spread out like a great tree. But as Robert Alter observes, the list of David's children, as impressive as it is, also "bristles with future disasters" (Alter 1999: 208). Amnon will rape his half-sister Tamar; Absalom will kill Amnon, rebel against his father, and find himself dangling helpless by his hair from a tree; and Adonijah will be put to death by Solomon. So it goes with the family of Israel, chosen and blessed by Yahweh and always ready to devolve into murderous internecine violence.

As David establishes himself in Hebron, we hear that Abner is "making himself strong in the house of Saul" (2 Sam. 3:6). Saul's son Ishbaal, already a weak and vacillating character, apparently is being gradually co-opted and outmaneuvered by his military commander—a familiar enough scenario in the history of politics. Abner evidently is not particularly interested in being king himself, but he is, like many behind-the-scenes players across the ages, deeply interested in holding the reins of power. One of the ways that he seeks to consolidate his authority is to take as his own a former concubine of King Saul (Alter 1999: 209). In the context of the time, this constituted far more than a man satisfying his sexual desire or his need for intimacy; it was an aggressive political act, for to take a woman of the king was to assert one's superiority over the king. In the same way Absalom, having taken Jerusalem from his father, has sex with a whole harem of David's concubines. This is precisely why Ishbaal takes exception to Abner's move, asking him, "Why have you gone in to my father's concubine?" Abner responds with indignation and, given that he is talking to the king, alarming boldness: "Am I a dog's head for Judah?" (2 Sam. 3:7–8). The dog, of course, is regularly invoked in the biblical literature as a figure of contempt, the opposite of the regal lion (Alter 1999: 209).

That Abner obviously felt that he could get away with such disrespectful speech is perhaps the clearest indication of the weakness of Ishbaal's personality and the precariousness of his political situation. So deeply insulted is Abner that he drops another rhetorical bomb on the king, promising to go over to David and accomplish for him "what the Lord had sworn to David . . . to transfer the kingdom from the house of Saul, and set up the throne of David over Israel and over Judah, from Dan to Beer-sheba" (2 Sam. 3:9–10). It becomes clear here that word of Samuel's anointing of David as king had, to some degree and in certain circles, gotten out. Saul himself, to his infinite chagrin, seems to have been aware that his successor had already been chosen, and now we learn that Saul's military commander was also privy to this disturbing and fascinating truth. There is almost an air of fatalism in Abner's acknowledgment that he has been fighting for the losing side and that he might as well work in accord with God's inevitable purpose. Throughout the Deuteronomistic History, the players on the ground, even as they operate according to perfectly understandable political or psychological motives, are also like pieces on a chessboard, moved by a higher power and for a mysterious purpose. Abner, Saul, and Jonathan seemed to have known that no matter what transpired through their own wills and machinations, David would become king, since that is what Yahweh desired. We will return to this famously complex theme and attempt to make sense of it theologically a bit later in this commentary. In the face of this challenge, all Ishbaal can do is cower in silence. The once mighty house of Saul has dwindled to this frightened forty-year-old king unable to discipline his own military commander.

Abner, as appears to be his wont, acts quickly, sending messengers to David at Hebron, basically promising to bring all of the north over to the son of Jesse. David responds affirmatively but cannily, insisting on the proviso that Abner must return Michal to her husband. After David had fled from Saul, Michal had been given by Saul to another man, Paltiel. Why did David want her back? There might have been some personal interest (though this seems unlikely, given Michal's coldness toward David later in the story), but the dominant concern was clearly political. Tellingly, Michal is referred to here as the "daughter of Saul." By reestablishing his tight relationship with the family of the fallen king, David was shoring up his respectability and his right to make a claim to Saul's crown. After conveying his demand to Abner, David boldly repeats it to Ishbaal himself, reminding the timid king that he (David) had effectively paid for his bride with a hundred Philistine foreskins! Outmaneuvered and abandoned by Abner, Ishbaal meekly acquiesces and takes Michal from the hapless Paltiel in order to mollify David. In one of the most pathetic and touching scenes in the Samuel literature, Paltiel walks behind Michal for quite some time as she is taken away, and all the supplanted husband can do is weep. Finally, Abner barks at him, "Go back home!" (2 Sam. 3:16), and the poor man does as he is told. With typically beautiful understatement, the author, in a few deft lines, draws a contrast between the real affection that Paltiel had for Michal and David's coldly calculating use of her for his own political purposes. This is a harbinger of the surpassingly cold manipulations of both Bathsheba and Uriah, moves that will send David and his kingdom into a tailspin. In line with the typically moralizing exegesis of the church fathers, Augustine provides an interpretation of this scene that more than glosses over David's cruelty. Augustine argues that David, who is willing to take back a wife who had gone over to another man, is a *typos* of Christ, who was compassionate to the woman caught in adultery.[2] I propose that particular reading as a good example of an eisegesis oblivious to the texture, context, and plain sense of the text in question.

Abner is then presented as acting as an agent for David among the elders of Israel, which is to say, the leaders of the northern tribes. He tells them, "For some time past you have been seeking David as king over you. Now then bring it about" (2 Sam. 3:17–18). Is his first statement true? Every indication is that Saul and his allies were in active opposition to David, and one can only guess that at least some in the north were suspicious of the upstart giant killer from Bethlehem who seems to have advanced himself at the expense of Saul. At the same time, the sly Abner might have been appealing to real feelings of resentment against the house of Saul, especially given its failure against the perennial enemy, the Philistines. This could help to explain the thrust of Abner's argument: "For the LORD has promised David: Through my servant David I will save my people Israel from the hand of the Philistines, and from all their enemies" (2 Sam. 3:18). As we have seen, one of the principal tasks of the Adamic king was precisely the holding off of enemies, the clearing away of threats to the flourishing of the garden, and David appears to be a man capable of taking on this responsibility. Robert Polzin indicates that this section of 2 Samuel is marked by comings and goings, criss-crossings of all kinds, journeys in the physical sense that suggest a sort of knitting together of the country (Polzin 1993: 39). After speaking to his own people in the north, Abner also speaks "directly to the Benjaminites; then Abner went to tell David at Hebron" (2 Sam. 3:19). Performing a kind of shuttle diplomacy, Abner reconnects the tribes in anticipation of David's ascension to leadership. The visit of Saul's former commander to David's seat at Hebron is the culmination of this diplomatic and political tour de force.

Sensing the importance of what Abner has accomplished as well as appreciating the risks that Ishbaal's underling had taken, David throws a great banquet for his erstwhile rival. The meal, of course, is an enduring biblical symbol for the coming together of God's people.[3] In the Genesis telling, trouble began with a bad meal: the eating of the fruit of the tree of the knowledge of good and evil. Peppered

2. Augustine, "Adulterous Marriages 5," in *Joshua, Judges, Ruth, 1–2 Samuel*, ed. John R. Franke, Ancient Christian Commentary on Scripture: Old Testament 4 (Downers Grove, IL: InterVarsity, 2005), 338.

3. Robert Barron, *Eucharist*, Catholic Spirituality for Adults (Maryknoll, NY: Orbis Books, 2008), 32–33.

throughout the scriptures, meals are evocations of God's fellowship with us and of our communion with one another. Think of the meal prepared by Abraham for his three mysterious visitors at the oaks of Mamre (Gen. 18:1–8), the Passover meal of the escaping Israelites (Exod. 12:1–20), the sumptuous meal of pure choice wines and juicy red meats spread out by God on his holy mountain in Isaiah's prophecy (Isa. 25:6), or Jesus's open table fellowship and his last meal of fellowship with his apostles. All of these represent undoings of the dysfunctional eating on display in the garden of Eden. Thus, the sharing of food between David and Abner is a sacrament of unity, a symbol and cause of the gathering of the tribes around one figure.

Understandably pleased that his dream of kingship had at last come true, David sends Abner home "in peace," a phrase repeated, to ironic effect, three times in this section (Alter 1999: 212). Quite often in the biblical narratives, the work of unity is invariably shadowed by the threat of violence and division. Even as Jesus sits in fellowship with his disciples at the Last Supper, he says, "But see, the one who betrays me is with me, and his hand is on the table" (Luke 22:21). Just after Abner left "in peace," a number of David's men arrive bearing spoil from a raid. With them is Joab, the son of Zeruiah and brother of Asahel, whom Abner had killed at Gibeon. Filled with righteous indignation that David had allowed this killer to go free, Joab confronts the king: "What have you done? . . . You know that Abner son of Ner came to deceive you, and to learn your comings and goings and to learn all that you are doing" (2 Sam. 3:24–25). Is Joab really concerned that Abner might be a spy, or is he perhaps fearful that his northern counterpart might usurp him as head of the military in David's new kingdom? Is he still smarting over the death of Asahel? The sons of Zeruiah are always hotheaded, but there is more than intemperance here. Joab is speaking in the cadences and tones of the serpent, unduly planting suspicion and stirring up dissension without cause. He is nullifying the unifying effects of David's banquet and hence anticipating the role played by Judas at a banquet offered by the one called "the Son of David."

After delivering this threatening and disrespectful speech, Joab simply leaves the presence of David unrebuked and apparently unrestrained. A cynical reading of this passage might suggest that the clever David, who had dealt with the machinations and duplicities of Saul and certainly understood that Joab had motives for doing harm to Abner, was quietly allowing his nephew to do his dirty work even as the king retained plausible deniability.[4] On the other hand, there seemed to be little for David to gain from the death of Abner, a man who was in a position

4. Robert Pinsky, *The Life of David* (New York: Schocken, 2005), 76–77.

to rally much-needed northern support for David and who had clearly grown exasperated with Ishbaal. Therefore it is probably safest to conclude that David was sincerely attempting to work with Abner and was, if anything, guilty of not sufficiently reining in his headstrong nephew. This "bad fathering" on the part of David—a trait he shares, to some degree, with Eli—is a theme to which we will return later in the commentary (Polzin 1993: 52–53). At any rate, unbeknownst to David, Joab sends messengers ahead to track down Abner and invite him back to Hebron. Pretending that he wants to speak with his counterpart privately, Joab takes Abner into a gateway and stabs him in the abdomen. "So he died for shedding the blood of Asahel, Joab's brother" (2 Sam. 3:27). Though Joab pretends this is a case of "an eye for an eye," or "belly stab for belly stab," there is actually little in common between the two slayings. Abner killed Asahel on the field of battle after repeatedly warning the younger man to turn aside; Joab murdered Abner in cold blood after deceptively insinuating friendship. Later, the imprudent Joab will commit a similar murder, the killing of the rebellious Absalom, against the express wish of David. Though they run counter to David's intentions, Joab's rash moves serve to advance the king's cause and, indirectly, God's own purposes. Once again God's transcendence makes possible a noncompetitive synergy with finite freedom, even when that freedom is twisted in sin.

David's immediate reaction to the murder is to distance himself from it in no uncertain terms: "I and my kingdom are forever guiltless before the Lord for the blood of Abner son of Ner" (2 Sam. 3:28). This doubtless was good politics, but it was also utterly congruent with David's stance of nonviolence toward the house of Saul. Though he is assuredly a man of war, David exhibits a strange streak of peacefulness, especially in regard to his coming to power. He goes so far as to walk behind the funeral bier of Abner and compose an elegy for his fallen rival—not as fine, of course, as his song to Saul and Jonathan, but impressive enough in its sincerity and concision of expression. He laments that Abner, who had never fallen captive during his career as a warrior, was made to "die as a fool dies" (2 Sam. 3:33). Ambrose and other church fathers praise the tremendous magnanimity displayed in David's attitude toward his fallen rival, so unlike Saul's petty resentment: "He [David] admired Abner, the bravest champion of the opposing side, while he was their leader and was yet waging war. Nor did he despise Abner when suing for peace, but honored him by a banquet. When killed by treachery, David mourned and wept for him."[5] It is impossible for Christians to miss the link to Jesus, whose

5. Ambrose, "Duties of the Clergy," in Franke, *Joshua, Judges, Ruth, 1–2 Samuel*, 339.

coming to power is thoroughly marked by a nonviolent engagement of those who would block him and whose "reign" reaches its fulfillment as he suffers on an instrument of torture and offers forgiveness to his killers.

That David is not utterly devoted to the path of nonviolence, however, becomes plain in the next verse, as he utters a "first-class curse" (Alter 1999: 214) against Joab: "May the guilt fall on the head of Joab, and on all his father's house; and may the house of Joab never be without one who has a discharge, or who is leprous, or who holds a spindle, or who falls by the sword, or who lacks food!" (2 Sam. 3:29). He is wishing the worst things that could befall a male in the culture of that time: a painful infection of the penis, a skin disease that would distance him from community life, reduction to woman's work, death in war, and starvation. Despite this horrific curse, David does not move against Joab in any significant way; rather, he keeps him on as his chief military commander. The blood guilt that Joab bore for the killings of Abner and Absalom would one day fall on Joab's head but only after the death of David. Because Joab backed Adonijah in the period after David's demise, Solomon, once be became king, hunted down Joab and had him put to death. In his speech justifying this bloody act, Solomon explicitly mentions Joab's murder of "a man more righteous than himself," Abner (1 Kgs. 2:32). Once again, that relentless, even dreadful, biblical law of karma is at work. Though it might take time and might not manifest itself as one would reasonably expect, God's justice prevails. The biblical authors certainly do not turn a blind eye to human wickedness, but they are, for the most part, convinced that a deep moral order grounded in God's providence obtains in the world.

2 SAMUEL 4

All of twelve verses long, the fourth chapter is the shortest one in 2 Samuel, and its function is transitional, for it recounts the clearing of the last hurdle before David's accession to kingship of a united Israel, which will be the focus of the fifth chapter. As the chapter opens, we are reintroduced to Ishbaal, who, having heard of the murder of Abner, is more frightened and ineffectual than ever. The author says, with delicious understatement, "His courage failed, and all Israel was dismayed" (2 Sam. 4:1). There is an interesting and contrasting parallel here to the coming together of the nation that will occur around the courage, vision, and virtue of David. Both Ishbaal and David are heads of "mystical bodies" that participate in the qualities of their respective leaders—the first to dissolution, the second to organic unity. Ishbaal's cowardice and bad leadership conduce toward dissension and civil strife (as will be the case later with David himself). Two of Ishbaal's own captains, Baanah and Rechab, sensing the inevitability of David's rise, conspire to kill their own king.

But before we read the story of their attack on Ishbaal, the author compels us to consider Mephibosheth, the son of Jonathan, who was crippled as a child when he fell from his nurse's arms as she hastened to flee after hearing the dreadful news from Mount Gilboa. One might wonder why this figure is mentioned precisely at this point in the narrative. The author probably wants to make clear that, with the death of Ishbaal, there would be an heir of Saul fit to assume command. Both the pusillanimity of Ishbaal and the physical disability of Mephibosheth function as apt expressions of the collapse of the house of Saul. The author is also preparing us for one of the most touching stories within the Samuel literature, the account of David's kindness to the grandson of his mortal enemy and the son of his best friend.

After this interlude concerning Mephibosheth, the author returns to the story of the murder of Ishbaal. Baanah and Rechab sneak up on the king as he is taking his midday siesta. The image of sleeping in the middle of the day suggests weakness, even corruption. We will see in just a few chapters that David's adultery with Bathsheba follows immediately upon a lengthy nap that the king enjoyed, even as his troops were out fighting a war without the benefit of his leadership. One might also recall Eli, slumbering in the temple, inattentive both to the complaints of his people and to the voice of God (1 Sam. 3:2). The murder itself is simply and graphically described: "Now they had come into the house while he was lying on his couch in his bedchamber; they attacked him, killed him, and beheaded him" (2 Sam. 4:7). The double mention of the fact that Ishbaal is asleep serves to remind us of the nefariousness and cowardliness of the act by Baanah and Rechab. The two murderers, eagerly currying favor with the new king but obviously oblivious to what David does to those who bring him news of the death of his enemies, hurry through the night, carrying the head of Ishbaal to Hebron. They present the severed head to the king, announcing that Yahweh had "avenged my lord the king this day on Saul and on his offspring" (2 Sam. 4:8). In the Bible it is almost invariably a bad idea to seek to do the work of God's justice on one's own. The apostle Paul speaks for the mainstream of the scriptural tradition when he says, "Beloved, never avenge yourselves, but leave room for the wrath of God; for it is written, 'Vengeance is mine, I will repay, says the Lord'" (Rom. 12:19). Like the Amalekite who finished off Saul, these two killers take it upon themselves to attack the anointed of Yahweh, but at least the Amalekite's act took place on a battlefield against an armed soldier. Baanah and Rechab murder a defenseless man while he sleeps in his own home. Therefore David orders their immediate execution and goes a step beyond, commanding the mutilation of their corpses: "They cut off their hands and feet, and hung their bodies beside the pool at Hebron" (2 Sam. 4:12). The macabre display with which this brief chapter ends is meant to suggest that these figures are forces of dissolution who cut up the mystical body of Israel, which David will attempt to assemble (Alter 1999: 219).

Once more, David's unwillingness to attack any members of the house of Saul signals his patient acceptance of Yahweh's plan, however confounding and slow in development it might prove to be. David consistently submits to the demands and rhythms of the theo-drama rather than press the agenda of his own ego-drama.

2 SAMUEL 5

With Saul dead, Mephibosheth crippled, and both Abner and Ishbaal out of the picture, David emerges naturally as the inevitable king of a united Israel: "Then all the tribes of Israel came to David at Hebron" (2 Sam. 5:1). He does not force the issue through conquest or threats; they come to him, drawn magnetically. David becomes the still point around which the entire nation composes itself, like the medallions of a rose window around the center. This theme of a gathered nation is central to the biblical narrative, for Israel's unity in praise and purpose is the condition for the possibility of the gathering of the entire world around the true God. It represents the reversal of the centrifugal force of the original sin, which sent Adam and Eve out of the garden. From an extraordinary abundance of texts dealing with the ingathering of Israel and the world, I will choose just a handful: "He will raise a signal for the nations, and will assemble the outcasts of Israel, and gather the dispersed of Judah from the far corners of the earth" (Isa. 11:12); "Do not fear, for I am with you; I will bring your offspring from the east, and from the west I will gather you" (Isa. 43:5); "Then I myself will gather the remnant of my flock out of all the lands where I have driven them, and I will bring them back to their fold, and they shall be fruitful and multiply" (Jer. 23:3); "I will let you find me, says the LORD, and I will restore your fortunes and gather you from all the nations" (Jer. 29:14); "Thus says the Lord GOD: I will gather you from the peoples, and assemble you out of the countries where you have been scattered" (Ezek. 11:17); "Thus says the Lord GOD: when I gather the house of Israel from the peoples among whom they are scattered, and manifest my holiness in them in the sight of the nations, then they shall settle on their own soil that I gave to my servant Jacob" (Ezek. 28:25). To be sure, these passages make more or less explicit reference to the gathering in of postexilic Israel and hence to a period chronologically well past the time narrated in 2 Samuel. Nevertheless, the motif of united Israel/united world is clear and consistent throughout the Old Testament.

Having come to David, the elders of the tribes say, "Look, we are your bone and flesh" (2 Sam. 5:1). They cannot mean a physical, tribal connection, for these are not men of Judah, but they do indeed assert that David is the head under which a kind of mystical body can form. No one familiar with the Bible can miss the connection between this language and the words used by Adam of Eve: "This at last is bone of my bones and flesh of my flesh" (Gen. 2:23). What the elders of Israel are proposing is a sort of marriage between themselves and David, a joining together of what had become separated, a union that will result in fruitfulness. Most Christians will recognize the link between this description of David's relationship to Israel and Paul's description of Jesus's relationship to the church: "He [Christ] is the head of the body, the church" (Col. 1:18); and "now you are the body of Christ and individually members of it" (1 Cor. 12:27). David is more than a skilled political leader who protects and directs his people, and Jesus is more than a prophet or rabbi who inspires the nation; both are the agents by which a people finds its cohesiveness, sacraments that effect what they signify. As N. T. Wright argues, one of the principal messianic tasks that Jesus, the Son of David, undertook was none other than the gathering of the scattered tribes.[1] When Jesus used language about the coming of the kingdom of God, he was understood to mean that the tribes of Israel, exiled by the Assyrians and then by the Babylonians and divided by their own sinfulness, were coming back together. In fact, much of the ministry of Jesus—his open table fellowship; his outreach to sinners, the sick, and the marginalized; his conversations with the woman at the well, Zacchaeus, and Matthew the tax collector; his journeys into Samaria, the decapolis, and the region of Caesarea Philippi; and his consistent offer of forgiveness—can be construed as a mission to knit the unraveled nation back together. Furthermore, the Israel united under Jesus was meant to become the vehicle for the unification of the world, which explains precisely what Paul was up to. Hurtling around his world as energetically as he could, Paul announced to the Gentiles that they had a new Lord; *Iēsous Kyrios* (Jesus [is] Lord) is his gospel in a nutshell.[2] David becoming king in Hebron is both a new Adam coming to

1. N. T. Wright, *Jesus and the Victory of God*, Christian Origins and the Question of God 2 (Minneapolis: Fortress, 1996), 104.

2. Robert Barron, *Catholicism: A Journey to the Heart of the Faith* (New York: Image, 2011), 34.

reign over a reconstituted Eden and a prototype of the Christ, destined to reign over a mystical body encompassing, in principle, all the world.

Revealing that they know something of Samuel's anointing of the shepherd boy of Bethlehem, the elders say, "For some time, while Saul was king over us, it was you who led out Israel and brought it in. The LORD said to you: It is you who shall be shepherd of my people Israel" (2 Sam. 5:2). It is not primarily David's military prowess that recommends him to them but rather the fact that he was charismatically chosen. Once more the author signals the subtle and noninvasive manner in which God works his purpose out: precisely through the affairs of human beings, which are utterly explicable on ordinary psychological and political grounds. The trope of shepherd is picked up throughout the scriptures, most notably by Ezekiel, who speaks of the wicked shepherds (kings) of Israel who have left the sheep wandering leaderless on the hillsides. It is of supreme importance that Ezekiel imagines Yahweh himself coming in time to shepherd his flock, a view reflected in Ps. 22. Reading these passages together with the references to the kingship of David and his descendants, an extraordinary conclusion emerges: Yahweh becomes king through an earthly king.[3] The good rule of David (and his definitive son, Jesus) is the means by which the good rule of Yahweh expresses itself in the world.

David, we are told, was thirty years old when he was anointed by the elders at Hebron. Is there any great significance in the age of the king? In Numbers 4:3 we learn that God instructed Moses and Aaron to choose priests from the Kohathites, a subset of the Levites, and he specified that they must be no younger than thirty years old. The author of 2 Samuel seems to be hinting that from the moment of his anointing as king, David was also identified as a priest; indeed, the priestliness of David is especially emphasized in the stories concerning his taking and dedicating of Jerusalem, which follow immediately.[4] Moreover, the Christian reader will recognize a link to Christ. In the Gospel of Luke we hear that "Jesus was about thirty years old when he began his work" (Luke 3:23), a work that would be decidedly kingly and priestly. And speaking of numbers, the author goes to the trouble of specifying that David's reign in Hebron covered seven years and six months, and his reign in Jerusalem covered another thirty-three years, giving him forty years as king overall. Though the mention of the extra six months in Hebron compromises this schema a bit, it is clear that these are symbolically important numbers, for

3. N. T. Wright, *How God Became King: The Forgotten Story of the Gospels* (New York: HarperOne, 2012), 185–96.

4. A. A. Anderson, *2 Samuel*, Word Biblical Commentary 11 (Dallas: Word, 1989), 77.

both "seven" and "forty" are evocative of perfection and completeness. "Seven" is the Sabbath number and the figure associated with the cutting of covenants, and "forty" is used to designate the fullness of time that Moses spent with God on Mount Sinai, that the Israelites wandered in the desert before entering the promised land, and that many of the judges ruled. The clear implication is that David's government is not simply the reign of a political lord of Israel from the Late Bronze Age but also a mystical reign; it references both the rule of Adam, which was meant to be perfect but was interrupted by sin, and also the definitive rule of the one whose governance would transcend time (Alter 1999: 221).

What follows immediately in the narrative is of tremendous historical and theological significance. David's first move upon being made king of a united country is to establish himself in a new capital city: "The king and his men marched to Jerusalem against the Jebusites" (2 Sam. 5:6). Why would David be so interested in this particular city? First, the experienced warrior would have recognized the obvious tactical advantages of establishing himself in high-ridged Jerusalem, a natural citadel. Second, the one who wanted above all to unite north and south would have appreciated the geographical value of Jerusalem, which lies more or less on the dividing line between Israel and Judah. But I would like to tease out some other, more symbolic reasons why this town was of such significance to David and the author of the Samuel books. Prior to this reference, there are only a few scattered mentions of Jerusalem in the Deuteronomistic History, mostly having to do with the stubborn opposition that the inhabitants of Jerusalem offered against the invading Israelites. Though the invaders managed to conquer most of the land around it, Jerusalem remained unvanquished and in the hands of the Jebusites. Therefore David's eventual victory over this famously resistant city symbolically represents the completion of the incursions that Joshua led several hundred years before.[5]

There is one curious reference to Jerusalem in 1 Samuel. Just after the slaying of Goliath, David joins the Israelites in pursuing the fleeing Philistines, but upon his return, he "took the head of the Philistine and brought it to Jerusalem" (1 Sam. 17:54). Was this a threat? Was it a sign that the Jebusites there were at least somewhat sympathetic to David? Was Jerusalem an ally of Israel in the struggle against the Philistines? We are given no indication in the text concerning how to answer these questions. Perhaps the author means it to be an anticipation of David's eventual conquest of the city and as a rather bold affirmation of David's kingly

5. Ibid.

willingness to put to death that which threatens the flourishing of the garden of Israel. Adam did not crush the head of the serpent, but David cut off the head of Goliath and placed it as a kind of trophy in what would be the capital city of the new Eden. Another reason why Jerusalem is singled out is, perhaps, its association with the mysterious figure of Melchizedek, identified as a "king of Salem" and "priest of God Most High" (Gen. 14:18). Though it is not entirely clear from the language of Genesis, the connection between Salem and David's Jerusalem is made in Psalms: "His abode has been established in Salem, his dwelling place in Zion" (Ps. 76:2). Melchizedek is both a king and a priest, for we hear that he "brought out bread and wine" and blessed Abraham in the name of the "maker of heaven and earth" (Gen. 14:18–19; Hahn 2012: 53).

Once more David, precisely as the conqueror of Melchizedek's city, is presented as both political and cultic leader of the nation, an association famously celebrated in Ps. 110. As the new king is crowned, the psalmist sings, "The LORD has sworn and will not change his mind, 'You are a priest forever according to the order of Melchizedek'" (v. 4). Political and spiritual ordering are the tasks of the Davidic priest-king of Salem, and they will be the tasks of the definitive priest-king of Salem, Jesus Christ. The author of the Letter to the Hebrews makes this link explicit: "Although he was a Son, he learned obedience through what he suffered; and having been made perfect, he became the source of eternal salvation for all who obey him, having been designated by God a high priest according to the order of Melchizedek" (Heb. 5:8–10). I agree with Scott Hahn, who speaks of David (and Christ) as leaders of a "liturgical empire," a kingly order based upon the right praise of God (Hahn 2012: 58–61).

As David and his men approach the walls and ramparts of the Jebusite city, they are met by a curious taunt: "You will not come in here, even the blind and the lame will turn you back" (2 Sam. 5:6). The scholarly consensus is that the Hebrew here is more than a little ambiguous; consequently, the meaning of the taunt is muddy. Does it mean that even the blind and lame will be strong and skilled enough to defeat David? Or is it perhaps a sort of curse implying that David's men will be like those unfortunates if they dare to attack? At any rate, we are left with a curious impression of Jerusalem, a city in which the severed head of Goliath rests and on whose walls stand a ragtag band of the sightless and the crippled. Are we meant, once more, to have the sense that Jerusalem is a place of dysfunction and disorder, a sad holdout against righteous Israel, a microcosm of the fallen world? Despite its fortifications and its geographical advantage, Jerusalem falls easily to David, whose men make their way up the underground water supply into the city.

The Chronicler adds the historically plausible detail that David offers a reward to the first man able to breach the defenses of the city, which inspires Joab to make a special effort, resulting in his being rewarded with command of David's army (1 Chr. 11:6). This certainly jibes with the general sense one has of Joab as a daring, even rash, adventurer, and it helps to explain David's loyalty to him despite his nephew's consistent tendency to question and challenge the king.

Having overtaken Jerusalem, David "occupied the stronghold, and named it the city of David," and he "built the city all around from the Millo inward" (2 Sam. 5:9). Eden was meant to be defended ground, but the first king failed to keep out what should have been kept out. The ark of Noah was strongly built and covered in bitumen both inside and out in order to keep the floodwaters at bay and preserve the life within; now David's capital, meant to be the focal point of a properly ordered new creation, has to be fortified, defended, and clear in its distinctive identity. The maintenance of the walls of Jerusalem emerges as a key biblical motif: when Israel allowed those walls to be breached—most infamously at the time of the Babylonian captivity—it lost its integrity and hence found its mission on behalf of the wider world fatally compromised. When Nehemiah led the restoration of the nation after the Babylonian exile, he commanded, first and foremost, the rebuilding of the walls of Jerusalem (Neh. 2:17), and his priestly counterpart, Ezra, read the law to the people who gathered behind those rebuilt defenses (Neh. 8:1–8). Both were essential acts of reintegration, recapitulations of David's act of fortifying his capital city.

The account of David's conquest of Jerusalem concludes with the simple observation, "And David became greater and greater, for the LORD, the God of hosts, was with him" (2 Sam. 5:10). This tagline is properly characterized as the pithy conclusion to the story of David's rise, which commenced with the anointing by Samuel and led, through endless twists and turns, to the establishment of David as undisputed and adequately defended king of a united Israel. In a sense, this is the end to a much longer and more complex story that began with the expulsion of the first king from his poorly defended kingdom and led through Abraham, Isaac, Jacob, Joseph, Moses, Joshua, the judges, Samuel, and Saul to the point where a new Adam could become king of a new Eden.

Once Jerusalem is established as the capital of a united nation, it begins to have its magnetic effect: "King Hiram of Tyre sent messengers to David, along with cedar trees, and carpenters and masons who built David a house" (2 Sam. 5:11). Read along purely political lines, Hiram's gift might be seen as a subtle diplomatic move, an attempt to mollify a powerful neighbor. But read through a theological lens, the gift represents one of the first indications that the Adamic mission of Israel—the Edenization of the world—is being successfully carried out. The precise nature of Hiram's donation is interesting for at least two reasons. First, by helping to build the palace of David, he provides the most vivid indicator of the king's establishment and staying power; he, a foreigner, writes a fitting climax to the story of David's rise to power as king of Israel. Second, the "house" of David is an absolutely central theme in the Samuel literature, since it calls to mind both the dynasty that would flow from David and the great house of Yahweh, the temple that Solomon would build. (Indeed, if this Hiram of Tyre is the same king who provided supplies for Solomon's building project, the incident described must have taken place somewhat late in David's career and hence is out of place this early in the story.) The foreignness of Hiram is an important sign that non-Jews would in time be summoned to worship at the house of Yahweh.

In the immediate wake of the construction of his palace, "David then perceived that the LORD had established him king over Israel, and that he had exalted his kingdom for the sake of his people Israel" (2 Sam. 5:12). Had he not perceived this when the elders came together at Hebron? Or when he conquered Jerusalem? Why would the building of his house particularly trigger David's awareness of his sovereignty? It had to be the "international" quality of Hiram's gift. David knew that he was king of the nation intended to gather the world precisely when a non-Israelite king acknowledged him. A further sign of the consolidation of David's kingship is the numerous concubines and wives he takes, which results in a small army of children. Along with the six children mentioned earlier whom David fathered in Hebron, we now hear of eleven more offspring whom David fathered while he was king in Jerusalem: "Shammua, Shobab, Nathan, Solomon, Ibhar, Elishua, Nepheg, Japhia, Elishama, Eliada, and Eliphelet" (2 Sam. 5:14–16). Besides demonstrating the love for lists of names evident throughout the Bible, the author, in this context, bothers to spell out each of David's offspring in order to show as concretely as possible how the king is fulfilling the command to Adam to go forth and multiply as well as ratifying the covenant promise to Abraham that he would be the father of innumerable descendants. As is typical of the author of the Samuel literature and indeed of the Old Testament authors in general, this high theological observation is coupled with a keen sense of the realities on the ground. David's somewhat irresponsible choice of numerous wives and concubines results in at least the seventeen children who are explicitly named. This large coterie of offspring, whom David never manages adequately to discipline, will be the source of unremitting suffering in the wake of the Bathsheba incident. Once more David is presented as the Adamic king in both his prefall and postfall phases.

None of David's moves has, of course, gone unnoticed by the Philistines. After the battle of Mount Gilboa, the Philistines surely felt that Israel was finished as a political and military rival. Furthermore, they had at least some confidence that the most charismatic leader remaining in Israel was in fact one of their vassals. David's anointing at Hebron and his taking of Jerusalem would have disabused them of both of these notions. Accordingly, "all the Philistines went up in search of David" (2 Sam. 5:17). Though valid, this purely political reading does not constitute a sufficient account of this opposition. We have come to expect from the sweep of the Old Testament narrative that whenever Israel is strengthened or united or under powerful leadership, it should expect opposition. The serpent, the floodwaters, Pharoah, the Amalekites, and the Philistines, along with many others, represent the powers opposed to the purposes of God (Beale 2011: 58–63). The kings of Israel are meant to succeed where the first Adam failed; that is, they are meant to protect the garden from invasion by destructive forces. Therefore, David springs into action.

When, some thousand years after the events described here, a new David appears, he is met immediately with opposition: "When King Herod heard this, he was frightened, and all Jerusalem with him" (Matt. 2:3). So acute was this fear and so violent this opposition that Herod tried to stamp out the invader, killing every child in Bethlehem under the age of two. Herod attacked David's city and attempted to crush under his heel any infant messiah, any pretender to the throne of David, who might threaten him. In Luke's account of the nativity we find a similar motif. Luke commences his story the way one would expect an encomium or poem in the ancient world to begin, with the mention of mighty political and military players: "In those days a decree went out from Emperor Augustus that all the world should be registered. This was the first registration and was taken while Quirinius was governor of Syria" (Luke 2:1–2). But Luke pulls an extraordinary reversal, for his story is not about those worldly leaders; rather, it concerns an ordinary couple making their way from one unknown outpost of Augustus's empire to another. Luke proposes the child born of Mary in David's city as a rival emperor, not ensconced in a palace but born in a cave; not rangy in freedom but wrapped in swaddling clothes; not well-fed but placed in a manger; not supported by a worldly army but by an angelic host. Augustus and his servants are presented as the latest iteration of the Philistines, Egyptians, and

Amalekites—enemies of God's purposes.[6] The life of this son of David unfolds as an unremitting struggle against these opponents until it culminates with his execution by order of the Roman emperor's local representative. Jesus allowed the darkness of the world—cruelty, hatred, betrayal, denial, institutional injustice, and plain stupidity—to overwhelm him, but then he swallowed up that darkness in the infinite ocean of the divine mercy. That is precisely how he fought, employing a sort of divine aikido, the martial art that cunningly redirects an opponent's aggression and momentum back against the opponent.[7] All of the moves of the kings of Israel that preceded Jesus's move were but foreshadowings, imperfect anticipations of the final and victorious strategy.

We hear that the Philistines established themselves in the valley of Rephaim, which is just to the west of Jerusalem. David's first move is to ask for God's guidance: "Shall I go up against the Philistines? Will you give them into my hand?" (2 Sam. 5:19). Throughout his career, David invoked Yahweh, which was the key to his success. He consistently situated his own decision making within the framework and under the aegis of God's holy purpose. Like all of the other great heroes of Israel, he implicitly grasped the truth of Isaiah's claim, "O LORD, you will ordain peace for us, for indeed, all that we have done, you have done for us" (Isa. 26:12). Precisely because of the divine transcendence, God's activity is not competitive with ours; rather, it grounds and enhances finite freedom. Upon receiving word of God's support, David goes forth with confidence and breaks through the Philistine line, inspiring him to comment, "The LORD has burst forth against my enemies before me, like a bursting flood" (2 Sam. 5:20). But David's conquest is much more than a military victory; it is also a kind of theological triumph, for we hear that the Philistines "abandoned their idols there, and David and his men carried them away" (2 Sam. 5:21). For the biblical authors, the principal problem is always idolatry—that is, suspension of orthodoxy, bad worship. I will say much more about this in the next chapter, but for now suffice it to say that the improper orientation of the heart toward a good other than God leads necessarily to a disintegration of the self, a falling apart and a falling away. All sin is predicated finally upon this primordial dysfunction. At this point in the narrative David is a man of right praise and hence able consistently to triumph over an idolatrous people. The king's troubles will come, as we will see, precisely from his heterodoxy.

Despite their reversal, the Philistines regroup and face David again in the valley of Rephaim. The king once more turns to Yahweh, who offers some canny

6. Wright, *How God Became King*, 129–47.
7. Barron, *Catholicism*, 50.

military advice: "You shall not go up; go around to their rear, and come upon them opposite the balsam trees" (2 Sam. 5:23). We see here the typical cleverness of the one who had outmaneuvered Goliath and successfully evaded the army of Saul, but David's humble willingness to be instructed by Yahweh is also on display, even in matters of detail. Yahweh tells David to strike when he hears the sound of marching in the branches of the balsam trees. David obeys and strikes down the Philistines. One might interpret this as a wind blowing through the trees, which successfully masks the sound of the marching Israelite army. One might construe it as heavenly aid, or perhaps as both, since God works through secondary causes. The fundamental point, which is made by spiritual writers across the centuries and across cultures, is that spiritual aid comes to those who have surrendered to the will and purpose of God. When you throw in your lot with God, God will fight for you and with you.

2 SAMUEL 6

With the defeat of the Philistines in the valley of Rephaim, David's consolidation of kingly leadership is, from a political standpoint, more or less complete. He emerges as the new Adam, leader of a properly defended Eden. But there was more to Adam than kingliness. The first man was presented by the rabbis of the intertestamental period and by the church fathers as priest as well as king. Walking in easy fellowship with Yahweh, Adam naturally occupied the stance of adoration, a word derived from *adoratio* (*ad ora*; literally, "to the mouth").[1] To adore is to be mouth to mouth with God, breathing in his divine life and breathing out praise. The opening line of Song of Songs—"let him kiss me with the kisses of his mouth!" (Song 1:1)—can be seen not only as a cry of erotic desire but also as a longing of the soul for worship.[2] Mouth to mouth, one is "reconciled" to God, and eyelash to eyelash with him as well. So aligned, everything in the worshiper becomes properly ordered.[3] In the attitude of adoration, Adam was, accordingly, the first priest, and the ordered garden that surrounded him can be construed as the primordial temple. Right praise (orthodoxy) leads to the right ordering of the person who gives praise, and it also conduces toward the right ordering of the family, community, society, and cosmos that surrounds that person. In this context, we can understand a remark often associated with Dorothy Day and Peter Maurin, the founders of the Catholic Worker Movement: "Cult cultivates

1. Robert Barron, *Catholicism: A Journey to the Heart of the Faith* (New York: Image, 2011), 21.
2. Bernard of Clairvaux, "Sermons on the Song of Songs," in *Bernard of Clairvaux: Selected Works*, trans. G. R. Evans (New York: Paulist Press, 1987), 213.
3. Barron, *Catholicism*, 271–73.

the culture."[4] Business, finance, politics, sports, the arts, entertainment, and so on—all these find their proper place and realize their proper finality when they are grounded in the praise of God. One could read the liturgical prayer, "Glory to God in the highest, and on earth peace to people of good will," not only as a word of praise but also as a kind of formula: when glory is given to God above all things, then peace breaks out among us.

I have shown that the original sin can be appreciated as the result of bad kingly leadership on the part of the first king; in light of the clarifications just made, it might also be appreciated as the suspension of right praise, the consequence of a failure in priesthood. When Adam and Eve listened to the voice of the serpent and disobeyed the command of God, they fell out of the stance of adoration and ordered their hearts away from the unconditioned good. This led to interior disintegration: the falling apart of mind from flesh, soul from body, intention from action, and so on. It also gave rise, as I pointed out earlier, to the disintegration of community and alienation from nature. The expulsion of Adam and Eve from the garden should not be interpreted as a sentence passed by an insulted deity but rather as the inevitable consequence of bad praise. When something other than God is given glory in the highest, the garden turns into a desert. Therefore the entirety of the biblical narrative could be read as the story of God's attempts to lure his people back into right praise, not because God needs such devotion but precisely because such devotion is tantamount to human flourishing.[5]

When sin resulted in the destruction of the entirety of the created order, God sent a rescue operation in the form of a great ship on which a microcosm of Eden was preserved.[6] This is why Noah can be read as a priestly figure presiding over a tiny remnant where right praise was practiced. Once the floodwaters receded, Noah the priest offered a sacrifice to Yahweh and allowed the good order that he had preserved to flood the world, reconstituting it as a temple. As Yahweh shaped his people Israel, he consistently coupled covenant with sacrificial worship.[7] Thus Abram, having heard the promise that his descendants would be more numerous than the stars, was asked to sacrifice five animals to Yahweh, cutting their bodies in two. Moses received the word of Yahweh on Mount Sinai and then slaughtered bulls and sprinkled their blood on the altar and on the people. In

4. Dorothy Day, *The Long Loneliness: The Autobiography of Dorothy Day* (Chicago: Thomas More, 1952), 203.

5. Matthew Levering, *Ezra and Nehemiah*, Brazos Theological Commentary on the Bible (Grand Rapids: Brazos, 2007), 19.

6. Barron, *Catholicism*, 150.

7. Levering, *Ezra and Nehemiah*, 51–52.

Exodus, Leviticus, and Deuteronomy we read detailed prescriptions governing the offering of sacrifice to Yahweh, oblations that took place in a tabernacle or tent sanctuary that accompanied the wandering people in the desert. Why was the worship that Yahweh demanded sacrificial in form? Prior to the fall, adoration was effortless; but after the tumble into sin, right praise came only at a cost. This is because heterodoxy twisted the human person out of shape, setting mind against will, body against spirit, passion against passion, and so on. The recovery of one's spiritual equilibrium, therefore, was necessarily painful. The action of bringing an animal to the tabernacle (and later to the temple) for sacrifice was an implicit statement that what was happening to that animal should by rights be happening to the offerer of sacrifice.[8]

At the heart of the tabernacle was the ark of the covenant, the gold-plated box of acacia wood that housed the remnants of the tablets of the law, the rod of Aaron, and some pieces of manna—all reminders of the exodus journey and the Sinai covenant. This ark became the focus of Israelite worship, both a sign of Yahweh's presence among his people and a pledge of the people's obedience. Like Noah's ark, it was a microcosm of Eden, creation rightly ordered around the praise of God. This is precisely why the ark was carried by Israel into battle. In the book of Numbers we hear, "Whenever the ark set out, Moses would say, 'Arise, O LORD, and let your enemies be scattered, and your foes flee before you'" (Num. 10:35). The task of the kingly and priestly people of Israel was to Edenize the world, and hence they would carry this emblem of Eden before them when they met the enemies of Yahweh. One of the central tragedies of Israelite history is described in 1 Samuel, the loss of the ark during a disastrous battle with the Philistines: "So the Philistines fought; Israel was defeated, and they fled, everyone to his home. There was a very great slaughter, for there fell of Israel thirty thousand foot soldiers. The ark of God was captured; and the two sons of Eli, Hophni and Phinehas, died" (1 Sam. 4:10–11). This represents a collosal failure of the kingly and priestly mission of Israel, the collective Adam.

But in the somewhat comical section of 1 Samuel commonly referred to as the "ark narrative," we see that the power of the true God is greater than that of the false gods that can beguile the human heart. When the ark of the covenant is brought into the "house of Dagon," the shrine to the gods of the Philistines, the idols collapse before it: "But when they rose early on the next morning, Dagon had fallen on his face to the ground before the ark of the LORD" (1 Sam. 5:4)

8. Margaret Barker, *The Great High Priest: The Temple Roots of Christian Liturgy* (London: T&T Clark, 2003), 53.

(Murphy 2010: 43–44). This is much more than an affirmation that one particular ancient Near Eastern god is more powerful than another; it is a showing forth of this absolutely central theme that human flourishing is a consequence of right praise. The central battle of Israel's God is always against idolatry, for everything that is dysfunctional in the human heart and in society flows finally from that primordial skewing. In this regard, the story of the ark's triumph over Dagon is not unlike the account in 1 Kings of Elijah's victory over the priests of Baal.

This brief summary provides, however inadequately, a background for the decisively important sixth chapter of 2 Samuel. Having become king, David knows that he must become a priest, for he is to preside over a liturgical kingdom. In the book of Exodus we hear that Yahweh will form an "orthodox" nation, a people who worship aright: "Now therefore, if you obey my voice and keep my covenant, you shall be my treasured possession out of all the peoples. Indeed, the whole earth is mine, but you shall be for me a priestly kingdom and a holy nation" (Exod. 19:5–6). The prescriptions given to Moses and the sons of Aaron, as well as the mobile tabernacle with the ark, were the provisional means by which Yahweh shaped this priestly people during the years of wandering and during the period of consolidation. But David intuited that these strands had to be gathered, and that, above all, the ark had to come to rest in his new capital city, providing thereby an unambiguous center for the nation, a still point around which all of its various elements could arrange themselves. This is why David's establishment of the ark in Jerusalem represents a certain climax to the narrative that began with the fall and led through the formation of the priestly people, the cutting of covenants, the giving of the law, and the invasion of the promised land.

The sixth chapter commences on a triumphant note: "David again gathered all the chosen men of Israel, thirty thousand. David and all the people with him set out and went from Baale-judah to bring up from there the ark of God" (2 Sam. 6:1–2). The king chose a veritable army of his best men in order to seize an apparently undefended piece of sacred furniture and bring it back to Jerusalem. One can see the enormous importance that David attaches to this mission. As Robert Polzin astutely observes, an echo is heard of the thirty thousand who were lost when the ark was taken by the Philistines (Polzin 1993: 60–61). Baale-judah, or Baalah in Judah, is a synonym for "Kiriath-jeraim," which is mentioned in 1 Sam. 7 and beautifully invoked in Ps. 132: "He [David] swore to the LORD and vowed to the Mighty One of Jacob, 'I will not enter my house or get into my bed; I will not give sleep to my eyes or slumber to my eyelids, until I find a place for the LORD. . . .' We heard of it in Ephratha; we found it in the fields of Jaar"

(Ps. 132:2–6). This lyrical passage captures well the holy obsession of David to ground and center his liturgical empire through right praise. In the account of this scene in 1 Chronicles we hear that David consults with the entire people before making this move and that they enthusiastically support him (Hahn 2012: 56). Hence, we see the liturgical people gladly shaping themselves around the ark and the priest-king. The ark of the covenant, we are told, is in the house of Abinadab, an Israelite who presumably took it in when it was returned by the Philistines many years before, convinced that it bore a curse. Abinadab's dwelling is said to be "on the hill," which probably carries the implication of a holy place or shrine of some kind. Of some interest is why, during the long years of Saul's reign and the civil war, the ark was more or less forgotten. Was this perhaps emblematic of the fact that suspension of right worship and the dissolution of Israel always go hand in hand?

Once he finds the ark, David endeavors to bring it back. He places it in "a new cart" (2 Sam. 6:3)—that is, a cart that had never been used before for any secular purpose—and he commences the journey back to Jerusalem (Alter 1999: 225). We hear that Uzzah and Ahio, the sons of Abinadab, are directing the cart and that David and his entourage are dancing with reckless abandon before the ark of Yahweh. When the festive liturgical procession reaches "the threshing floor of Nacon," the oxen stumble and the ark is jostled. Uzzah, innocently enough, reaches out to steady it, at which point he is struck dead by an angry God. There is probably no story in 2 Samuel that puzzles and irritates a contemporary reader more than this one. To conceive of God's ark as the bearer of a deadly electric charge and to conceive of God as a cruel tyrant capable of an utterly disproportionate reaction to a minor and unintentional liturgical infraction seems primitive at best and dangerous at worst. Much of the liberal, enlightened theologizing of the last two hundred years, in fact, militates against this sort of construal of God's relationship with humanity. The problem for liberal theology is that this story in 2 Samuel is hardly egregious. The Bible is filled with accounts of God's anger, justice, and punishment, and often enough, the biblical authors present a divine retribution that appears, at least to us, to be disproportionate or exaggerated.

What sense can be made of this? The One who created the whole of the cosmos—"the heavens and the earth" in more scriptural terminology—cannot be determined by any of the limitations or ontological conditions that circumscribe creatures. The One who gives the entirety of the being of the world cannot, for example, be characterized as standing in need of any further existential realization. This in turn entails the immutability of the Creator. It is crucially important to note that this has nothing to do with God being cold or indifferent to the world that he made and continues providentially to direct.[9] God's immutability means that God cannot change in a creaturely way—that is, in the manner of a finite being moving beyond its limits toward greater perfection of being. From God's unchangeability, it can be deduced that God does not pass in and out of emotional states, shifting, as we do, from contentment to discontentment, from joy to anger, from anticipation to disappointment, and so on. As the author of 1 John clarifies, "God is love" (1 John 4:8), implying that the very to-be of God is identical with the stance and attitude of love. Mutable as we are, we creatures fall in and out of love; we love to varying degrees; we love and then we do not love. But this cannot be the case in regard to the God who stands beyond the ontological vagaries of the created realm.

But how does this divine love manifest itself? To answer that question adequately, we have to be clear on what love is. For the mainstream theological and spiritual tradition, love is not an emotion or a sentiment; rather, it is the act of willing the good of the other as other.[10] This means that love expresses itself in a variety of ways depending upon the object of love. If I love someone who is on a self-destructive path, my willing of that person's good will doubtless appear harsh, angry, even punitive, for I am trying to get that person rightly aligned. Therefore, God's anger could be construed as a symbolic expression of God's passion to set things right, as the dark face of his love. We might think of God's love as a pure white light, which, upon passing through the prism of creation and history, breaks into a variety of colors. The language of the biblical authors, drawn as it must be from psychology and general experience, gestures analogically toward the various ways that the one divine love manifests itself in the world. Storytellers tend to express themselves in bold and exaggerated ways, and the biblical narrators are no exception. To give just two examples, think of the ages of the patriarchs or the numbers of warriors mustered for or killed in battle. When they want to gesture toward the divine passion to set things right, they often present a God raging in anger or burning with indignation or even putting thousands to death. Rather than literalizing this language either historically or psychologically, we should construe it as a poetic indication of the dark face of a love that remains essentially mysterious to us.

With those clarifications in mind, let us return to this particular story of Uzzah and the ark of the covenant. Why would Yahweh be angry at Uzzah's attempt to

9. Matthew Levering, *Scripture and Metaphysics: Aquinas and the Renewal of Trinitarian Theology* (Oxford: Blackwell, 2004), 94–96.

10. Barron, *Catholicism*, 48.

prevent the sacred ark from falling to the ground? The key issue seems to be liturgical impropriety. In Exodus 25 we hear of God's explicit instruction regarding the construction of the ark: "You shall make poles of acacia wood, and overlay them with gold. And you shall put the poles into the rings on the sides of the ark, by which to carry the ark. The poles shall remain in the rings of the ark; they shall not be taken from it" (Exod. 25:13–15). God wanted the ark designed in a very particular way, and he ordained that it be carried in a very particular way. The principal problem with David's first attempt to carry the ark into his capital city is that he was hauling it by cart rather than carrying it by the poles. It was this faster but more precarious form of transport that caused the ark to tip and Uzzah to react. Once more the temption is to conclude that a God who would respond with deadly violence to such a minor violation of liturgical law is surely unbalanced.[11] Yet we have to keep the symbolic nature of the language in mind and get to the spiritual truths the author is endeavoring to communicate. The entire purpose of liturgy is to restore humanity to right order, *adoratio* leading to the harmonizing of self and society. Over the course of many centuries, Yahweh had been forming his people in the ways of orthodoxy; at the heart of this right praise is a decentering of the self, a twisting away from the ego and a turning toward God. As we saw, the founder of Israel was a man who listened to God, and the whole of Israelite life—covenant, worship, prophecy, and so on—was a systematic attempt to help the people to attend to Yahweh: "Hear, O Israel, the LORD is our God, the LORD alone" (Deut. 6:4). It was indeed more convenient to convey the ark by means of an oxcart, but Yahweh had instructed that it be carried by poles. A small matter? Perhaps, but obedience is the hinge on which Israelite life turns. God was angry not because Uzzah's act personally offended him (in point of fact, the one who needs nothing from the world cannot, even in principle, be offended) but rather because it represented a compromising of the liturgical attitude.

The church fathers are eminently clear on this score. Chrysostom says, "As the wrath of God was drawn down on Uzzah for intruding on an office that was not his own, God's wrath will likewise advance against those who subvert the gospel."[12] Salvian remarks, "Uzzah's punishment for steadying the ark shows that nothing may be considered lightly when it pertains to God."[13] Pacian of Barcelona com-

11. David Rosenberg and Harold Bloom, *The Book of J* (New York: Grove Weidenfield, 1990), 304.

12. John Chrysostom, "Commentary on Galatians 1," in *Joshua, Judges, Ruth, 1–2 Samuel*, ed. John R. Franke, Ancient Christian Commentary on Scripture: Old Testament 4 (Downers Grove, IL: InterVarsity, 2005), 344.

13. Salvian the Presbyter, "The Governance of God 6.10," in Franke, *Joshua, Judges, Ruth, 1–2 Samuel*, 344.

ments, "So great a concern was there of reverence toward God that God did not accept bold hands even out of help."[14]

Another theological theme emerges from this odd tale that is worthy of some careful consideration: divine inscrutability and sublimity. The Creator of the universe cannot be categorized in any conventional philosophical system. God cannot be deftly defined or set in easy contrast to other beings or states of affairs. Thomas Aquinas catches the sheer strangeness of God when he comments that God is not in any genus, even the genus of being.[15] Further, the providential range of God includes the whole of creation, which means the totality of space and time. All of this implies that God's activities and purposes in the world necessarily remain inscrutable to a finite mind: "O the depth of the riches and wisdom and knowledge of God! How unsearchable are his judgments and how inscrutable his ways!" (Rom. 11:33). The strangeness of God and his actions has nothing to do with capriciousness on God's part; rather, it is a function of God's absolutely unique manner of being and our limited consciousness. The author of the book of Job makes much the same point in his magnificently constructed dialogue between a frustrated human sufferer and the providential Lord of the entire cosmos. The utilization of a Kantian conceptual framework is helpful when speaking of the sublimity of God—that is, God's overwhelming of the human sensorium and intellect.[16] Hans Urs von Balthasar speaks of God as a raging Alpine torrent, which utterly smashes any receptors designed to channel it and convert it to human use. This divine sublimity is, by turns, thrilling and terrifying. The prophet Isaiah can exult in the overwhelming beauty of God manifested in a temple vision of cloud and angels (Isa. 6:1–3), but as the Letter to the Hebrews has it, "It is a fearful thing to fall into the hands of the living God" (Heb. 10:31). A one-sided stress on the latter quality gives us an arbitrary God, but a unilateral stress on the former gives us a superficial and manipulable God.[17] Without for a moment rescinding any of the clarifications that I made above, I will also say this: Yahweh's striking down of Uzzah is finally inexplicable, for it expresses and participates in the sublimity of God.

The sheer weirdness of God's act helps to explain why "David was angry because the LORD had burst forth with an outburst upon Uzzah" (2 Sam. 6:8). Robert

14. Pacian of Barcelona, "On Penitents 6.3," in Franke, *Joshua, Judges, Ruth, 1–2 Samuel*, 345.

15. Thomas Aquinas, *Summa theologiae: Latin Text and English Translation, Introductions, Notes, Appendices, and Glossaries*, ed. Thomas Gilby et al., 61 vols. (New York: McGraw-Hill, 1964–81), 2:35.

16. Immanuel Kant, *Critique of Judgment*, trans. Werner S. Pluhar (Indianapolis: Hackett, 1987), 119–23.

17. Robert Barron, *And Now I See: A Theology of Transformation* (New York: Crossroad, 1998), 163.

Alter renders the Hebrew here as "afraid of the Lord." The ambivalence is eloquent, for both anger and fear are understandable reactions to the disorienting sublimity of God (Alter 1999: 226). In a pastoral context, the Christian minister discovers that anger at and fear of God are very common states of soul among those who are striving to believe in God. On account of this anger/fear, David resolves not to bring the ark into his capital and instead has it sent to the "house of Obed-edom the Gittite," most likely a Philistine from Gath who attached himself to David during the time when David was a vassal of the king of Gath. In the earlier sections of the "ark narrative," the presence of the ark of the covenant in the temple of the Philistines caused the foreign gods to fall. However, while the sacred vessel resides in the house of a Philistine within Israel, "the LORD blessed Obed-edom and all his household" (2 Sam. 6:11). Is this a foreshadowing of the ingathering of the nations, a hint of the blessings that would come to the peoples of the world when they ordered themselves around the right praise of God?

Inspired by this benediction of Obed-edom's house, David endeavors anew to bring the ark into its proper house in Jerusalem. What ensues is one of the richest and most festive liturgical processions described in the Bible. The king is careful not to repeat the mistake of hauling the ark by oxcart. This time, he arranges for bearers to carry the ark by poles set through rings, as specified in the book of Exodus. Further, he orders that when the bearers take but six steps, they will sacrifice "an ox and a fatling." There is some ambiguity here: Does the author mean to insinuate that the procession stopped every six paces to sacrifice or simply that they did so at the beginning of the march? If it was the former, the parade would have been endless, and Israel would have been emptied of oxen (Alter 1999: 227)! In either case, the point is made that the ark is conducted in a festive but sacrificial attitude and that the people are aware both of their blessing and their sin. In the killing of the animals is the anticipation of the thousands upon thousands of sacrifices that would take place over the centuries in the Jerusalem temple. Though the practice is utterly alien to us, the logic of sacrifice is quite straightforward.[18] One returns to God some aspect of creation in order to signal one's gratitude for the whole of creation, for a blessing received, or in reparation for sins committed. The Creator of the universe cannot possibly need anything in the universe; however, the offerer of the sacrifice needs the act of sacrifice in order to become rightly oriented to God. Further, sacrifices involve the death of an animal so that the inner pain of this reorientation might be adequately symbolized. This great sacrificial procession,

18. Barker, *Great High Priest*, 47.

evocative of the entire sacrificial history and attitude of Israel, was presided over by the one who is not only king but priest as well.

The priesthood of David is unmistakably referenced in the garb that the king dons for the parade: he "was girded with a linen ephod" (2 Sam. 6:14; Alter 1999: 227). In Exodus, in the description of the priestly vestments to be worn by Aaron and his sons, the ephod is mentioned a number of times (Exod. 28:15, 35; 29:5). And in Leviticus we hear that Moses "brought Aaron and his sons forward, and washed them in water. He put the tunic on him, fastened the sash around him, clothed him with the robe, and put the ephod on him" (Lev. 8:6–7). Most tellingly for our purposes, Saul, having invaded the sanctuary of Nob in search of David, ordered Doeg the Edomite to kill the priests, and we are told that "on that day he killed eighty-five who wore the linen ephod" (1 Sam. 22:18). In putting on the garment of the priesthood, David decides to assume the role and take up the task of those fallen victims of Saul. But he is also hearkening back to Samuel, Eli, and the Aaronic priesthood as well as to the priesthood of Adam, the first one to assume the stance of adoration. Only in light of the connection to Adam can we fully understand the energetic dance of the king before the ark of Yahweh. Before the fall, Adam walked in easy fellowship with Yahweh, thinking his thoughts, feeling his feelings, moving as he moved. He danced in unison with Yahweh. Sin is nothing but a falling out of step with God, an insistence upon dancing to one's own rhythm. The whole of the history of salvation might be characterized as Yahweh's attempt to restore the sacred dance, to get his human creatures to move with him. Accordingly David, dancing with energy before the ark, is humanity dancing with Yahweh, recovering the effortless harmony of Eden. Some argue that the gestures and movements of the priests in the Jerusalem temple were intended to mimic, in a stylized way, the exuberant dance of King David. And since the ritual moves of the Byzantine and Catholic Masses trace their origins to the temple, the conclusion could be made that the processions, gestures, and bows of Christian priests today participate in the priesthood of the king who wore the ephod as he danced before the ark.

I would wager that there is still another element of this story that makes it puzzling for most moderns: why David and his people would be dancing before the law. As we saw, the ark contained manna and the staff of Aaron, but it contained, most importantly, the tablets of the Ten Commandments, the rather strict provisions and prohibitions given by Yahweh to Moses on Mount Sinai. Most reasonable people in the West today accept the law—from traffic regulations to income tax—as a necessary evil, something that, in the best of all possible worlds, they can do without. Therefore it would be difficult indeed to imagine anyone dancing with joy before the tax code or the latest motor vehicle statutes, or even before the U.S. Constitution. To understand the coherence of David's dance, one needs to grasp the sea change that occurred from biblical to modern times in regard both to law and to freedom. On the modern reading, freedom is primarily choice and self-determination. The roots of this view stretch back to the late medieval period, to the speculations of the English Franciscan William of Occam. For him, human freedom is utterly autonomous, for it is the capacity to choose, on the basis of no constraint, either interior or exterior. The sheer independence of the will, he argues, can be proved by an act of suicide committed by a sincere religious believer, for such a move against the supreme good is made in the presence of the supreme good.

The contemporary Thomist Servais Pinckaers refers to this Occamist notion as "the freedom of indifference," for it is predicated on the assumption that the free agent hovers indifferently above the yes and the no.[19] An implication of this way of construing freedom is that each moral act is monadic, something like a Whiteheadian actual occasion. Precisely because the truly free choice is determined by nothing whatsoever, neither the character of the agent nor the succession of the agent's previous moral moves have a determining influence on a present ethical choice. On this interpretation, law must be seen as a limitation on freedom and hence as a necessary evil at best. Freedom, perforce, chafes against the law, and law, by its very nature, sets limits to unruly freedom. Moreover, when Occam extrapolates theologically from this construal of freedom, he arrives at an understanding of God as a supremely arbitrary power.[20] And since the divine freedom is as unconstrained in its essence as human freedom, infinite and finite liberty necessarily confront one another as opponents, and their relationship is mediated only by a divine law powerfully imposed. Many argue that this account of the God-human relationship conduces by a few short logical steps to atheism, for such a God is inevitably seen as a threat to human flourishing. Hence Feuerbach concludes, "The no to God is the yes to man," and Sartre formulates the pithy syllogism, "If God exists, I cannot be free; but I am free; therefore, God does not exist."

But prior to Occam, there was a very different notion of freedom, what Pinckaers calls *liberté de qualite* (freedom for excellence). Here, freedom is not primarily

19. Servais Pinckaers, *Morality: The Catholic View*, trans. Michael Sherwin (South Bend, IN: St. Augustine's Press, 2001), 72–75.

20. Robert Barron, *The Priority of Christ: Toward a Postliberal Catholicism* (Grand Rapids: Brazos, 2007), 14.

choice and self-creation but the disciplining of desire in order to make the achievement of the good first possible and then effortless. One becomes a free player of the violin, capable of playing any type of music, precisely in the measure that one submits to a range of disciplines, laws, and practices. Or one becomes a free swinger of the golf club, able to respond effortlessly to the shifting demands of the game, inasmuch as one has internalized the laws and rules that govern a good swing. On this interpretation, law is not the opponent to freedom but rather the condition for its possibility. A most important concomitant of this notion is a view articulated in the philosophical anthropology of Thomas Aquinas: will is a function of intellect. For Aquinas, the will emerges at the moment when the mind understands the good as good, and this entails that the objective good never stands over and against freedom as a constraint but rather informs it and guides it at every turn.[21] The theological implications are significantly non-Occamist. God is free not inasmuch as he stands in sovereign indifference to the yes and the no but inasmuch as he can only say yes—that is, in the measure that his will is utterly congruent with the goodness of his being. With God and freedom so construed, the divine will is not a threat to human flourishing; quite the contrary, the sacred law is something in the presence of which a grateful humanity might be moved to dance.

I would like to make a final set of observations and associations before turning from David's dance. A connection that the church fathers make with particular enthusiasm is between the ark of the covenant, which bore the divine law, and Mary of Nazareth, who bore the divine presence in the fullest possible sense. Maximus of Turin says, "But what would we say the ark was if not holy Mary, since the ark carried within it the tables of the covenant, while Mary bore the master of the same covenant?"[22] One of the many artistic depictions of this patristic association is the relief of a juxtaposed Mary and the ark, which is carved in stone over the left portal at Notre Dame Cathdedral in Paris. A number of symbolic echoes can be heard. David arose and went to get the ark, which was in the house of Abinadab, situated on "a hill" (probably a shrine) in the country of Judah. In the Gospel of Luke we are told that just after the angel Gabriel's annunciation to Mary, "Mary set out and went with haste to a Judean town in the hill country, where she entered the house of Zechariah and greeted Elizabeth" (Luke 1:39). In other words, the supreme ark, like its prototype, situates itself on a hilltop shrine in Judea. I do not say "shrine" casually here, for Zechariah is a

21. Aquinas, *Summa theologiae*, 11:229–31.
22. Maximus of Turin, "Sermon 42.5," in Franke, *Joshua, Judges, Ruth, 1–2 Samuel*, 346.

temple priest and Elizabeth a descendant of Aaron, the first priest. Further, after the death of Uzzah, David asks, "How can the ark of the LORD come into my care?" (2 Sam. 6:9). Upon receiving her cousin, Elizabeth asks, "And why has this happened to me, that the mother of my Lord comes to me?" (Luke 1:43). Both David and Elizabeth are unworthy to be in the presence of the bearer of the Lord. The king danced with all his might before the ark, and "when Elizabeth heard Mary's greeting, the child leaped in her womb" (Luke 1:41)—the unborn John the Baptist performing an infant's dance in the presence of the true ark. Finally, an intriguing detail: after the Uzzah incident David sent the ark, as we saw, to the home of Obed-edom, where it stayed for three months. After proclaiming her great song, the Magnificat, "Mary remained with her [Elizabeth] about three months and then returned to her home" (Luke 1:56). There can be little doubt that Luke is consciously echoing these stories of the ark in order to highlight Mary's identity as *Theotokos*, the "God-bearer."

As the procession winds its way into the city, it catches the attention of Michal, the daughter of Saul and first wife of David, who watches from a window high above the scene. We are told that "she despised him in her heart" (2 Sam. 6:16). One can only begin to imagine the texture of her feelings at this point in the narrative. She had witnessed the deaths of her father and brother and the fall of Saul's kingdom; her husband had gone on to marry several other women and fathered children with them while she remained childless; and David had her beloved second husband torn away from her as part of a cynical political game. Certainly she had a right to feel angry and resentful toward the one she knew as an upstart shepherd boy and who had now become king in place of Saul and instead of Jonathan. Significantly, Michal is referred to in this short section not as the wife of David but consistently as "daughter of Saul," signaling that she represents the fading house of the former king. That she gazes down from a window rather than participating in the celebration indicates that she represents the Saulide past (Polzin 1993: 69). From her height, she regards David with the same haughty disdain that her father once showed to his rival.

Before resuming the story of Michal, the narrator lingers over David's performance of a variety of priestly and kingly tasks. First, he establishes the ark in its "tent" or "tabernacle" within the holy city, thus anticipating the eventual installation of the ark in a proper temple by his son Solomon. Next, he offers up "burnt offerings" and "offerings of well-being," two prototypes of what would become temple sacrifice. Finally, he blesses the people "in the name of the LORD of hosts" (2 Sam. 6:18). Going into the tent, offering sacrifice, and then returning to bless the assembled crowd, David is echoing the moves of the high priest on the Day of Atonement, reconciling Yahweh and Israel and establishing a new garden of Eden (Beale 2011: 70–72). Finally, David performs a distinctively kingly act, feeding the "whole multitude of Israel, both men and women, to each a cake of bread, a portion of meat, and a cake of raisins" (2 Sam. 6:19). Here he is Moses, who promised to give the people food and drink during their sojourn in the desert; he is Joshua, who pledged to bring Israel to a land flowing with milk and honey; and he is Adam, sharing the fruitfulness of the garden. The ark, which was constructed in the shadow of Mount Sinai, finally finds a resting place, and Jerusalem is thereby established as the center of Israelite worship, the still point around which the nation could turn.

After performing these priestly and kingly functions, David returns home to his less-than-contented wife. Astonishingly, the conversation that follows is the only dialogue between Michal and David recorded in the Samuel literature. In 1 Sam. 19 she urgently instructs David to flee from Saul, but we hear nothing of David's response to her in that episode. When we finally hear them speak to one another, we perceive only sarcasm, anger, and recrimination. Not content to wait for her husband to come in, Michal goes out with energy to meet him and then pours invective into his ear: "How the king of Israel honored himself today, uncovering himself today before the eyes of his servants' maids, as any vulgar fellow might shamelessly uncover himself!" (2 Sam. 6:20). The Hebrew verb for "uncover" clearly has a sexual connotation, reflecting Michal's insinuation that David crudely offered his nakedness for the delighted contemplation of lowly slavegirls. There is more than a hint of sexual jealousy in Michal's observation as well as a foreshadowing of dangers to come through David's sexual imprudence. But the king's willingness to expose his nakedness even in that most public of settings also hearkens back to the garden and the time before the fall, when Adam and Eve walked unself-consciously naked in one another's presence and in the sight of God. That the nakedness of David is revealed precisely in the act of worship only reinforces the connection to the Adam of innocent, prelapsarian *adoratio*. The king's response to his first wife is both psychologically devastating and theologically interesting: "It was before the Lord, who chose me in place of your father and all his household, to appoint me as prince over Israel, the people of the Lord, that I have danced before the Lord" (2 Sam. 6:21). With these words, David puts to rest the notion that the house of Saul will have any say in the governance of Israel. It had perhaps been the hope of Saul, in his more lucid moments, that his house would endure precisely through the son of David and

Michal, but Saul himself, when the wicked spirit was upon him, had so interrupted their marriage that no progeny came from it. Now David definitively shuts the door on that possibility and thereby shuts down the Saulide line. Moreover, the decision of David is given quasi-divine sanction, since a sort of curse settles upon her from that moment: "And Michal the daughter of Saul had no child to the day of her death" (2 Sam. 6:23).

I said that David's rejoinder is also theologically interesting, and this is for several reasons. First, we see the paradox that a person's debasement before God is tantamount not to dimunition but to elevation and enhancement. For human beings to debase themselves before one another is indeed humiliating and dehumanizing, because a competitiveness or zero-sum dynamic naturally obtains among finite things. But the Creator God is not one being, however supreme, among many, and therefore no ontological competition exists between him and creatures. God does not stand over and against the world but instead exists precisely as the ground of the world's existence. Accordingly, the debasement of a human being before God results not in that person's annihilation but rather in his or her fulfillment. It is this very paradoxical quality of the biblical God's relationship with humanity that permits Irenaeus to assert, "The glory of God is a human being fully alive."[23] And this is why David can honor Yahweh through an exuberant dance in the spirit of joy.

Second, this episode sheds considerable light on the relationship between political power and the authority of God. King David's obeisance before God is a clear indication that he realizes that his worldly rule must be situated in the context of God's providence and placed upon the foundation of moral principles derived from God. Once more the correlation to the kingship of Adam is illuminating. The first man functioned as a good ruler of Eden as long as he was obedient to the divine word and responsive to the promptings of the divine spirit. But his kingship foundered the moment he seized for himself the prerogative of determining the difference between good and evil, when he arrogated to himself the power to establish the moral foundation for his kingly choices. This move, which is functionally equivalent to abandonment of orthodoxy, leads inevitably to expulsion from the garden and to loss of rule. Once more, the whole of the biblical narrative from Genesis to the account of David's kingly dance might be construed as the story of humanity struggling to recover the right relationship between human authority and divine authority. Again

23. Irenaeus, *Against Heresies* 4.7.

and again the biblical authors tell us that earthly kings are rightly conceived as under the aegis of God, and they consistently show us the devastation, both personal and societal, that follows from the laying aside of this truth. The lords of the tower of Babel, the pharaoh of the exodus, the kings of the Amalekites and Philistines—all of them recapitulated the sin of Adam and set themselves up as the criterion of good and evil. But Israel, in principle, was meant to be the countersign, a corporate Adam, a people whose political and cultural life unfolded according to God's principles.

In his treatise on law Thomas Aquinas teaches that positive law, the concrete prescriptions by which a society is governed, is derivative from the natural law, the first principles of morality and their immediate applications. Natural law in turn is grounded in the eternal law, which is none other than the reasonability of the divine mind itself.[24] When this nesting relationship is overlooked, positive law becomes but an expression of the will to power of the legislator, and the moral integrity of a society so governed is fatally compromised. At least a vestige of this Thomistic understanding can be discerned in the American Declaration of Independence, precisely in its affirmation of humans' rights to life, liberty, and the pursuit of happiness, explicitly recognized as "endowed by their Creator." The implication is that the positive laws that govern the United States must be correlated to objective moral principles, articulated as rights, which in turn are implanted in us by God. Joseph Ratzinger proposes a reading of Jesus's conversation with Pontius Pilate, which is apposite in this context. Under pressure from the restive crowd, Pilate both abdicates moral responsibility and confesses ignorance of any objective ground for moral decision making: "What is truth?" (John 18:38). Having severed any possible link between positive law and natural law, he surrenders to the whim of the crowd, asking them to decide whether an obviously guilty man or an obviously innocent man should be released. This, Ratzinger argues, is the prototype of the moral governance by public opinion poll so prevalent in contemporary society. But what the severance of positive, moral, and eternal law inevitably results in is the ultimacy of the legislator's will to power. Thus Pilate bullyingly says to Jesus, "Do you refuse to speak to me? Do you not know that I have power to release you, and power to crucify you?" (John 19:10). To which the One who came to testify to the truth responds, "You would have no power over me unless it had been given you from above" (John 19:11). Pilate's authority, the legitimacy of which Jesus does not question, is nevertheless subalternate to

24. Aquinas, *Summa theologiae*, 28:105–7.

the higher authority of God. David, the king who dances with joyful reverence before God, is an apt iconic representation of this truth.

A third theological implication of David's response to Michal is that in a properly religious context, the ecstatic trumps the rational and moralistic. In a certain sense, Michal is right in criticizing the king for his somewhat imprudent display. It would not be hard to find altogether respectable and reasonable moral categories according to which David's dance could be characterized as inappropriate. Perhaps he truly scandalized some in Jerusalem that day and was the occasion for lustful thoughts in others. The prim, downward-looking Michal aptly symbolizes the moral dimension that is legitimately part of religion. She is a sort of ancient Israelite version of Immanuel Kant, for whom religion was entirely a matter of morality, rationally construed. Kant's programmatic text *Religion within the Limits of Reason Alone* gives away the nature of the project. But as Paul Tillich argues, real religion can never be captured with the limits of reason alone, precisely because it involves the honoring of the unconditioned.[25] Whatever can be grasped by reason is ipso facto conditioned. Therefore the relationship to the properly unconditioned must involve the bursting of the bounds of reason, an ecstatic leap outside the self and beyond the controlling aspect of the mind. John Henry Newman speaks of the kingly, prophetic, and priestly dimensions of the church. In its kingly mode, the church is marked by order, authority, and discipline; in its prophetic mode, it is rational, inquisitive, and engaged in a dialogue with the wider culture; and in its priestly mode, it is prayerful, contemplative, and mystical. Without the leavening of the priestly, Newman contends, the prophetic dimension devolves, in short order, into a dry rationalism.[26] The moralizing Michal might be read as the prophetic side of religion and the dancing David as the priestly side of religion, which refuses to be constrained by reason alone.

25. Paul Tillich, *Systematic Theology*, 2 vols. (London: Nisbet, 1953–57), 1:229.

26. John Henry Newman, "The Three Offices of Christ," in *Sermons Bearing on Subjects of the Day* (London: Longmans, Green, 1891), 60–61.

2 SAMUEL 7

The seventh chapter of 2 Samuel is of extraordinary importance because it represents simultaneously the end of a major part of the story of Israel and the beginning of another. It looks back through Israelite history all the way to the garden of Eden and forward toward the definitive messianic fulfillment of God's salvific plan. It presents King David as a hinge, a center, an indispensible point of reference indicating whence Israel has come and where Israel is tending. Because of the prophecy of Nathan (which I will consider in detail presently), the first Christian evangelists and theologians looked with intense interest at this chapter, and Christians to the present day continue to find considerable illumination in its pages. Some of the literary archaeologists of this text discover the heavy hand of the Deuteronomistic editor, since the language of the seventh chapter—hortatory, majestic, courtly—is so different from that of the surrounding narratives (McCarter 1984: 215–31). Be that as it may, the present chapter does have a distinct quality vis-à-vis the rest of 2 Samuel, and this alone should summon particular theological attention.

The chapter begins in a domestic space and in a peaceful mood: "Now when the king was settled in his house, and the LORD had given him rest from his enemies all around him . . . " (2 Sam. 7:1). Through enormous effort—including the slaying of Goliath, the outmaneuvering of Saul, the conquest of Ishbaal's kingdom, and the defeat of the Philistines—David managed to create a garden space where God's people could live in peace, their lives centered on the praise of God in Jerusalem. Now he comes to a kind of Sabbath rest, and his thoughts appropriately turn to the things of God (Hertzberg 1964: 284). To his court prophet Nathan (introduced for the first time here) he says, "See now, I am living in a house of cedar, but the ark of God stays in a tent" (2 Sam. 7:2). Just as he listened to God in order to know how to act during time of war, now he turns to God in time of peace in order to worship. This is an altogether appropriate way to spend Sabbath time, which is not for indolence but rather for that heightened activity that has no end extraneous to itself. It represents the proper trajectory of all the warlike activity of Israel over the centuries, for all of that violence and toil was meant finally to establish a people who know how to worship God. We will see the contrast between this use of Sabbath time and the use that David makes of his leisure time in the eleventh chapter, when he orchestrates the elaborate seduction of Bathsheba. It is none other than the difference between Adam's proper and improper exercise of regal authority in the garden.

Impressed by David's success and the obvious sincerity of the king's request, Nathan concurs: "Go, do all that you have in mind; for the LORD is with you" (2 Sam. 7:3). I see no reason whatsoever to ascribe either to David or Nathan base political or questionable personal motives for their concurrence on this score. That David sought consistently to honor Yahweh is apparent from the whole of the Samuel literature, and that Nathan is no sycophantic "court prophet" becomes eminently clear in the eleventh chapter. Both men are at a relatively early stage of the process, but they discern that the building of a temple is indeed God's holy will and not just their own. However, that very night, God speaks to Nathan and tells him that David's building plan is not in accord with the divine will. Some suggest that this prohibition represents an anti-temple ideology predating the time of Solomon, but it seems much more likely that it is an attempt to explain the somewhat puzzling fact that David, given all his accomplishments, was not the one who constructed the mighty temple (McCarter 1984: 197). Robert Alter argues that the likeliest historical reason is simply that David was too occupied with establishing himself militarily and politically to take on the massively complex task of building a temple (Alter 1999: 232). In 1 Chr. 22 David himself explains why God did not allow him to construct the temple: "The word of the LORD came to me, saying, 'You have shed much blood and have waged great wars; you shall not build a house to my name, because you have shed so much blood in my sight on the earth'" (1 Chr. 22:8; Hahn 2012: 99–101). From a theological point of view, this is fascinating because it appears to refute those who say that the God of the Old Testament is ruthlessly bloodthirsty. Though God certainly sanctioned the rise of David, it appears as though God was not entirely pleased with all or even any of David's wars. At the very least, he did not want a shedder of blood to be the builder of the place where divinity and humanity were to be liturgically reconciled. Staying with the text of 2 Samuel, one gathers that God's principal objection has to do with human presumption, namely, David's taking it upon himself to conceive and pursue a project of enormous theological significance. At his best, David asked Yahweh's permission and guidance before undertaking any endeavor, but here, as with the transportation of the ark by oxcart, he takes matters into his own hands.

There are times when a person might set out on a course that is obviously at cross-purposes with God's providential plan, but there are other times when a person resolves to act not in a selfish manner but according to an honest discernment of God's will. And often it is the people in the second category who find the divine opposition most unnerving. A person's plan might be bold, beautiful, magnanimous, and popular but still not be God's plan. A person's ambition might be admirable and selfless but still not be congruent with God's ambition. The fact that David was compelled to surrender his plan to the greater purposes of Yahweh is still another illustration of the biblical principle that our lives are not about us. Though this often runs counter to our intuitions and convictions, God's plans for us are always greater, more expansive, and more life-giving than our plans for ourselves. As Joseph Campbell comments, many people "have climbed to the top of the ladder and found it's against the wrong wall."[1] A major preoccupation of the Ignatian spiritual exercises is precisely the cultivation of a detachment from our own program of life in order to allow God to work effortlessly in us. This decentering of the ego—"It is no longer I who live, but it is Christ who lives in me" (Gal. 2:20)—is the condition for the possibility of becoming a conduit of God's grace to the world. According to Catholic theology and spirituality, God does indeed welcome human cooperation with noncompetitive divine grace, yet grace has to come first and condition the human response at every turn. This is precisely what God emphasizes in the word that Nathan relays to the king: "I took you from the pasture, from following the sheep to be prince over my people Israel; and I have been with you wherever you went, and have cut off all your enemies from before you; and I will make for you a great name, like the name of the great ones of the earth" (2 Sam. 7:8–9). God acts through grace, and his people cooperate—in that order. This graceful interaction between divinity and humanity will produce, God promises, none other than the Eden lost through bad kingship long before: "And I will appoint a place for my people Israel and will plant them, so that they may live in their own place, and be disturbed no more; and evildoers shall afflict

1. Joseph Campbell, *The Hero's Journey: Joseph Campbell on His Life and Work* (New York: Harper & Row, 1990), 63.

them no more as formerly, from the time that I appointed judges over my people Israel" (2 Sam. 7:10–11).

What follows is a delicious reversal. David proposes to build God a house, but God responds by promising to build David a house, the contours of which the king of Israel can scarcely imagine, a dynasty that will stretch out majestically over time and even into eternity: "The LORD will make you a house. When your days are fulfilled and you lie down with your ancestors, I will raise up your offspring after you, who shall come forth from your body, and I will establish his kingdom. He shall build a house for my name, and I will establish the throne of his kingdom forever" (2 Sam. 7:12–13). We must be particularly careful in our reading of this and the verses that immediately follow, for they constitute some of the most famous and pivotal texts of the entire Bible. There is a very proximate promise ingredient in this oracle: a son of David (the yet unborn Solomon) will literally build the temple (the house) that David envisioned. But there is a far greater range to Yahweh's covenant, for it promises that the kingly line, begun with Solomon, will extend through the ages. Moreover, unlike the other covenants that Yahweh made with Israel—with Noah, Abraham, and Moses—this one is unconditional: "I will be a father to him [both Solomon and the presumed "eternal" king], and he shall be a son to me. When he commits iniquity, I will punish him with a rod such as mortals use, with blows inflicted by human beings. But I will not take my steadfast love from him, as I took it from Saul" (2 Sam. 7:14–15). God will chastise wicked behavior—and this provides the indispensible hermeneutical lens for reading the stories of the far-less-than-stellar descendants of David who will occupy his throne over the centuries—but he will not give up on the line of David. No matter how fully the sons of David repudiate the commands of Yahweh, he will not go back on his promise to maintain the Davidic dynasty.

What is truly astounding about these texts is that they were finally edited, by common consensus, sometime during the postexilic period, after the death of the last of the Davidic kings, Zedekiah, who was blinded and forcibly carried off into captivity by the Babylonians. In other words, they were composed at a time when it was eminently clear that the Davidic line, which had endured for an impressive four hundred years, nevertheless had come clearly to an end, undermining, it seemed, God's promise. There must have been a mystical sense in the mind of the editor that God, *per impossibile*, would guarantee the endurance of David's line. Here one can see a similarity to Abraham's confidence, born of what Kierkegaard terms "the passion for the impossible"—that God would fulfill his promise of fruitfulness even as he commanded the death of the one through whom that fruitfulness would come.[2]

That this pledge fascinated the mind of Israel is evident in the numerous references to it throughout the Old Testament. Psalm 110, most likely a song commemorating the coronation of one of David's successors in Jerusalem, speaks of the newly anointed king as priest, thus hearkening back to David's priestly dance before the ark. And it affirms, curiously, that the priesthood of this king will endure unto eternity: "The LORD has sworn and will not change his mind, 'You are a priest forever according to the order of Melchizedek'" (Ps. 110:4). As we saw, Melchizedek, the mysterious figure who came out to meet Abraham, was presented as both a sacrificing priest and the king of Salem, a place roughly identified with Jerusalem. Hence the Davidic offspring, whose reign will be unending, is linked to the very beginnings of the formation of a people Israel through the faith of Abraham. My attempt to encapsulate the teaching implicit in this densely textured psalm is as follows: the promise made to the great patriarch, which recapitulates the command made to Adam to be fruitful and multiply, will be brought to fulfillment through the Davidic king, who will bring all peoples under his feet and whose reign is eternal.

Similarly, Psalm 89 celebrates the assurance that came to David through Nathan: "You said, 'I have made a covenant with my chosen one, I have sworn to my servant David: "I will establish your descendants forever and build your throne for all generations"'" (Ps. 89:3–4); and, "I will make him [David] the firstborn, the highest of the kings of the earth. Forever I will keep my steadfast love for him, and my covenant with him will stand firm. I will establish his line forever, and his throne as long as the heavens endure" (Ps. 89:27–29). At the same time, the tension alluded to above is evident even in this triumphant psalm, for the author seems to know that the Davidic line has, in fact, been broken: "You have removed the scepter from his hand, and hurled his throne to the ground. You have cut short the days of his youth; you have covered him with shame" (Ps. 89:44–45). This terrible discrepancy between promise and reality calls forth the deepest anguish of the author: "How long, O LORD? Will you hide yourself forever? . . . Lord, where is your steadfast love of old, which by your faithfulness you swore to David?" (Ps. 89:46, 49). Once again, in the Kierkegaardian spirit, the promise is not rejected, even though the reality on the ground seems utterly to contradict it.

Also, Psalm 132, which I have referenced in connection with the finding of the ark, speaks unambiguously of the prophecy conveyed by David's court prophet:

2. Søren Kierkegaard, "Fear and Trembling," in *A Kierkegaard Anthology*, ed. Robert Bretall (Princeton: Princeton University Press, 1946), 131–34.

"The LORD swore to David a sure oath from which he will not turn back: 'One of the sons of your body I will set on your throne. If your sons keep my covenant and my decrees that I shall teach them, their sons also, forevermore, shall sit on your throne'" (Ps. 132:11–12). What sets this citation off from the others is the clearer conditionality of the promise, though this might be construed as compatible with Nathan's insistence that God will indeed punish the wrongdoing of David's descendants (McCarter 1984: 225, 485).

The prophet Isaiah also knows of Nathan's prophecy. In the magnificent messianic hymn in the ninth chapter, Isaiah sees the day of a child who will be named "Wonderful Counselor, Mighty God, Everlasting Father, Prince of Peace" and whose authority will increase until he brings about "endless peace" (Isa. 9:6–7). Moreover, the throne that this child will occupy is "of David and his kingdom," and he will remain in power "from this time onward and forevermore" (Isa. 9:7). Two chapters later, we learn that "a shoot shall come out from the stump of Jesse, and a branch shall grow out of his roots" (Isa. 11:1). This Davidic paragon will possess the complete range of spiritual gifts—wisdom, understanding, counsel, might, and the fear of the Lord—and he will establish righteousness in his kingdom. So complete will be his rule that even the animal kingdom will come to harmony: "The wolf shall live with the lamb, and the leopard shall lie down with the kid. . . . And the lion shall eat straw like the ox. . . . And the weaned child shall put its hand on the adder's den" (Isa. 11:6–8). It does not require a great deal of imagination to see that this is the Davidic king as the new Adam, the one who tends the renewed garden of God's creation. The basic mark of this king is that he presides over the reconciliation of heaven and earth, the healing of the profoundest division prompted by sin: "They will not hurt or destroy on all my holy mountain; for the earth will be full of the knowledge of the LORD as the waters cover the sea" (Isa. 11:9). Through this Davidic king, God will come to reign on earth as in heaven. This cosmic dimension of messianic kingship was given splendid expression in the construction of Solomon's temple, which in every detail brought together the elements of creation in a harmonious design. In and on the temple were cedar, carvings of gourds and open flowers, cherubim, gold, olivewood, cypress, sculptures of palm trees, pomegranates, a "molten sea," depictions of lions and oxen, and more (Beale 2011: 67–68). In a word, the temple of Yahweh was Eden, presided over by Yahweh in the person of the son of David.

When the first Christian preachers and evangelists tried to make sense of Jesus the Messiah *kata ta grapha* (according to the scriptures), it was only natural that they turned to these texts and ideas that cluster around the promise conveyed to

David through Nathan. Matthew commences his Gospel with a detailed genealogy of Jesus, "the son of David, the son of Abraham" (Matt. 1:1; Hahn 2012: 82). By referring to those two figures specifically, Matthew is implicitly identifying Jesus as the One through whom the mission of Israel to bring their God to all the nations would be accomplished. He lays out three sets of fourteen generations: from Abraham to David, from David to the Babylonian captivity, and from the captivity to Jesus. According to the tradition of associating a number to each letter of the Hebrew alphabet, the consonants of David's name, *d-w-d*, correspond to fourteen.[3] Therefore, what Matthew is communicating to those who have eyes to see is that Jesus is a treble David, David cubed, David perfected and intensified. The lengthy genealogy at the beginning of Matthew's Gospel surely mimics and is meant to call to mind the even longer genealogy with which the books of Chronicles commence (Hahn 2012: 42). The first ten chapters of 1 Chronicles are essentially a list of the antecedents of King David, beginning with Adam himself and leading through hundreds of other figures and events to Saul and Jonathan and their tragic end on Mount Gilboa. What the Chronicler is not so subtly insinuating is that all of human history has in a very real sense been a preparation for David and his gathering of the tribes in Hebron and then in Jerusalem. By inaugurating his Gospel with a genealogy conducing toward the new David, Matthew is indicating that the human story finds its truest fulfillment in Jesus. Furthermore, when the angel visits Joseph and urges him to take Mary as his wife, he refers to Joseph pointedly as "son of David" (Matt. 1:20), and when the magi from the east arrive in Jerusalem, inquiring as to the whereabouts of the newborn "king of the Jews," they are told the word of the prophet that the Messiah would be born in "Bethlehem in the land of Judah," David's city. The very fact of prominent foreign personages seeking the king of the Jews is, of course, an echo of David's attraction not only to the tribes of Israel but also, as we will see, to the surrounding nations.

The Gospel of Luke is a text thoroughly drenched in Davidic themes. Luke's narrative begins with two "temple" persons: Zechariah, "who belonged to the priestly order of Abijah," and his wife, Elizabeth, who is characterized as a "descendant of Aaron" and hence of priestly stock (Luke 1:5). The first thing we hear about Zechariah is that he serves as priest in the Jerusalem temple, offering incense in the sanctuary. David's dream was to build the temple in which Zechariah serves, and Zechariah's gestures are a ritualized mimicking of the moves of the king who

3. Michael Dauphinais and Matthew Levering, *Holy People, Holy Land: A Theological Introduction to the Bible* (Grand Rapids: Brazos, 2005), 139–40.

danced before the ark. While in the sanctuary, we are told, Zechariah is visited by the angel Gabriel, who tells him that Elizabeth, despite her advanced years, will give birth to a son who will, like Elijah, prepare the way for the Messiah. The temple locale and the announcement of the birth of a child against all expectations brings us back to the beginning of 1 Samuel and Hannah's pregnancy, which resulted in the birth of Samuel, who would serve as forerunner to David. Indeed, Elizabeth's words upon conceiving ("This is what the Lord has done for me when he looked favorably on me and took away the disgrace I have endured among my people" [Luke 1:25]) powerfully evoke Hannah's frame of mind when she, after many tears and much prayer, finally became pregnant.

That same angel Gabriel made a subsequent appearance to Mary, a virgin residing in Nazareth and betrothed to Joseph, "of the house of David" (Luke 1:27). Gabriel announced that this young woman would give birth to a son to whom she must give the name "Jesus." When Mary voiced her perplexity, the angel offered this further clarification: "He will be great, and will be called the Son of the Most High, and the Lord God will give to him the throne of his ancestor David. He will reign over the house of Jacob forever, and of his kingdom there will be no end" (Luke 1:32–33). The Davidic line, which had come to an end politically with the death of Zedekiah, had gone, as it were, underground, continuing through Zerubbabel, a Davidide at the time of the return from exile, and then through a series of unknown figures for over five hundred years until it surfaced with Joseph and Jesus. Only with the angel's clarification that this Jesus would be "Son of the Most High" can one begin to understand something about the Nathan promise that has always been puzzling: the eternal quality of the reign of the son of David. Did this mean that the line would continue, temporally, forever, or that one member of that line would somehow sit on the throne forever? If the descendant of David referred to by Gabriel is in fact a figure not only human but also divine, his reign can be seen as properly transtemporal. Upon declaring herself "the servant of the Lord" and acquiescing to the angel's request, Mary became the definitive ark of the covenant, the bearer of Yahweh's presence. Upon visiting her cousin Elizabeth, Mary delivered an exultant prayer reminiscent in almost every detail of the prayer uttered centuries before by Hannah upon the birth of Samuel. Surely Luke is thereby bolstering his claim that Jesus is the long-awaited Son of David, the fulfillment of Nathan's prophecy.

Once this association with David is established, the work and ministry of Jesus can be understood with much greater clarity. From beginning to end of his preaching career, Jesus's central theme was the arrival of the kingdom of God.

What his original audience would have understood by this phrase was, doubtless, the ingathering of the scattered tribes of Israel, and what becomes eminently clear in all of the Gospels is that this coming together would happen in and through Jesus himself, much as the knitting together of ancient Israel happened in the person of David.[4] In going out to the woman at the well, Zacchaeus, the man born blind, and the Syrophoenician woman, and in offering open table fellowship to saints, sinners, prostitutes, and Pharisees alike, Jesus undertook the kingly task. It is most important to grasp that he was not simply exemplifying the virtue of "inclusivity" in the contemporary sense; he was doing what the Davidic Messiah was expected to do.

Jesus's activities in regard to the Jerusalem temple at the climax of his life are intimately tied up with the promise of Nathan as well. As we saw, Yahweh turned down David's offer to build a house for him and then promised that he himself would construct a house for David, playing on the ambiguity of the term. Yahweh did indeed build a physical house for David through the ministrations of Solomon and then constructed a dynasty for David across many centuries, culminating in Jesus, the king who surfaces after the Davidic line went underground for many years. That Son of David enters the descendant of Solomon's temple, declares judgment upon its corruption in the manner of the great prophets from Hosea and Amos to Isaiah and Ezekiel, and then, when asked for a sign to justify what he has done, responds, "Destroy this temple, and in three days I will raise it up" (John 2:19). The evangelist adds this illuminating gloss: "He was speaking of the temple of his body" (John 2:21). In short, Jesus announces himself to be the definitive fulfillment of Yahweh's promise to David that he would raise up a house for the king. In his own body, Jesus is the place of right praise, the dwelling place of Yahweh on earth. And this is why Jesus could say something in reference to himself that doubtless struck his original audience as breathtaking in its audacity: "I tell you, something greater than the temple is here" (Matt. 12:6). He himself is the "house" that David wanted to build for God and that God instead built for David.[5]

One of the clearest and most explicit invocations of the Davidic quality of Jesus is found in the Acts of the Apostles. On the day of Pentecost, Peter, in the grip of the Holy Spirit, delivers his first great kerygmatic sermon to a crowd gathered from all over the world. He speaks of the resurrection of Jesus and the coming of the Spirit as the "last days" of which the prophet Joel had spoken, a time when "your

4. N. T. Wright, *Jesus and the Victory of God,* Christian Origins and the Question of God 2 (Minneapolis: Fortress, 1996), 104.

5. Ibid., 343.

sons and daughters shall prophesy, and your young men shall see visions, and your old men will dream dreams" (Acts 2:17). He tells his audience thereby precisely where they stand in the great story of Israel. Then he speaks of the resurrection in a distinctively Davidic key. Some of the very people whom Peter addresses had contributed to the death of Jesus—"you crucified and killed [him] by the hands of those outside the law" (Acts 2:23)—but God raised him up and freed him from death. Peter makes sense of this by referencing Psalm 16, which the apostle presumes to have been authored by David: "For you will not abandon my soul to Hades, or let your Holy One experience corruption" (Acts 2:27). Displaying considerable exegetical creativity, Peter observes that since King David himself died and was corrupted, the author of the psalm must have seen past himself toward a descendant who would not see corruption—a son, moreover, who had been promised to David by oath. Therefore the resurrected Jesus, whose body *is* the final temple, must be the fulfillment of the Nathan promise, the ratification of the angel's word to Mary.

Whenever Jesus is presented in the Gospels in the role or attitude of king, he is being presented, at least implicitly, as the new David. A case in point is the story of Jesus's encounter with the blind Bartimaeus by the walls of Jericho. For any first-century Jew shaped by the biblical tradition, Jericho carried the overtone of sin and corruption since it was the city whose walls Joshua and his priest-led army caused to fall at the commencement of Israel's conquest of the promised land. Therefore, the man sitting in blindness by the walls of Jericho is evocative of the human race, compromised by sin, unable properly to see, without direction. The very geographical location of Jericho, at the bottom of a long decline from the heights of Jerusalem, evokes the fall. Hearing that Jesus is passing by, Bartimaeus calls out, "Jesus, Son of David, have mercy on me!" (Mark 10:47). Addressing Jesus by this Davidic title, Bartimaeus certainly is seeking healing but also, if I can put it this way, proper leadership. He is seeking to be led from the city of sin up to Zion, the city of the king. He is fallen Adam petitioning entry into the new Eden. Jesus calls, questions, and then heals him, at which point Bartimaeus "followed him along the way" (Mark 10:52), and the way that Jesus is walking is precisely toward Jerusalem, which becomes clear in the verses that immediately follow the Bartimaeus narrative.[6]

Furthermore, when Jesus enters Jerusalem on the foal of an ass just as Zechariah predicted the Messiah would do, he is greeted by festive crowds shouting,

6. Robert Barron, *Catholicism: A Journey to the Heart of the Faith* (New York: Image, 2011), 155.

"Hosanna! Blessed is the one who comes in the name of the Lord! Blessed is the coming kingdom of our ancestor David!" (Mark 11:9–10). Who could miss here the association with David's own dancing entry into his capital city as he was surrounded by enthusiastic throngs? Jesus is clearly presenting himself as the new priest-king leading his people to unity through right praise. And his kingship emerges with greatest clarity and irony when he enters into his passion. Upon being brought before the Sanhedrin, Jesus is asked whether he is the "Messiah, the Son of the Blessed One" (Mark 14:61). Any reference to the *māšîaḥ*, the "anointed one," is at least implicitly a reference to David, whom Samuel anointed as king. When Jesus calmly responds, "I am," the high priest tears his robes, for how could a shackled criminal possibly be the kingly descendant of David? Mark is insinuating that Jesus is a king, but a strange and deeply puzzling version of a king. Upon being presented to Pilate, Jesus is asked the functionally equivalent question: "Are you the King of the Jews?" Again a blandly affirmative answer comes: "You say so" (Mark 15:2). This leads the soldiers to mock him, placing a purple cloak on his shoulders and a crown of thorns on his head and shouting, "Hail, King of the Jews!" (Mark 15:18). Mark does not want us to miss the irony that, precisely as the King of the Jews and the Son of David, Jesus is implicitly king to those soldiers, for the mission of the Davidic king is the unification not only of the tribes of Israel but also of the tribes of the world. In the Gospel of John, Pontius Pilate places over the cross of Jesus a sign declaring the crucified to be "the King of the Jews," and the Roman governor makes sure that it is printed in the three great languages of that time and place (John 19:19–20). This makes Pilate, despite himself, the first great evangelist, the one who declares to the whole world that it has a new king. What commenced with David's gathering of the tribes of Israel would now reach completion in the criminal raised high on the cross, thereby drawing all people to himself (John 12:32).

Returning to the text of 2 Samuel, we find one of the most striking and beautiful prayers in the entire Bible. Having heard the promise that Yahweh made through Nathan, David "went in and sat before the LORD" (2 Sam. 7:18). The "going in" is doubtless a reference to the tabernacle where the ark of the covenant was kept. In utter and sincere humility, the king wonders, "Who am I, O Lord GOD, and what is my house, that you have brought me thus far?" (2 Sam. 7:18). David knows that whatever he has is in gift form. He realizes that the God of Israel owes him nothing, that there is no ontological parity in their relationship. He cannot manipulate God or enter into games of mutual obligation or exchange with him. What undergirds David's prayer is the fundamental biblical principle of the primacy of grace, which dictates that God's love always comes first. Whatever human beings do or say takes place through that grace and in response to it. This distinctive understanding of God informs the king's poignant prayer: "What more can David say to you? For you know your servant, O Lord GOD!" (2 Sam. 7:20). The God of Israel knows all things, even the deep interiority of human beings, not because he is an especially powerful observer of affairs but because he has known the universe in its entirety. His knowledge of the universe is not posterior and derivative but anterior and creative. As Thomas Aquinas specifies, God does not know things because they are, but rather things are because God knows them.[7] There is no clearer scriptural affirmation of this divine onmiscience than Psalm 139: "O LORD, you have searched me and known me. You know when I sit down and when I rise up; you discern my thoughts from far away.... Even before a word is on my tongue, O LORD, you know it completely" (Ps. 139:1–2, 4). And the psalmist clearly understands the metaphysical ground for this intimate knowledge: "For it was you who formed my inward parts; you knit me together in my mother's womb.... My frame was not hidden from you, when I was being made in secret" (Ps. 139:13, 15). As in Aquinas's account, the universality of God's knowledge of the world follows from the universality of God's creative reach.

The primacy of grace and the omniscience of God are finally grounded in God's absolutely unique metaphysical identity, which is obliquely but beautifully stated in the following invocation of David: "Therefore you are great, O LORD God; for there is none like you, and there is no God besides you, according to all that we have heard with our ears" (2 Sam. 7:22). This manner of theological speech is remarkably similar to what we find scattered throughout Deutero-Isaiah: "To whom then will you liken God, or what likeness compare with him?" (Isa. 40:18); "'To whom then will you compare me, or who is my equal?' says the Holy One" (Isa. 40:25); "I am the LORD, and besides me there is no savior" (Isa. 43:11); "I am the first and the last; besides me there is no god. Who is like me?" (Isa. 44:6–7); "Is there any god besides me? There is no other rock; I know not one" (Isa. 44:8); "There is no other god besides me, a righteous God and a Savior; there is no one besides me.... For I am God, and there is no other" (Isa. 45:21–22). What is being affirmed here with almost tiresome repetitiveness is that the God of Israel is not to be understood as one God, however great, however supreme, among many. If Yahweh were simply the greatest of the gods, then he could indeed be

7. Thomas Aquinas, *Summa theologiae: Latin Text and English Translation, Introductions, Notes, Appendices, and Glossaries*, ed. Thomas Gilby et al., 61 vols. (New York: McGraw-Hill, 1964–81), 4:29–31.

compared with them as a higher number is compared to a lower number or a more perfectly constructed building to an awkwardly constructed one. The metaphysical implication of the more prayerful and poetic language of both Deutero-Isaiah and 2 Samuel is that God exists in such a way as to be properly incomparable to creatures. The God of Israel is not simply somewhere else but somehow else; not merely other but "otherly other."[8]

This distinctiveness is directly correlative to another fundamentally biblical claim: God is the Creator of all finite existence. Almost as numerous in Deutero-Isaiah as the references to God's incomparability are references to God as Creator: "Lift up your eyes on high and see: Who created these? He who brings out their host and numbers them" (Isa. 40:26); "Thus says God, the LORD, who created the heavens and stretched them out" (Isa. 42:5); "But now thus says the LORD, he who created you, O Jacob, he who formed you, O Israel" (Isa. 43:1); "I am the LORD, your Holy One, the Creator of Israel, your King" (Isa. 43:15); and perhaps most tellingly, "For thus says the LORD, who created the heavens . . . who formed the earth and made it . . . : I am the LORD, and there is no other" (Isa. 45:18). The one who fashioned the whole of finitude—in biblical language, both "heaven and earth"—cannot himself be ingredient in the finite world in either its material or immaterial expression. The later theological tradition speaks of *creatio ex nihilo*, creation from nothing, which is the implication of this Isaianic claim that Yahweh made all of finitude and remains incomparable to it. For if God made the world out of some preexisting reality, then he could in principle be categorized alongside of that Equiprimordial stuff.

As his prayer continues, David effects a fascinating correlation between the uniqueness of God's way of being and the utter distinctiveness of the people this God has chosen for his own: "Who is like your people, like Israel?" (2 Sam. 7:23). Israel should not be understood as one people among many, even one "religious" tribe among many. The Creator God, who is not a being among beings, can enter into the life of a people in such a way that he neither ceases to be God nor undermines the integrity of the people he touches. This essential noncompetitiveness permits God to make covenants with his people that are not demeaning or oppressive but life-giving: "And you established your people Israel for yourself to be your people forever; and you, O LORD, became their God" (2 Sam. 7:24). In order to understand the uniqueness of the God-Israel relationship hinted at in David's great prayer, it might be instructive to contrast the story, in Greek

8. Robert Barron, *The Priority of Christ: Toward a Postliberal Catholicism* (Grand Rapids: Brazos, 2007), 205.

mythology, of Zeus's encounter with Semele and the image of the burning bush in the book of Exodus. In the Greek tale, Zeus appears in disguised form to the beautiful young woman, but when he discloses himself in his true nature, the unfortunate girl bursts into flame and is consumed.[9] The clear lesson is that the chief of the gods is ontologically incompatible with a creature of finite nature: when he asserts himself with full power, she has to give way. But in the Exodus story, something else altogether is on offer. Yahweh appears in a bush that burns but is not consumed. This implies that the drawing close of the noncompetitive God enhances a finite nature and makes it radiant, transfiguring it but not consuming it. The play of the enhancing God and transfigured creation comes to its fullest expression in the incarnation when two natures, divine and human, come together "without mixing, mingling, or confusion" as the Council of Chalcedon states it—Jesus's humanity is fully itself precisely in relation to his divinity. What appears completely in the person of the new David is anticipated in the subtle theological assumptions informing the prayer of the original David. This deeply biblical notion of the God-humanity relationship evident in both Testaments is the foundation for the long tradition of Christian humanism, perhaps given no better expression than in Irenaeus's axiom, *Gloria Dei homo vivens*: "The glory of God is a human being fully alive."[10]

9. Edith Hamilton, *Mythology* (Boston: Little, Brown, 1942), 63–64.
10. Irenaeus of Lyons, *Adversus Haereses* 4.20.7.

2 SAMUEL 8

After the rich and theologically resonant content of the sixth and seventh chapters, the eighth chapter of 2 Samuel might strike us as a bit of an anticlimax. Only eighteen verses long, it recounts a number of military victories of David as well as the expansion and consolidation of his empire. But one must always remember to squint at these texts through theological lenses, for the author is telling a very important story indeed: the beginning of the process by which the promises to Adam and Abraham are being concretely fulfilled. David is being presented here not simply as a victorious general and canny politician but as an agent of God's project of expansion and empire building (Hahn 2012: 19).

Some commentators suggest plausibly enough that the eighth chapter picks up a narrative thread that was dropped at the end of the fifth chapter in order to insert the story of the arrival of the ark and the Nathan promise. Indeed, the fifth chapter closes with the assertion that David "struck down the Philistines from Geba all the way to Gezer" (2 Sam. 5:25), and the eighth chapter commences, "Some time afterward, David attacked the Philistines and subdued them" (2 Sam. 8:1). The Philistine victory over Saul at Mount Gilboa, located quite a bit to the north and east of their home territory, signaled the supremacy of that nation in the region. David struggled throughout his military career to wrest control from this stubborn enemy, and the brief description of his battle at the beginning of the eighth chapter probably is communicating his victory in symbolic language: "David took Metheg-ammah out of the hand of the Philistines" (2 Sam. 8:1). Scholars search in vain for a clear geographical referent for "Metheg-ammah" and so try to explain the term metaphorically as either the "bridle" of the Philistines or their "mother city" (Alter 1999: 236). The point is that David finally deals with this ancient foe, pushing them out of Israelite territory as Adam should have pushed the serpent out of the garden.

The defeat of the Philistines frees David to engage other enemies of the nation further afield. We are told that he conquers the Moabites and treats their army with particular brutality, killing two-thirds of the soldiers chosen by a kind of random lottery. David had strong familial connections to the Moabites through his father, who was the grandson of Ruth the Moabite. Moreover, during the period when he was being pursued by Saul, David entrusted his own parents to the care of the Moabites. One might wonder, therefore, why he was so cruel to them. One could speculate that this was an example of David's willingness to engage in some rather crude realpolitik, but I think it wisest to interpret this in the theological context. When it comes to the tending of the garden and the eradication of those forces opposed to God's creative intention, one must be clear and undivided in purpose. Not even family connections and ties of affection should get in the way of performing one's moral and spiritual duty. We are reminded of Jesus's seeming cruelty in advising a prospective disciple who wanted to bury his father first before following the Lord: "Let the dead bury their own dead" (Luke 9:60). Having been conquered on the battlefield, the Moabites "became servants to David and brought tribute" (2 Sam. 8:2). This is the first indication that the newly constituted Israelite kingdom is becoming an empire and that the nations, however constrained militarily and politically, are beginning to come toward Zion (Polzin 1993: 90). What Isaiah prophetically envisioned—"In days to come the mountain of the LORD's house shall be established as the highest of the mountains . . . all the nations shall stream toward it" (Isa. 2:2)—and what the journey of the magi represented—"Then, opening their treasure chests, they offered him gifts of gold, frankincense, and myrrh" (Matt. 2:11)—is anticipated in this Moabite tribute to David.

With Moab under control, David turns his attention to Aram-Zobah, which Robert Alter describes as "the large and dominant kingdom of Mesopotamia, to the north and east of biblical Israel" (Alter 1999: 237). The Hebrew of this passage is ambiguous. One could read it as suggesting that David invaded Zobah when its king, Hadadezer, was sojourning to the Euphrates in search of a captured "monument" or stela. Or one could interpret it as suggesting that David engaged Hadadezer when David was venturing far north and east of Jerusalem in order to plant his own monument by the river. In any case, the king of Israel decisively defeats the king of Zobah and takes prisoner seventeen hundred horsemen and twenty thousand infantry. We are told that David "hamstrung all the chariot horses, but left enough for a hundred chariots" (2 Sam. 8:4). It would be incorrect to interpret this simply as an act of cruelty. Rather, it represents a canny military decision on David's part. We saw that in the battles with the Philistines, the Israelites were at a significant disadvantage whenever their enemy met them on the open plain with chariots. David wisely eliminates from this new foe a weapon with which Israel is poorly equipped to contend. Sprinting to the defense of their Aramean allies, armies from Damascus come against David. The king of Israel defeats them and subsequently places garrisons in the region of Damascus to ensure his imperial hold. Those conquered people then imitate the Moabites in bringing tribute to David. Here, one can see how extensive David's imperial ambitions are. Ranging far outside of the traditional home territories of either Israel or Judah, David certainly imposes his political authority. More important for the author of our text, he extends the reach of the God of Israel. In a move that anticipates the influx of wealth and *matériel* for the temple later in his reign, David arranges for a good deal of gold and bronze to be brought to his capital as well. Isaiah would later sing of this ingathering of the best of the nations to the world's true center: "Rejoice with Jerusalem, and be glad for her, all you who love her. . . . For thus says the LORD: I will extend prosperity to her like a river, and the wealth of the nations like an overflowing stream" (Isa. 66:10, 12).

Next we hear of King Toi of Hamath, a region to the northwest of the kingdom of Aram-zobah in present-day Syria, who is so impressed by David's victory over Hadadezer that he sends his son Joram to congratulate the Israelite king. On his visit to Jerusalem, Joram brings "articles of silver, gold, and bronze," and David immediately dedicates them to Yahweh. What would upend Israelite kings in the centuries that follow David was, among other moral failings, a tendency to accumulate wealth for its own sake. At least at this stage of his career, David was willing to put wealth at the service of a higher good, the conditioned for the sake of the unconditioned. Thomas Aquinas comments that the four great substitutes for God—the finite idols that we seek in place of the truly ultimate good—are power, pleasure, honor, and wealth.[1] All are good in themselves, but none is the infinite value that alone can satisfy the infinite longing of the heart. When any one of the four is sought in place of God, it becomes in short order the object of an addiction, and it will, in time, turn on and destroy the seeker. This is why there is extraordinary spiritual power to the image of David dedicating to Yahweh the wealth gained through his military exploits. The specific mention of

1. Thomas Aquinas, *Summa theologiae: Latin Text and English Translation, Introductions, Notes, Appendices, and Glossaries*, ed. Thomas Gilby et al., 61 vols. (New York: McGraw-Hill, 1964–81), 16:31–57.

the conquest of the Amalekites and the establishment of garrisons throughout Edom is meant to show that David had control of the regions south of Israel as well, giving him economic access to Egypt, the Sinai, Arabia, and Africa. All of this military expansion would give Solomon an extraordinary range of influence just a generation later and would provide further confirmation of David's Adamic and Abrahamic significance.

What is being communicated in just a few breathless verses in the short course of the eighth chapter is doubtless the work of many years that took up the prime of David's career. We are given the rather clear impression that he was a military, diplomatic, and political figure operating at the very height of his powers. At the same time, it is twice stressed during this chapter that the credit belonged to Yahweh: "The LORD gave victory to David wherever he went" (2 Sam. 8:6, 14). Once more we see the theme, present throughout the Samuel literature, that God does not so much intervene interruptively as operate congruently and noncompetitively with ordinary human agency. I will develop this central idea at much greater length below.

Finally, it is in this brief and seemingly nondescript chapter of 2 Samuel that we find the line that represents, in many ways, the very climax of the Old Testament story of Israel, the point toward which Israelite history had been tending and the point from which, tragically, that history declined: "So David reigned over all Israel; and David administered justice and equity to all his people" (2 Sam. 8:15). This is the reign of the new Adam presiding over a renewed Eden, having eliminated from the garden all those forces that stood opposed to God, guiding his people toward right praise, and preparing for the expansion of this sacred order to the rest of the world. What follows, as immediately as the eleventh chapter of 2 Samuel with the story of Bathsheba, is the tumble from this equity and right order into the chaos of sin. With the possible exception of the earliest years of Solomon, Israel never again attained the height represented by David's just rule over Israel described in the eighth chapter. At this stage of his career David was a messiah in full, for he had gathered the tribes at Hebron, established the ark in Jerusalem, dealt with the enemies of the nation, and was just beginning to bring the good order of Israel to the wider world. N. T. Wright and others argue that these four tasks—gathering the tribes, cleansing the temple, dealing with the enemies, and reigning as sovereign of the nations—are precisely the tasks that Jesus, the new David, fulfilled in an entirely different and more elevated key.[2]

2. N. T. Wright, *Jesus and the Victory of God*, Christian Origins and the Question of God 2 (Minneapolis: Fortress, 1996), 224.

2 SAMUEL 9

After the chronicling and grand summaries of the eighth chapter we return in the ninth chapter to the ruminations of a thoughtful king and to a much smaller, more carefully drawn scene, one extremely rich both psychologically and spiritually. David inquires of his staff, "Is there still anyone left of the house of Saul to whom I may show kindness for Jonathan's sake?" (2 Sam. 9:1). The typical laconism of the author of the Samuel literature requires the unpacking of this somewhat puzzling question. The Hebrew word behind "kindness" here is *ḥesed* (heartfelt compassion, grace), a term frequently used to describe Yahweh himself. The king wonders whether there is any member of Saul's family left upon whom he could lavish something like the love of God, a grace given without consideration of merit, a pure love. We recall, of course, that this is the family of the man who ruthlessly pursued David and sought his life, the family that, in principle, poses a permanent threat to David's rule. Normally in the tough, militaristic society of David's time and place, a king, having come to power, routinely eliminated anyone in the family of the previous ruler. This explains why the narrator of 2 Samuel is so very careful to indicate time and again that David was not responsible for the deaths of his Saulide rivals.

David specifies precisely why he wants to show this grace to the house of Saul: "for Jonathan's sake" (2 Sam. 9:1). This clue sends us back to 1 Samuel, more specifically to two promises that David made—one to his beloved friend and the other to that friend's father. When David was fleeing from Saul but obviously was destined to become king one day, Jonathan said,

> But if my father intends to do you harm, the LORD do so to Jonathan, and more also, if I do not disclose it to you, and send you away, so that you may go in safety.

> May the LORD be with you, as he has been with my father. If I am still alive, show me the faithful love of the LORD; but if I die, never cut off your faithful love from my house, even if the LORD were to cut off every one of the enemies of David from the face of the earth. (1 Sam. 20:13–15)

And so David swore a "covenant" with Jonathan precisely in these terms. Again, what Jonathan assumed was that, once in power, David would be naturally inclined to eliminate the family of Saul. Later, having for the second time experienced the mercy of David, Saul said, "Now I know that you shall surely be king, and that the kingdom of Israel shall be established in your hand. Swear to me therefore by the LORD that you will not cut off my descendants after me, and that you will not wipe out my name from my father's house" (1 Sam. 24:20–21). David dutifully swore to these terms. These promises, made to two men now dead, haunt the mind of the king as the ninth chapter of 2 Samuel commences.

With so many of the house of Saul dead, no one in David's immediate entourage is able to answer the king's plaintive query about remaining members of that house. A functionary from the circle of Saul is summoned, and he tells David that a son of Jonathan remains—the young man Mephibosheth, whose story we heard earlier. As a descendant of Saul, Mephibosheth posed a certain danger to David, especially if the king brought the young man into his inner sanctum. Moreover, as someone crippled in both feet, he would hardly be an ornament to the Jerusalem court, nor would he easily find a place among the beautiful children of David. But David is not interested in finding someone who would prove advantageous to him; he is trying to find someone upon whom he can show *ḥesed*, "tender mercy." If love is willing the good of the other, a sure test of love is compassion toward someone who cannot repay one's kindness. As Jesus himself said, "If you love those who love you, what reward do you have? Do not even the tax collectors do the same? And if you greet only your brothers and sisters, what more are you doing than others?" (Matt. 5:46–47). Upon hearing of Mephibosheth, David asks but one question: "Where is he?" The usually canny and calculating king is not sizing up the situation, weighing advantages and disadvantages, determining the political fallout of his decision; he simply wants to find a recipient of his grace. In that, he is a beautiful Old Testament icon of the God who "makes his sun rise on the evil and on the good, and sends rain on the righteous and the unrighteous" (Matt. 5:45).

David is told that Mephibosheth is living in the house of Machir son of Ammiel at a place called Lo-debar, located in the northern Transjordan, a region to which other members of the Saulide clan had fled. The town name in Hebrew means, literally, "no pastureland," and therefore it can probably be assumed that Mephibosheth had repaired, for his own safety, to a remote and desolate area far from David's immediate sphere of influence, a place no one would be particularly tempted to visit. One might think of Mephibosheth like someone in a witness protection program today; perhaps only Ziba knew where he was ensconced. One can only imagine Mephibosheth's terror when an agent of King David arrives at his door in Lo-debar. He must have thought that the end had come. And this explains why, upon being ushered into the king's presence, he "fell on his face and did obeisance" (2 Sam. 9:6); he doubtless thought that he had to beg for his life. Sensing the young man's understandable fear, David says, "Do not be afraid, for I will show you kindness for the sake of your father Jonathan; I will restore to you all the land of your grandfather Saul, and you yourself shall eat at my table always" (2 Sam. 9:7). Expecting the worst, Mephibosheth receives an abundance of grace; crippled and prostrate before the one who had supreme power over him, he finds himself lifted up and lavished with benefits, even to the point of being invited to share the family table of his master.

It is not difficult to see why this scene is described as a stunning icon of the divine grace, of God's willingness to raise to his own splendor someone utterly undeserving of it. Psalm 23 speaks of the God who prepares a table for his subject and invites him to dwell in the royal house (Ps. 23:5–6). Jesus consistently invited both the worthy and the unworthy to sit at table with him, graciously drawing them into the divine fellowship. Sensing the sheer surprise and paradox of what was happening to him, Mephibosheth cries out, "What is your servant, that you should look upon a dead dog such as I?" (2 Sam. 9:8). Classical Christian tradition, both Protestant and Catholic, teaches that salvation cannot be merited or earned through the exertions of the will and that human beings stand before God in a state of sin and helplessness. We are "dead dogs," in the words of Mephibosheth, but we have received an amazing grace from the God who condescended to invite us into his household and to share the treasury of his intimacy and regard. Mephibosheth was hid in fear of the king; likewise we sinners, alienated from God by our own refusal to accept the divine love, conceal ourselves from God as Adam and Eve hid themselves in the underbrush of Eden after the original sin. But David did not wait for Mephibosheth to come to him or impress him with a show of loyalty; rather, he sought out the young, misshapen man and made him a member of the royal company. In our case God does not expect us to earn our way into his friendship but rather offers that friendship as a sheer gift, even to us who are misshapen by sin. To be sure, the Protestant and Catholic theological traditions diverge at this point, for Catholics see this unmerited grace as the origin and root of justification but not as justification tout court. The Council of Trent speaks of justification and increase in justification, which is to say, the deepening of friendship with God that comes through active cooperation with the divine grace.[1] This increase corresponds to what Jesus spoke of as "remaining" in the love of God, which is freely given but which can be participated in to varying degrees.

There is, of course, a more cynical reading of this scene, which suggests that David wanted to identify the last of the Saulides so that he could keep him under close surveillance, essentially, as Robert Alter comments, "under a luxurious house arrest" (Alter 1999: 243). The repeated mention of Mephibosheth eating at the king's table could be construed by the more skeptical observer as an attempt clearly to publicize David's benefaction. Lending credence to this darker interpretation is the fact that Mephibosheth will eventually turn on David, joining the Absalom rebellion against the king. Finally, the frequent reference to the crippled feet of Jonathan's son, including the last line of the chapter—"Now he was lame in both his feet" (2 Sam. 9:13)—might be read as a somewhat triumphalistic reminder that the house of Saul, though still in existence, is attenuated and deeply compromised. Who could miss the contrast between David dancing his way on extremely nimble feet into his capital city and the grandson of Saul limping his way to David's table (Alter 1999: 243)?

1. H. J. Schroeder, trans., *Canons and Decrees of the Council of Trent* (St. Louis: B. Herder, 1941), 36.

2 SAMUEL 10

We find an interesting link between the ninth and tenth chapters, for both deal with David's desire to show compassion on the son of someone who had been kind to him. In the present case, the object of David's generosity is Hanun, the successor to Nahash, king of the Ammonites, who had been good to David, probably during the time of the civil war with Saul. In these two chapters, David is at the height of his powers, relatively secure as king of Israel, having subdued most of the rival nations around him. At peace, he can radiate peace and kindness. Once again, although these gestures make perfect sense in ordinary political, military, and psychological terms, they are also intended to be iconic representations of what the anointed of Israel properly means for the rest of the world: a source of blessing and well-being.

In accord with his benificent inclinations, David sends a delegation to console Hanun on the death of his father. But the Israelite envoys are perceived by wary Ammonite observers as potential spies, sent to reconnoiter the territory in advance of an Israelite takeover: "Do you really think that David is honoring your father just because he has sent messengers with condolences for you? Has not David sent his envoys to you to search the city, to spy it out, and to overthrow it?" (2 Sam. 10:3). Ancient walled cities often had clandestine tunnels and underground conduits that could be detected only by careful inspection from inside the city. Indeed, precisely this kind of spy work might explain how David learned of the well by which his men were able to take Jerusalem. Given this and David's recent military sorties into a variety of neighboring regions, this Ammonite suspicion is, to say the least, understandable. In fact, their attitude precisely mirrors that of Joab regarding the visit of Abner to Hebron during the war with Ishbosheth.

So the offer of condolence and good will is refused in a most dramatic fashion: "Hanun seized David's envoys, shaved off half the beard of each, cut off their garments in the middle at their hips, and sent them away" (2 Sam. 10:4). The shaving of half the beard was meant not merely to produce a ludicrous effect but to deeply insult the masculinity of the ambassadors; the vertical cutting of the garment so as to reveal one buttock was meant to shame, even sexually so. In the culture of that time and place, it would be hard to imagine actions more demeaning and humiliating. We recall that David, when he had the opportunity to kill his persecutor, instead sliced off a small piece of Saul's garment, and even earlier that Saul, desperate to stay in the good graces of Samuel, tore off a piece of the prophet's mantle. In all of these cases the ripping of another's clothes was at the very least offensive and inappropriate, even aggressive. Moreover, the garments in question in the tenth chapter are not ordinary clothes; they are *madim*, which carries the sense of clothes worn in performance of an official function. Therefore the Ammonites, by this mocking gesture, are not simply humiliating the ambassadors personally; they are consciously insulting the one who sent them (McCarter 1984: 270). Deeply sensitive to their shame, David instructs the envoys to remain in Jericho, likely the first place of habitation between the Ammonite capital and Jerusalem, until their beards grow back.

The callous, even violent, rejection of ambassadors calls to mind for any Christian Jesus's parable of the vineyard owner who sends a series of representatives to hostile tenant farmers. After these envoys had been mistreated, the owner finally sends his son, confident that they will respect his heir. But they kill the son and hence offer the deepest possible affront to the owner, prompting his destructive wrath. Jesus's story is, of course, an allegory of Israel's relationship with the prophets sent to them generation after generation and with the Son whom the Father sent in the last days. Might this peculiar tale from the tenth chapter of 2 Samuel be construed in a similar manner as a figure of Yahweh's rapport with the wider world through the ministration of Israel? When the representatives of God's way of being arrive in a world distorted by sin, they are regularly mocked and rejected, and this mockery invites God's chastisement. In this sense, David is the new Adam seeking to spread the influence of a restored Eden and meeting with the resistance of those who prefer the path of disobedience.

Once they understood how angry David is, the Ammonites steel for war, drawing to them as allies Arameans from both Beth-rehob and Zobah as well as the forces of the king of Maacah and the king of Tob. The somewhat achronological narrative style of the author is revealed here, for we heard in the eighth chapter that David had already subdued the Arameans. In any case, the consistent and organized resistance to God's way, which is evident in the biblical story from Adam and Eve to the Philistines, is the focus here. In response to this mustering of enemy troops, David springs into action. This is the same David who, as a boy, killed the lion threatening his flock of sheep; who, as a young man, severed the head of the giant; who, in the prime of his life, deftly engaged the jealous Saul; who, as king, gathered the tribes and held off the Philistines. In a word, this is still the David of decision and deed, an Adam who knows how to defend the garden. However, just the slightest indication of a shift in attitude, which will become tragically apparent in the next chapter, is on display in the description of the king's action: "When David heard of it, he sent Joab and all the army with the warriors" (2 Sam. 10:7). Robert Alter points out that throughout the tenth chapter David is depicted as "sending" others on mission rather than taking action himself. He is becoming less the martial leader and more the sedentary king. That this change might be due to David's increasing age is likely, but a theological reading compels us to notice a moral and spiritual issue as well: the king's growing unwillingness to engage evil directly and personally (Alter 1999: 246).

When Joab arrives at the gates of the Ammonite capital, he finds himself in a dicey situation. The Ammonites had arrayed themselves before the walls of their city, and one set of their allies, the Arameans of Zobah, were arriving from the northeast while another, the men of Tob and Maacah, were moving in from the south. The Israelite commander intuits immediately that he has been drawn into a trap, caught between two rocks and a hard place. At this point, the author does something fairly rare in the biblical literature. He lays out in some detail the precise military maneuvers undertaken by the Israelite commander. We hear how Joab takes an elite corps of his troop against the Arameans and sends the rest of the Israelite army, under the command of Abishai, against the Ammonites and establishes a subtle coordination between the two armies. The result is a resounding victory for Israel. To be sure, the scriptural authors exult in recounting the numbers of the dead after a decisive battle, but they hardly ever delve into the tactical details of how generals, Israelite or otherwise, bring about a great victory. Why the attention to strategy in this case? Perhaps the author is preparing us for the following chapter, in which Joab's military acumen is again on full display, even as David languishes at home, falling into his disastrous flirtation with Bathsheba. Once more, the paradigmatically good king is undergoing a gradual metamorphosis, anticipating the centuries of bad kings who would follow him.

However, just prior to his great fall, David does indeed rouse himself to one last mighty military exploit. Stung by the Israelite victory, the Arameans regroup, this time with reinforcements from beyond the Euphrates. When David hears of this, he does not send anyone, but rather "he gathered all Israel together, and crossed the Jordan, and came to Helam" (2 Sam. 10:17). This is the David of Hebron and Jerusalem, the uniter of the nation; this is the David of the Philistine wars. So impressive is his kingship and so skillful his military strategy that he "killed of the Arameans seven hundred chariot teams, and forty thousand horsemen" (2 Sam. 10:18). When the kings arrayed against him see this slaughter, they surrender to David and willingly become his vassals. But this display of resolve and power is a kind of twilight of David's kingship, a last, glorious manifestation of the leader he was.

Robert Polzin makes the fascinating observation that "halves" play a great role in this tenth chapter: the ambassadors to the Ammonites have half their beards cut away and half their garments ripped, and Joab splits his army in two in order to hold off the enemies of Israel (Polzin 1993: 108). Building on Polzin's insight, Robert Alter speculates, "One wonders whether this narrative dynamic of mitosis, even though it is a saving strategy in Joab's case, might be a thematic introduction to all the inner divisions in court and nation, the fractures in the house of David, that take up the rest of the narrative" (Alter 1999: 246). The time of David's consolidated reign as king in Jerusalem will prove tragically short—as brief as Adam's reign over a sinless Eden, as brief as Solomon's lordship over kingdom and temple. The climb toward the high point of David's reign was slow and ragged indeed, and the fall from it would be long and steady. But that brief, shining moment was enough to beguile the imagination of Israel for a thousand years, animating a messianic hope that carried the people through national disaster, exile, and conquest until the arrival of a new David whose kingdom, an angel from heaven declared, would last forever. But why should David's Edenic moment have been so short? Why is it so impossibly difficult for human beings to remain in right relationship with God? The eleventh chapter, which deals largely with the episode between David and Bathsheba, explores those questions.

SERIES THREE

DAVID AND BATHSHEBA

2 SAMUEL 11

The Samuel literature constitutes one of the most narratively sophisticated and psychologically penetrating texts that has come down to us from the ancient world. But the artistry of the author is on fullest display in the two chapters, eleven and twelve, that deal with the Bathsheba incident and its immediate aftermath. The development and interweaving of key themes, the economical manner of suggesting motive through the language that the characters employ, the sinuously subtle relationship between commands and responses—all of it comes together in a story as beautiful, moving, and sad as the best of Shakespeare's tragedies. This tale has intrigued the imaginations of some of the greatest artists in the Western tradition. One has only to think of Rembrandt's depiction of the face of Bathsheba as she reads a letter from David. Has any artist ever managed to convey a more complex set of emotions and perceptions? But Rembrandt's artistry is simply a vague imitation in oils of what the author of the Samuel literature communicates in words.[1]

Moreover, Robert Alter certainly is right when he suggests that "the story of David and Bathsheba . . . is the great turning point of the whole David story" (Alter 1999: 249). For indeed, practically everything that follows in 2 Samuel is conditioned by this epic fall from grace. David wrestled with this sin for the rest of his life, and both his public and private affairs were permanently marked by it. Most important, Israel was changed for the worse by this event, in a manner analogous to the change for the worse visited upon the human race by the sin of Adam. What is perhaps most remarkable is that the Bible contains this story at all. The book of 1 Chronicles, which reproduces most of the events of David's career

1. Kenneth Clark, *Civilisation: A Personal View* (New York: Harper & Row, 1969), 206.

mentioned in the books of Samuel, piously leaves out any reference to Bathsheba; almost any other hero's story from any culture would edit out a scene as embarrassing to the hero as this one. Why does the author so openly undermine the greatest king in Israelite history? Perhaps he wants to communicate the simple truth that divine grace, and not human virtue, is finally what counts, that reliance upon ethical perfection and heroic effort results inevitably in disappointment and tragedy. It is indispensible that we do not forget that the David who fell with Bathsheba was none other than the slayer of Goliath, the friend to Jonathan, the loyal servant of Saul, the man after Yahweh's heart, and the sweet singer of Israel. He is not presented as a sexual pervert or a self-involved, power-hungry tyrant; quite the contrary, he is a remarkably good man, one of the best that Israel ever produced, a new Adam. And yet, like the old Adam, he sinned. Thereupon hangs a tale of enormous theological importance.

The eleventh chapter opens with the seemingly bland remark that it was the spring of the year, the time when kings usually sallied forth to do battle, once the torrential rains of the winter had subsided and military operations were feasible. The observation becomes more pointed when we hear that King David, instead of leading the campaign himself, sends Joab to reengage the Ammonites about whom we heard in the preceding chapter. Why, precisely at the moment when ardent fighters sally forth, was the great David sending someone else? Perhaps he had simply grown too old. Though it is difficult to determine intervals of time within this narrative to any degree of exactitude, David is probably around fifty years old as this episode commences. On the other hand, in the previous season he was fully engaged in the battle with the Ammonites. It would be hard to imagine that David was lacking in courage, for that quality has been on steady display throughout both books of Samuel. I wonder whether the best explanation is that the king had grown lazy—a bit fat and sassy. Earlier, we heard that upon becoming king in Jerusalem, David took on many new wives and concubines. The author of Samuel does not comment on this negatively, but the author of Deuteronomy is eminently clear on the danger posed to Israelite kings through the taking on of many possessions, including women: "Even so, he [the king] must not acquire many horses for himself, or return the people to Egypt in order to acquire more horses, since the LORD has said to you, 'You must never return that way again.' And he must not acquire many wives for himself, or else his heart will turn away; also silver and gold he must not acquire in great quantity for himself" (Deut. 17:16–17). Sexual indulgence, the management (both financial and emotional) of a large harem, the intrigue that inevitably bubbles up among the intimates of a king—all of it distracts from the central concern of a monarch. He would become more preoccupied with maintaining peace in his court than defending and expanding the kingdom that God had entrusted to him. That telling word "send" occurs eleven times in this brief chapter, commencing with David's "sending" Joab to fight, and its connotations of withdrawal from action convey the heart of the story (Polzin 1993: 109–10). The sedentary king, with too much time on his hands and unclear in regard to his mission, begins to engage in manipulative and self-serving behavior. Indeed, the Hebrew term that is rendered "remained" in the New Revised Standard Version ("But David remained at Jerusalem" [2 Sam. 11:1]) literally means "sat" (Alter 1999: 250). Who could miss the contrast with the dashing and frenetically mobile David whom we have known to this point?

"It happened, late one afternoon, when David rose from his couch and was walking about on the roof of the king's house, that he saw from the roof a woman bathing; the woman was very beautiful" (2 Sam. 11:2). One might imagine that an afternoon siesta would commence not long after lunch, and even if David ate a very late lunch, his rising in the late afternoon indicates that he had enjoyed a rather lengthy *riposo*. The scriptures and the theological tradition often use sleep pejoratively to indicate lack of moral and spiritual awareness. Think of the three disciples, accompanying Jesus at Gethsemane, who could not manage to stay awake at the moment of the Lord's greatest need, and of the exhortation in Ephesians, "Sleeper, awake! Rise from the dead, and Christ will shine on you" (Eph. 5:14). Therefore to be asleep in the middle of the day, especially when soldiers are fighting a desperate battle on one's behalf, is a symbolic evocation of deep inattentiveness, drowsy indifference to the mission and to the demand of the moment. Chrysostom speaks of the "drunkenness" of David's soul at this moment: "Because, when the charioteer gets drunk, the chariot moves in an irregular, disorderly manner. What the charioteer is to the chariot, the soul is to the body. If the soul becomes darkened, the body rolls in mud."[2]

David's view from the roof, gazing down in an all-seeing way on the whole of his capital city, is a confirmation of Samuel's worst fears concerning kings: that they would be domineering, oppressive, superior, and self-absorbed. Strutting on top of his palace, David is a parody of God's providential presidency over the whole of creation. This is David having seized, Adam-like, the prerogatives of divinity, and what follows shows vividly the havoc that is wreaked when human

2. John Chrysostom, "Homilies on Repentance and Almsgiving 2.2.4–7," in *Joshua, Judges, Ruth, 1–2 Samuel*, ed. John R. Franke, Ancient Christian Commentary on Scripture: Old Testament 4 (Downers Grove, IL: InterVarsity, 2005), 356.

beings begin playing the role of God. Surveying the whole of his city, seeing what delights his eye, ordering about his underlings, David is the precise opposite of the pious young king who guilelessly asked God whether to go up to Hebron. The "look" of David, the regard from on high, is the gaze of the master that objectifies what it sees. The look of the lover is one that invites an answering look while the regard of the master pins the object of that regard to the table for examination.

He sees a woman of great beauty. Especially given the numerous associations between David and Adam that I have already noted, it would be difficult to miss the link between Bathsheba and Eve and between Bathsheba and the fruit of the tree of the knowledge of good and evil. On the one hand Bathsheba, comfortably naked in the garden of David's city, is Eve, the occasion for the king's sin; on the other hand, the very beauty of Bathsheba is like that Edenic fruit that was "good for food . . . and a delight to the eyes" (Gen. 3:6). Indeed, it would be naive in the extreme to construe Bathsheba as totally innocent—she just happens to be bathing nude within easy eyeshot of the king? David's first move is to send a messenger to find out about her. Once more buffers, indirection, and the use of others to do the dirty work is consistently characteristic of the king during this episode. The servant reports that she is "Bathsheba daughter of Eliam, the wife of Uriah the Hittite" (2 Sam. 11:3). Since it was unusual to identify a woman by both her father and her husband, some suggest that both Eliam and Uriah were prominent members of David's inner military circle. Eliam will play a role later in the story, but the emphasis is clearly on Uriah, explicitly identified as a foreigner, though he bore a stately Hebrew name meaning "Yahweh is my light." Likely, therefore, he was not so much a foreigner as a native or naturalized Israelite of Hittite extraction. The irony, obviously, is that this man of foreign origins shows far greater loyalty to the customs and traditions of Israel than the Israelite king who murders him.

Instead of approaching Bathsheba directly and personally, David once again sends intermediaries: "So David sent messengers to get her, and she came to him, and he lay with her" (2 Sam. 11:4). The matter-of-fact, even rat-a-tat-tat, rhythm of that sentence conveys the coldness of kingly command. David is in charge. He has seen what he wants, and he gets it. This scene is reminiscent of Jezebel's cold-hearted and swift action against Naboth, who rebuffed King Ahab's request to buy Naboth's vineyard. With a few deft administrative commands, and without a second thought for the morality of her moves, Jezebel eliminated her recalcitrant subject and secured the vineyard for her husband. Since David controlled the army and whatever "police" force there was, and since there were no real checks and balances built into the system, the king could do whatever he wanted. But the biblical authors are never pleased with this naked sort of power play. A possible mitigating factor is suggested by the subtle change in grammatical subject in the middle of the sentence under consideration. David indeed sends for Bathsheba and lays with her, but it is Bathsheba who comes to him. When the verb "come to" or "come into" is used with a masculine subject and feminine object, it invariably denotes active sexual penetration on the part of the male. But here the author makes the woman the subject of the verb, suggesting perhaps that Bathsheba was not an entirely passive victim of David's aggression and manipulation (Alter 1999: 251). This interpretation is given added weight by the author's dry observation that Bathsheba had been purifying herself—almost certainly the ritual bath after menstruation. According to the standard Jewish sensibility, a woman was particularly receptive to conception in the week or so just following menstruation. Therefore one might be justified in thinking that the rooftop bath was far from innocent but rather a none-too-subtle advertisement to the king that Bathsheba was interested in becoming pregnant. That Bathsheba is far from a merely passive object of manipulation is emphatically confirmed at the beginning of 1 Kings, where we learn that she cleverly and successfully lobbies the aged David to allow her son Solomon to succeed to the throne.

Just after her intercourse with the king, Bathsheba becomes pregnant and informs David of the fact. Astonishingly, her words "I am pregnant" (2 Sam. 11:5) constitute the only speech of Bathsheba in all of 2 Samuel. His feel for danger and instinct for decisive action intact, the king immediately moves: "So David sent word to Joab, 'Send me Uriah the Hittite.' And Joab sent Uriah to David" (2 Sam. 11:6). Again, the bang-bang rhythm of the sendings and commandings can be seen but also the detached, at-a-safe-distance nature of these instructions. This is a far remove indeed from the David who went out personally and boldly to meet Goliath, tore a piece from Saul's cloak, and cut off the foreskins of two hundred Philistines. Why, precisely, was David afraid? Though he exercised authority without the restraint of ordinary legal checks and balances, he knew that even the king is not *extra legem* in regard to the commands of God. Deuteronomy is utterly clear concerning the fate of those caught in adultery: "If a man is caught lying with the wife of another man, both of them shall die, the man who lay with the woman as well as the woman. So you shall purge the evil from Israel" (Deut. 22:22). Therefore, like so many powerful people before and since, David endeavors to effect a cover-up, concealing his sin rather than facing it.

When Uriah arrives at the palace, David inquires in good nature after the health of Joab and the success of Israelite arms in the battle against the Ammonites.

However, the king is utterly uninterested in the soldier's answers, and Uriah must have wondered why he had been summoned all the way to the capital simply to make some elementary observations. Then he hears this command: "Go down to your house, and wash your feet" (2 Sam. 11:8). Since feet often symbolize the male genitals, this is a delicately indirect way of saying, "Go home and have sex with your wife." Obviously, David is confident that this hastily arranged intercourse between Uriah and Bathsheba will quell any suspicion that someone other than Uriah is the father of her child. And given all of the sendings and deliveries of messages at the court of David, suspicion of the affair must have been rampant. To assure that the couple will be in a relaxed and amorous mood, David goes so far as to send a catered dinner to their home. But the king's best-laid plans unravel precisely because he chooses the wrong soldier to manipulate. Instead of lying with his wife, Uriah lays down to sleep with his fellow soldiers guarding the palace of the king, practicing along with them the sexual abstinence that was expected of Israelite fighters during wartime.

When David, in frustration, presses the Hittite and encourages him to go home, Uriah responds in the manner of a loyal Boy Scout: "The ark and Israel and Judah remain in booths; and my lord Joab and the servants of my lord are camping in the open field; shall I then go to my house, to eat and to drink, and to lie with my wife? As you live . . . I will not do such a thing" (2 Sam. 11:11). Uriah is a pure Kantian here, following the demand of the moral law despite any inclination in the contrary direction, including the inclination to obey a direct command of the king. He demonstrates the unconditioned love for the law David endeavored to demonstrate with his exuberant dance before the ark. Indeed, Uriah's reference to the ark remaining in a booth or tent must have cut David to the heart, for it was precisely that lowly housing of the ark that prompted the king to seek the building of a great temple (Baldwin 1988: 228). Uriah embodies the very values that David exemplified at his best and hence is, unwittingly, mocking the king and undermining his nasty little cover-up. Frustrated but still conniving, David orders Uriah to stay an extra day in the capital. That night, he invites the soldier for a night of eating and drinking at the royal palace. Having flattered Uriah and successfully made him drunk, David once more sends the soldier to spend the night with his wife, but he sleeps instead with the palace guard.

I just said that Uriah blocked the king's machinations unwittingly, but there is another way to read this section. Perhaps Uriah was not as innocent as he is often made out to be (Alter 1999: 252). Is it possible that his own cleverness, combined with the gossip that he would have picked up from his fellow soldiers at the palace gate, had revealed to him what David was up to and that he was very wittingly undermining the king's plan? And was that reference to the ark dwelling in a tent a pointed way to prick the heart of David? It seems congruent with the style of the author of this psychologically sophisticated text to leave the ambiguity in place.

At any rate, convinced finally that he cannot effect the cover-up through deception and manipulation, David has recourse to murder. Using Uriah himself as his courier (an act of particular cruelty), David sends a message to Joab at the front, commanding him to place Uriah in the thick of the fight and then abandon him to a certain death. Lending credence to the standard interpretation of Uriah's complete innocence of David's intentions, the king must have assumed that his dutiful soldier would not read the message entrusted to him. Joab does what David ordered him to do, but he hedges a bit. If he had followed David's directions exactly, it would have looked as though a setup had taken place. Thus Joab sends a large group of fighters against the Ammonites, but instead of leaving Uriah isolated, he allows many to be killed, including Uriah the Hittite. This means, of course, that David's sin is multiplied for now, in order to cover up the cover-up, many more besides Uriah are murdered. Laziness and self-absorption lead to misuse of power, which leads to adultery, which leads to crude deception, which leads finally to murder, indeed mass murder—sin piling on sin. And it appears as though this concatenation of sin, at least when perpetrated by a powerful and respected king, carries the day: Uriah is dead, and David is free to take the dead man's wife.

But no matter how powerful a tyrant is and no matter how thoroughly he is capable of manipulating external events, he cannot finally reach into the inner sanctum of the conscience. A moral agent can be browbeaten, cajoled, threatened, or deprived of worldly goods, but he cannot finally be compelled to act against his convictions. One has only to think of Thomas More, Maximilian Kolbe, or Jesus before Pilate to see this truth exemplified. In an obvious sense, David outmaneuvered Uriah and arranged things to suit his own purposes. But this narrative, echoing down the ages to the present day, continually reminds readers that Uriah in fact has won, for he shines as an exquisite moral exemplar over and against the squalid David. Vaclav Havel, the great twentieth-century Czech playwright and political dissident who spent many years in prison for his opposition to communism, comments that the truthful stance of the morally upright dissenter opens up a new space in which more people can stand. And their presence expands that space so that even more can enter. In time, their moral integrity effectively envelops and overwhelms even the most powerful opposition, who have no place to plant their feet.

That Joab fully understood the nefariousness of David's scheming is evident in the peculiar little scene between him and the messenger he sends to inform David of recent events. Joab cleverly lays out an imaginary scenario of David's reaction to the news that so many Israelite soldiers were killed during a raid near the wall of the beseiged city. He speculates that David will become angry and reminds the messenger of the lesson implied in the story of the death of Abimelech, which is narrated in the book of Judges. When that Israelite hero wandered too close to the wall of a beseiged city, he was killed by a rock dropped on him by a woman. Just before dying, Abimelech urged his armor bearer to run him through, lest it be said that he died at the hand of a woman. If David in his frustration brings up that cautionary tale, Joab counsels, the messenger should then tell him that Uriah the Hittite is among the dead. Is David's commander not-so-subtly insinuating first, that he knows that the king is especially interested in the death of this one man, and second, that he knows that a woman, however obliquely, is responsible for Uriah's death? When the messenger dutifully reports that Uriah is among the Israelite dead, David immediately worries about his field commander: "Thus you shall say to Joab, 'Do not let this matter trouble you, for the sword devours now one and now another; press your attack on the city, and overthrow it.' And encourage him" (2 Sam. 11:25). Though this seems like just a bit of commonsense military wisdom, a soldierly cliché, it is rather obvious that David knows that his commander knows, and that he is telling Joab, obliquely but unmistakably, not to pursue this matter any further. We will therefore watch Joab's actions and reactions in regard to David with a good deal of interest as this tragic story unfolds.

We are then told that Bathsheba mourns over her dead husband and immediately thereafter comes to David's bed. Robert Alter reminds us that since the usual mourning period at the time would have been seven days, Bathsheba was more precipitous than Gertrude after the murder of Hamlet's father! Obviously, both Bathsheba and the king were desperately concerned that they be married before the signs of pregnancy became all too apparent. Nevertheless, the speed and "convenience" of these events coupled with the activity of Bathsheba in and around the palace must have aroused suspicions to say the very least. But what concerns the author most is that the whole episode has unfolded under the watchful eye of God and that "the thing that David had done displeased the LORD" (2 Sam. 11:27). I spoke earlier of the omniscience of God, specifying that it is a function of God's unconditional mode of existence. God does not know passively and derivatively but actively and creatively. Moreover, precisely as the ground of finite being, God knows all dimensions of reality, both interior and exterior, both visible and invisible. Using all of his kingly power, David attempted to arrange things so as to conceal his interior intentions and decisions from a human audience; even in this regard he was only moderately successful. But he manifested an extreme narcissism or spiritual naivete in imagining that he could possibly have concealed his maneuverings from Yahweh.

This speaks to the issue raised at the outset of the chapter: how could this man after God's own heart, this paragon of Israel, have fallen so easily and so disastrously? The Council of Trent teaches that original sin—the primal dysfunction that affects the whole of the human race like an inherited addiction—conduces toward a skewing and disordering of the person, a setting at war of those elements that comprise the self.[3] Dissociated and disintegrated, none of the powers of body and soul operate properly or at their full capacity. Thus the fallen will does not choose properly, and the fallen mind does not see properly. Bernard Lonergan, who as a Jesuit was exquisitely sensitive to the discernment of spirits and the reading of interior states, knew that the fallen mind stands in constant need of conversion. Hence he formulated four great epistemological imperatives: be attentive, be intelligent, be reasonable, and be responsible.[4] He knew that the mind, conditioned by sin, tends to fall into lazy and self-absorbed patterns of not seeing, not thinking, not deciding, and not changing. Of course, any spiritual director or confessor could tell us that even very bright people can tumble into gross patterns of self-deceptive or self-serving thinking—seeing what they want to see, imagining escape routes that are not there, spinning out exculpating scenarios, and so on. David, the sweet singer of Israel, the celebrator of Yahweh's sovereignty over creation, seemed to imagine that his puny and deceptive moves could somehow conceal his sin from God. Surely David knew that even as he chose to take Bathsheba he was operating at cross-purposes with God's law and his own good. But David's mind and will were simply overwhelmed by an unruly sexual passion that had been allowed to break away from its center. Thomas Merton comments that the passions for sex, food, and drink are something like little children, demanding what they want when they want it. Not wicked in themselves, they are nevertheless to be disciplined by intellect and will lest they come, in time, to dominate the soul. During this sad episode, David is a person compromised by the fall, or to use more explicitly Catholic language, a man in the grip of concupiscence, the warping of mind and desire, which is the enduring consequence of original sin.

3. H. J. Schroeder, trans., *Canons and Decrees of the Council of Trent* (St. Louis: B. Herder, 1941), 21–22.
4. Bernard Lonergan, *Method in Theology* (Toronto: University of Toronto Press, 1971), 13.

Or is something else in play, something cooler, more calculating? If David's adultery with Bathsheba and the murder of Uriah are construed more or less as crimes of passion, then they are relatively forgivable. They might be categorized alongside of the sins committed by those on Dante's first circle of hell. But David got Uriah drunk and ordered the hapless soldier to go home and sleep with his wife. It seems clear that the king was far more interested in avoiding embarrassment than in taking Bathsheba for himself. He is not like Paolo burning lustfully for Francesca, or Romeo in a delicious fit of passion for Juliet; he is more, as Robert Pinsky argues, like a man trying to avoid a messy paternity suit.[5] And if this interpretation is right, it makes David's sins more sordid, more thoroughly self-absorbed. Did he take Bathsheba as his wife because he was hopelessly in love with her? Or did he do so at her insistence, lest she (and he) be exposed to humiliation and execution? On this reading, Dante (were he ever in mind to punish David for this particular crime) might have put the king not with the lustful on the first circle but with the fraudulent and treacherous on one of the lower levels of hell.

5. Robert Pinsky, *The Life of David* (New York: Schocken, 2005), 105.

SERIES FOUR

A SWORD WILL NEVER LEAVE YOUR HOUSE

2 SAMUEL 12

That chapters eleven and twelve are linked in a particularly tight way thematically is signaled by the single sentence that overlaps and connects the end of the former and the beginning of the latter: "But the thing that David had done displeased the LORD, and the LORD sent Nathan to David" (2 Sam. 11:27–12:1). The punishment outlined in the twelfth chapter follows hard upon the crimes described in the eleventh, and there is a fitting correspondance between the latter and the former. Robert Alter brilliantly observes that David's sin, in all of its complexity and multivalence, was expressed through a series of "sendings"; it is only appropriate, indeed an ironic comeuppance, that Yahweh's punishment commences through a sending of his prophet (Alter 1999: 257). Once more, the author indicates that there is a king more powerful even than David, someone whom David cannot manipulate or intimidate. In all of his sendings and orderings-about, David was recapitulating Adam's primal move of appropriating divinity for himself. In sending Nathan, which trumps all of the puny sendings that David commanded, Yahweh reminds the king of this most fundamental of metaphysical truths: "I am God; and you are not."

In accord with his divine mandate, Nathan simply comes to the king and speaks. It does not appear that he sought David's permission or fit himself into David's schedule. His speech is not prefaced by marks of deference, nor is it expressed in the language of court ceremonial. It is uttered with serenity, confidence, and even an air of command. Nathan stands very much in the tradition of Samuel, and he also anticipates the attitude of Isaiah, Jeremiah, Ezekiel, Elijah, and Hosea—all confronters of kings, troublers of the consciences of the powerful. Moreover, keeping in mind what David has done to those who bring him bad news, Nathan manifests a considerable amount of courage. Though the biblical authors do not typically dwell on the interiority of their characters—there are no Shakespearean soliloquies on the lips of Abraham, Moses, or David—I would speculate that Nathan's speech was exquisitely timed in order to correspond to the moment when the king was ready to hear it. For Nathan did not present himself directly after either the killing of Uriah or David's taking of Bathsheba for his wife; rather, Nathan speaks after David's conscience had some time to gnaw at him.

Presumably, Nathan comes into the presence of the king in order to procure the royal judgment in a particular case involving two men, one rich and the other poor. As he unfolds the story, an attentive listener would know that he was spinning a tale rather than recounting a real-life episode, for his speech is filled with literary conventions, rhythms, and thematic parallels. Nevertheless, David seems to accept Nathan's tale at face value, as a report of a real injustice that calls for kingly intervention. "The rich man had very many flocks and herds; but the poor man had nothing but one little ewe lamb, which he had bought. He brought it up, and it grew up with him and with his children; it used to eat of his meager fare, and drink from his cup, and lie in his bosom, and it was like a daughter to him" (2 Sam. 12:2–3). But when a traveler came upon him unexpectedly, the rich man "was loath to take one of his own flock or herd to prepare for the wayfarer . . . but he took the poor man's lamb, and prepared that for the guest who had come to him" (2 Sam. 12:4). What is especially powerful about this artfully constructed parable is that Nathan makes the rich man appear not only unjust but also remarkably crude in his self-absorption. Robert Polzin observes that the three verbs that Nathan uses to describe the poor man's relation to the ewe—eat, drink, lie—echo exactly what David tried to get Uriah to do with Bathsheba (Polzin 1993: 123). And Robert Alter points out that "lying in the bosom" or "in the lap" has, in Hebrew, not only the sense of parental sheltering but also the clear connotation of sexual intimacy (Alter 1999: 258). In other words, Nathan composes his story in such a way that it touches on the reality of David's situation with unnerving accuracy.

Why was David taken in? Why did the king not see through the artifice of the prophet's story? Perhaps his conscience was deeply bothering him, and perhaps, consciously or not, he was longing for relief. In presenting his story, Nathan appeals to the king's deep sense of moral responsibility for the weakest among his fellow Israelites. Perhaps David knew that he had violated that responsibility dramatically in the case of Uriah and desired, accordingly, to confess his guilt. Hence he allowed himself to be drawn into the moral universe created by Nathan's parable in order to find some catharsis. Gregory the Great catches some of this in his splendid comparison between Nathan and a cunning surgeon: "He [Nathan] came like a physician to a sick man . . . and concealed the knife under his coat, but drawing it out suddenly, pierced the wound, that the sick man might feel the knife before he saw it."[1] In any case, Nathan sets his trap magnificently, for David's anger is stirred up and he says, "As the LORD lives, the man who has done this deserves to die; he shall restore the lamb fourfold, because he did this thing, and because he had no pity" (2 Sam. 12:6). The king is carried away in his righteous indignation, for traditional Hebrew law dictated that a property thief was required to make a fourfold compensation. However, he was not subject to the death penalty. Ironically, of course, an adulterer was indeed subject to capital punishment. That being said, David has certainly taken the point of the parable and accurately identified lack of pity—massively displayed in his own case—as the hinge issue. At this point, the rhetorical trap is sprung, and Nathan delivers what has to be the most devastating condemnation in all of the Old Testament: "You are the man!" (2 Sam. 12:7). Adapting Chrysostom's metaphor, Augustine makes this magnificent remark: "To cut away diseased tissue in David's heart and heal the wound there, Nathan used David's tongue as a knife."[2] There is no discussion, no debate, no attempt on David's part to explain or exculpate himself. The king, who is usually so commanding and downright dangerous regarding those who bring him unwelcome reports, remains utterly silent and acquiescent as Nathan lays out the implications of David's deeds.

Without pause, Nathan relays a message designed to remind the king of some fundamental metaphysical and spiritual truths: "Thus says the LORD, the God of Israel: I anointed you king over Israel and I rescued you from the hand of Saul; I gave you your master's house, and your master's wives into your bosom, and gave you the house of Israel and of Judah; and if that had been too little, I would have added as much more" (2 Sam. 12:7–8). I have remarked already on the noncompetitive transcendence of God—that is, the Creator's unique capacity to relate in the most intimate but noninterruptive way with his creation. Isaiah's "O LORD . . . all that we have done, you have done for us" (Isa. 26:12) is the pithiest expression of this principle. In this particular case, it means that David has indeed been accomplishing all sorts of things through his ingenuity, skill, courage, and political canniness, but all the time it was Yahweh who, precisely as the giver and

1. Gregory the Great, "Pastoral Care 3.2," in *Joshua, Judges, Ruth, 1–2 Samuel*, ed. John R. Franke, Ancient Christian Commentary on Scripture: Old Testament 4 (Downers Grove, IL: InterVarsity, 2005), 358.
2. Augustine, "Explanations of the Psalms 50," in Franke, *Joshua, Judges, Ruth, 1–2 Samuel*, 360.

sustainer of those qualities in the king, was accomplishing them at a higher level. The awareness of this metaphysical state of affairs ought to conduce a spiritual transformation—a decentering of the self. The apostle Paul witnessed to such a change when he said, "And it is no longer I who live, but it is Christ who lives in me" (Gal. 2:20). As is especially clear in the case of Paul, this condition is tantamount not to a negation of an individual's peculiar and distinctive personality but rather the raising up and transfiguring of that personality. The irony is that David appears to have forgotten the very truth that he humbly acknowledged earlier: "Who am I that the Lord has done such favors to me?" (see 2 Sam. 7:18). Indeed, Nathan's speech in this chapter in many ways echoes Yahweh's speech to David in the earlier chapter: there is nothing you have that you have not received.

As Nathan continues to channel the words of Yahweh, he says, "You have struck down Uriah the Hittite with the sword, and have taken his wife to be your own wife, and have killed him with the sword of the Ammonites" (2 Sam. 12:9). David might have been able to confuse and deceive his courtiers and fellow Israelites (though even this, as we have seen, is open to question), but he certainly could not fool the sovereign God, who not only sees external events but also discerns the movements of the heart. John Henry Newman refers to the conscience as "the aboriginal vicar of Christ in the soul," in part because it mediates the presence of the God who knows and judges even the most intimate affairs of the heart.[3] The metaphysics that informs this sense of conscience is, once again, the ontology of creation from nothing. Since God is responsible for the whole of the being of the finite world and since he literally knows things into existence, nothing can escape his notice. All of the machinations of the human mind, as well as all of the complex chains of cause and effect that bring about worldly conditions, lie open to the divine perception.

What follows immediately upon this stark recitation of David's recent moral history is the pronouncement of a sentence that will absolutely condition the rest of the king's story: "Now therefore the sword shall never depart from your house. . . . I will raise up trouble against you from within your own house" (2 Sam. 12:10–11). There is, as I pointed out in an earlier episode, a sort of strict law of karma at work here, something similar to Dante's *Divine Comedy*: a balancing of sin and punishment, a harmony between offense and purification. David's sin was violence against the household of Uriah and, indirectly, violence against his own

3. John Henry Newman, "A Letter Addressed to His Grace the Duke of Norfolk on Occasion of Mr. Gladstone's Recent Expostulation," in *Certain Difficulties Felt by Anglicans in Catholic Teaching*, 2 vols. (London: Longmans, Greens, 1888), 2:248.

family. Hence, he will be chastised through violence that will relentlessly arise within his intimate family circle: brother against sister, brother against brother, son against father. This is not divine vindictiveness; it is the playing out of the dreadful truth that violence by its very nature begets violence, and betrayal by its very nature gives rise to betrayal. This is, if you will, the dark side of the metaphysics of communion. Since we are all connected to one another by a coinherence that goes to the very roots of our being, our negative behavior necessarily has a ripple effect around us in all directions. One thinks again of Dante. At the pit of hell Dante places Satan, buried to his waist in ice. The fallen angel beats great wings like a bat, which moves air over the ice, creating thereby the freezing meteorology of hell.[4]

Psalm 51, the famous *Miserere*, is given an uncommonly precise superscription in the Bible: "A psalm of David, when the prophet Nathan came to him, after he had gone in to Bathsheba." I will leave to the side the vexed issue of the authorship of the psalms, but suffice it to say that this memorable poem has been, probably from the moment of its composition, associated with this dark period of David's life and so represents a theological-poetical reflection on the nature of his sin. Its power is proved by the fact that this psalm has retained a prominent place in the liturgical and prayer life of the Jewish and Christian churches for millenia. Though the king desperately tried to conceal his malfeasance, the offense clawed at his conscience: "For I know my transgressions, and my sin is ever before me" (Ps. 51:3). This in itself is a good thing, for it proves that the transgressor is in the presence of God. G. K. Chesterton remarks, "There are saints indeed in my religion: but a saint only means a man who knows he is a sinner."[5] The saint orders his or her life toward the light of God, and this orientation brings the imperfections of the soul more readily to view. This helps to explain why the greatest saints are more, rather than less, aware of their sin, convinced even that they are the worst of sinners. Not a false modesty, this attitude reveals that the saint is in the light. On the other hand, those who blithely report that all is well with themselves are, almost perforce, looking away from God.

Furthermore, the spiritually serious person instinctually searches out the deepest root of his or her sin, not content to accept a superficial account of it: "Indeed, I was born guilty, a sinner when my mother conceived me" (Ps. 51:5). This is one of the clearest biblical texts supporting the doctrine of original sin, which teaches that there is something disordered and off-kilter in us, even before we perform any particular wicked acts. Why did David fall so readily with Bathsheba? In part it

4. Robert Barron, *And Now I See: A Theology of Transformation* (New York: Crossroad, 1998), 33.
5. G. K. Chesterton, "The High Plains," in *Alarms and Discursions* (London: Methuen, 1924), 142.

was because the harmony that ought to have obtained among the various elements of his self had been, from the beginning, compromised. He was bent toward sin. Is Paul not getting at the same confounding disorder when he comments, even after years as a follower of Jesus, "For I do not do the good I want, but the evil I do not want is what I do" (Rom. 7:19)? Paul is musing not about a particular iniquitous act but rather about an iniquitous state: "But I see in my members another law at war with the law of my mind, making me captive to the law of sin that dwells in my members. Wretched man that I am! Who will rescue me from this body of death?" (Rom. 7:23–24). This is why the author of Psalm 51 understands that his moral renovation will come not from his own efforts or from adopting a program of right habituation but rather from God alone: "Therefore teach me wisdom in my secret heart. . . . Wash me, and I shall be whiter than snow" (Ps. 51:6–7). Paul knows the same thing, which is why, after his anguished question, he cries, "Thanks be to God through Jesus Christ our Lord!" (Rom. 7:25). He does not need a program of ethical renewal; he needs to be re-created.

A point that bothers any number of commentators is the psalmist's insistence that his sin has offended only God: "Against you, you alone, have I sinned, and done what is evil in your sight" (Ps. 51:4). Surely Uriah, Bathsheba, the newly born child, and Joab—just to name the most obvious cases—were sinned against as well. But this is another expression, somewhat more oblique, of the noncompetitive transcendence that I have mentioned. Since God is the ground of being and the unconditioned act of goodness itself, God is in fact sinned against in every sin. It is not as though God can be isolated from an offense as if he were another being disconnected from the victim of sin. And it is not as though God can be divorced from any act of the will, since any move in the direction of a particular good, even the apparent good, is predicated finally on the will's orientation toward the unconditioned good.

The psalmist knows that all sin is essentially a form of idolatry, which is incorrect worship. This is why he confesses to God that, once purified of sin, his "tongue sing[s] aloud of your deliverance" and his "mouth will declare your praise" (Ps. 51:14–15). Augustine famously characterizes sin as the state of being *incurvatus in se*, caved in around oneself.[6] This is precisely the condition into which David fell during the Bathsheba incident: indifferent to the demands of God and utterly oblivious to the damage that he produced all around himself. *Curvatus in se*, one is by definition incapable of praise, for authentic worship is the most centrifugal act possible. The

6. Augustine, *The City of God against the Pagans*, ed. and trans. R. W. Dyson (Cambridge: Cambridge University Press, 1998), 609.

primary manner in which an ancient Israelite praised God was through sacrifice, and Psalm 51 gives us a wonderful theological account of what was going on, spiritually speaking, in that act: "For you have no delight in sacrifice; if I were to give a burnt offering, you would not be pleased. The sacrifice acceptable to God is a broken spirit; a broken and contrite heart, O God, you will not despise" (Ps. 51:16–17). The One who made the entire universe from nothing cannot possibly stand in need of any offering of created things. The God of Israel is not like the pagan deities that literally need the sacrifice and praise offered from earth. What God delights in is the attitude of the sacrificer, which is symbolically represented in the act of sacrifice. In the crushing of the animal, God sees the contrition (literally, "crushing," from *contritio*) of the heart of the one making the sacrifice. This pleases God, not because God is sadistic or emotionally needy but because the properly contrite spirit is attuned to its own good. Thomas Aquinas clarifies that the sacraments, the Mass, and other acts of worship benefit not God but rather those who engage in them.[7]

After the general assurance that a sword will never depart from David's house, God lays out in exquisitely painful detail what will happen to the king because of his sin. Here Yahweh, through Nathan, is a bit like the queen mother in Shakespeare's *Richard III*, who prophesies with unnerving accuracy the dire things that will happen to Richard and his cohorts: "I will raise up trouble against you from within your own house; and I will take your wives before your eyes, and give them to your neighbor, and he shall lie with your wives in the sight of this very sun. For you did it secretly; but I will do this thing before all Israel, and before the sun" (2 Sam. 12:11–12). Yahweh is referring, as we will see, to the horrific public humiliation visited upon the king by his own son when Absalom has sex with David's concubines on the roof of the royal palace, having chased his father from his own capital. One could also extrapolate from the threat of the sword never leaving David's house to the whole of Israelite royal history. In many ways, the corruption on such clear display in the Bathsheba-Uriah incident sets the tone for the centuries of corruption that will follow in the bedeviled house of David. This is why Robert Alter observes that the story of the rise of the dynasty of David is inextricably bound up with the story of its fall (Alter 1999: 259). The author of the Samuel books clearly admits the wickedness of the royal family even as he admits and celebrates its divine legitimacy.

When will the trouble cease? Only when Christ, the sinless Son of David, assumes his throne—a throne that would prove to be an instrument of torture

7. Thomas Aquinas, *Summa theologiae: Latin Text and English Translation, Introductions, Notes, Appendices, and Glossaries*, ed. Thomas Gilby et al., 61 vols. (New York: McGraw-Hill, 1964–81), 18:117–19.

willingly accepted. N. T. Wright argues, as I mentioned earlier, that the Gospels essentially tell the story of how Yahweh, through his Davidic representative, became king.[8] In his love, compassion, forgiveness, nonviolence, open table fellowship, and inclusivity, Jesus demonstrated an alternative path of governance, an entirely different way of being a ruler. "A dispute arose among them as to which one of them was to be regarded as the greatest. But he said to them, 'The kings of the Gentiles lord it over them; and those in authority over them are called benefactors. But not so with you; rather the greatest among you must become like the youngest, and the leader like one who serves'" (Luke 22:24–26). What commenced with David's abuse of power and continued through centuries of corruption would end only with the One who said, "Put your sword back into its place; for all who take the sword will perish by the sword" (Matt. 26:52). Violence stopped devouring the house of David only when the definitive Son of David answered his crucifiers with a word of forgiveness and the soldier's lance with blood and water.

Now it is to David's infinite credit that upon hearing the charge and sentence he immediately admits his guilt: "I have sinned against the LORD" (2 Sam. 12:13). The king played myriad games of deceit, subterfuge, indirection, and self-concealment, but when everything is laid bare, he surrenders. Jonah made the mistake of thinking that God is conditioned by space (when God said, "Go east by land," Jonah went west by sea); David made the mistake of thinking that God is conditioned in his knowledge. When Nathan disabuses him of that metaphysical confusion, David relents. It is helpful to keep in mind that the king assuredly knew the law of Israel that dictated that he and Bathsheba should both be put to death for their crime. Therefore this admission, though in one sense forced upon him, was by no means without consequence—much like the assurance from a contemporary politician who states the intention to "take full responsibility" for an offense. It must have been with an extraordinary sense of relief that the king heard the prophet's words, "Now the LORD has put away your sin; you shall not die" (2 Sam. 12:13). But this communication of undeserved grace is immediately tempered by the promise that the child conceived by their adulterous union would die.

At this point we are thrown back once again to a vexing question: Why was David treated so leniently, at least in comparison to Saul? David committed adultery and murder, but Yahweh neither abandoned nor deprived him of his kingship. Saul had been utterly rejected for not following certain liturgical prescriptions foisted upon him rather arbitrarily by Samuel and for not carrying out the ban

8. N. T. Wright, *How God Became King: The Forgotten Story of the Gospels* (San Francisco: HarperOne, 2012), 185–96.

on the Amalekites with thoroughness. Does this not seem a tad disproportionate? The decisive difference seems to be that David admitted his offense honestly, completely, and humbly, whereas Saul made excuses, tried to explain himself, wheedled, and begged. David is not unlike Peter, a bold sinner who wept bitterly when he fully realized his sin, whereas Saul is more like Judas, a sinner who, having been found out, fell into despair and self-loathing. The author of Psalm 51 identifies the hinge point: "A broken and contrite heart, O God, you will not despise" (Ps. 51:17).

David will not die, but his child will: "The Lord struck the child that Uriah's wife bore to David, and it became very ill" (2 Sam. 12:15). The very wording of this verse presents a bevy of theological problems. The mainstream of the theological tradition, beginning with Augustine and extending through Aquinas and an army of their disciples to the present day, maintains that God cannot be the direct cause of evil since God is unconditionally good. The standard formula, therefore, is that God "permits" certain evils in order to produce goods that could be arrived at in no other way. When this causal relationship is opaque to us, recourse is usually had to the great lesson of the book of Job: the purposes of God are too sublime and complex for a finite mind to adequately comprehend. But the Bible seems far less squeamish than the theological tradition to speak of God actively performing evil deeds. The prophet Isaiah speaks, for example, of the God who creates both weal and woe, both light and darkness (Isa. 45:7). And throughout the historical books of the scriptures God is regularly described as smiting and punishing various individuals and peoples. Perhaps most notoriously, the book of Genesis relays the story of Abraham's willingness to sacrifice Isaac at the express command of God. The rubric of divine permission simply seems inadequate to these examples. However, if God commands both weal and woe, he seems arbitrary, capricious, and utterly inscrutable—as likely to be a monster as to be the source of love. The philosophical articulation of this position is the voluntarism of Descartes, according to which moral acts are right and wrong in a purely relative sense only because God has, at least for the moment, according to the whim of his will determined that they be so.

Thomas Aquinas argues against voluntarist construals of God's acts, insisting that what God does can never be out of step with who God is, since the divine simplicity dictates that the divine mind and the divine will are substantially identical. But this same Thomas also holds that God was perfectly "within his rights" to command the sacrifice of Isaac, and his argument in this case might show a path through the thicket in which we find ourselves. Thomas broaches this thorny issue in the famous question 94 of the second part of the *Summa theologiae*, which treats the natural law. In article 5 of this question Thomas wonders whether the precepts of the natural law are ever changeable. The second objection proceeds as follows: "Further, the slaying of the innocent, adultery, and theft are against the natural law. But we find these things changed by God: as when God commanded Abraham to slay his innocent son; and when he ordered the Jews to borrow and purloin the vessels of the Egyptians; and when he commanded Osee to take to himself a wife of fornication. Therefore, the natural law can be changed."[9] Thomas's answer to this objection is conditioned by the subtle metaphysics of participation to which I have alluded a number of times in this commentary. The natural law arises from a reasoned reflection on certain basic goods that are at play in ordinary human affairs. Thus, it is indeed a precept of the natural law that innocent life ought never to be directly taken and that adultery is always counterindicated. However, the natural law is derivative from the eternal law, which is identical to the divine mind. Therefore, for his own purposes and according to his overarching justice, God can suspend or change the precepts of ordinary moral law. Aquinas answers the objector, "All men alike, both guilty and innocent, died the death of nature: which death of nature is inflicted by the power of God on account of original sin, according to 1 Samuel 2:6: 'The Lord killeth and maketh alive.' Consequently, by the command of God, death can be inflicted on any man, guilty or innocent, without any injustice whatever."[10] Here, the command of God is not arbitrary but rather grounded in that justice that is identical to the divine being. The changing or suspension of the natural law, therefore, is not the triumph of will over reason but rather the contextualization of mere human reason within a higher reason. Thus, to return to the David narrative, God's "striking" and eventual killing of Bathsheba's child was neither unjust nor capricious. It was a divine act that shaped human affairs in accordance with God's mind and will.

In response to his child's illness, the repentant David pleads with God, fasts, and lays all night on the ground, presumably before the ark of the covenant. The king's lying on the bare earth is reminiscent, appropriately enough, of Uriah's uncomfortable sleeping arrangement during his visit to Jerusalem (Alter 1999: 261). This intense petitionary prayer lasts for seven days, during which time David stubbornly refrained from eating. The king must have felt particularly deep distress given that the child was suffering because of the father's sins. Despite David's heroic effort at persuading God otherwise, the baby dies on the seventh

9. Aquinas, *Summa theologiae*, 28:93.
10. Ibid.

day of the king's ordeal. This episode prompts us to consider issues regarding the theology of prayer.

First, why would a believer in the Creator God pray in a petitionary way at all? The One who made and now sustains the universe in its entirety must know every detail pertaining to the finite world, and indeed this truth is laid out any number of times in 2 Samuel. The author of Psalm 139 gives strikingly eloquent expression to this theological conviction of the Israelites: "O LORD, you have searched me and known me. You know when I sit down and when I rise up; you discern my thoughts from far away. . . . Even before a word is on my tongue, O LORD, you know it completely" (Ps. 139:1–2, 4). And Jesus states the principle with typical laconisicm, "For your Father knows what you need before you ask him" (Matt. 6:8). On the other hand, Israelites are urged throughout the Bible to pray in a petitionary way. Abraham certainly seems to be bargaining with a God whose mind he endeavors to change, as he begs God not to destroy Sodom and Gomorrah. And the same Jesus who insists that the Father knows what we need even before we ask also counsels us to knock, seek, and ask with the relentlessness of the visitor seeking bread for his family or the widow desperately hungry for justice.

How can the dilemma be resolved? Clearly, the One who created the universe from nothing and who has known it into being cannot be "informed" by our prayer, as though he were ignorant and stands in need of enlightenment. Moreover, the One whose very nature is love cannot be thought of as a reluctant pasha whose attitude needs to be changed by particularly diligent and persuasive petitioning. Following the prompts of Thomas Aquinas, the contemporary theologian Herbert McCabe argues that since God is not a supreme being standing over and against the petitioner but rather the very ground of the petitioner's existence, the asking prayer itself should be interpreted as the work of God—God, as it were, prompting the pray-er from within.[11] Again, since God is not a competitor operating on the same metaphysical plane as the petitioner, this divine activity is neither interruptive nor domineering. It is instead the means by which the pray-er discovers his or her ownmost desire and purpose. Both Aquinas and McCabe find their inspiration in Paul's mysterious rumination in Romans: "Likewise the Spirit helps us in our weakness; for we do not know how to pray as we ought, but that very Spirit intercedes with sighs too deep for words. And God, who searches the heart, knows what is the mind of the Spirit, because the Spirit intercedes for the

11. Herbert McCabe, *God Still Matters*, ed. Brian Davies (London: Continuum, 2002), 71.

saints according to the will of God" (Rom. 8:26–27). God, as it were, prays to God through us, and we are expanded and rightly ordered in the process.

Second, what about those whose petitionary prayer is refused? What sense can be made, for example, of David's apparently fruitless seven days of prayer and fasting, which did not result in the saving of his child? Augustine's reflections in his letter to Proba are perhaps the most illuminating in regard to this problem. At times, God might refuse to answer a particular petition favorably in order to cause a sort of dilation in the heart of the petitioner, an expansion of soul that enables the pray-er to more fully receive the gift that God eventually wants to give.[12] Moreover, some prayers of petition are not, in fact, from the Holy Spirit and hence should not be answered by a gracious God. Finally, and this might apply most aptly in the case under consideration, God prompts an intensification of prayer in a person in order to effect some spiritual change. The David who wandered far from God during his period of surveying, commanding, sending, and manipulating had to be compelled to return to God, to reorient his life. Is this not precisely what happened during his painful seven days of fasting and prayer?

In point of fact, a spiritual alchemy can be discerned quite readily in David. His courtiers are terrified to tell him of his child's death, convinced that the king might do himself harm in a frenzy of grief. Or perhaps they remembered what happened to other people who had brought the king bad news. However, upon hearing the report, David simply rose from the ground, bathed, changed his clothes, and went into the sanctuary to worship. When he finishes with his prayers, they place food before him, and he ends his fast. When pressed as to why he accepted the news so blithely, David says, blandly enough, "While the child was still alive, I fasted and wept; for I said, 'Who knows? The LORD may be gracious to me, and the child may live.' But now he is dead; why should I fast? Can I bring him back again? I shall go to him, but he will not return to me" (2 Sam. 12:22–23). After hearing the speech of Nathan, David grimly and resolutely accepts the truth, his fate, and divine punishment. He makes no excuses; he does not hide; he does not complain. The Bathsheba-Uriah incident is marked, at every turn, by deception and concealment, with untruth. But God, the unconditioned source of being itself, is nothing but *the* truth. When God breaks into someone's life, that person begins to live stubbornly in the light and to remain impatient with falsehood. Post-Nathan, David is such a man.

12. Augustine, "Letter to Proba," in *Saint Augustine: Letters, Volume II (83–130)*, trans. Wilfrid Parsons (New York: Fathers of the Church, 1953), 397.

I would also argue that David exhibits here the relief of a man who knows that his sacrifice has been accepted. The king had committed a grave crime, and the prophet had communicated a sentence to him: the child must die. Now he is confident that all is square between himself and God. Of course, as one follows the rather terrible trajectory of this story, other sons of David fall because of this sin, the sword indeed never leaving the king's family.

The remaining chapters of 2 Samuel put to rest the concern that Yahweh was somehow "tougher" on Saul than on David. In point of fact, the punishment meted out to David is practically commensurate with the grace that rushed on him throughout his life. Also apparent is the enormous spiritual power that suffering often unleashes. To this point in the Bathsheba-Uriah story, all of David's words were politically motivated, cunning, and manipulative, born of an inflated sense of self. After the death of his child he speaks not with political or self-interested purpose but simply out of deep existential pain. The wielder of great power became vulnerable and self-reproachful, and this is essentially how he remains for the rest of the narrative.

Finally, David's behavior reveals the attitude of detachment so praised by spiritual teachers up and down the centuries. Attached to God and God's demands, a person can be utterly detached from any finite good that would claim ultimacy: wealth, pleasure, power, or honor. At rest in God, a soul can let go of all else, convinced that peace will follow—whether living a long life or a short one, whether wealthy or poor, whether admired or despised. Going in calmly to worship the God who has just taken the life of his child, David exemplifies this spiritual stance. He is not unlike Job who, after enduring every sort of misfortune, simply said, "Shall we receive the good at the hand of God, and not receive the bad?" (Job 2:10).

We hear that David then "consoled" his wife (the first time, by the way, that Bathsheba is referred to as David's wife) and that she bore a son who was given the name "Solomon" (*šĕlōmōh*, from *šālôm*, meaning "peace"). Why this name? Perhaps because he represents the calm after the storm, or perhaps because he will be, unlike his father, a man of peace and hence worthy to build the holy temple, the place where *šālôm* between God and Israel is effected. We are told, simply enough, that Yahweh loved Solomon and sent a message to Nathan to that effect, prompting the prophet to give the boy the added name "Jedediah," or "friend of Yahweh." This small detail gives rise to a major theological issue: whether God plays favorites or loves some more than others. Why should the Spirit of Yahweh have rushed upon David but not Saul, at least not to the same degree? Why, for that matter, did God favor Jacob over Esau? Why does John's Gospel speak of a disciple of Jesus who was, in a unique sense, the "beloved"? And why should Solomon, prior to any achievement on his part, have received the special favor of Yahweh? Though it most certainly offends one's egalitarian sensibilities, the Bible rather clearly defends the proposition that God loves some more than others.

Thomas Aquinas broaches this thorny problem in question 23 of the *Summa theologiae*, which addresses predestination. Having clarified that predestination is a resolution in the mind of God according to which God conducts some to eternal life, Thomas entertains the commonsense objection that this sort of discrimination seems repugnant to the universal love of God. In answering, Aquinas contends that God does indeed love everyone (indeed every existing thing) in the measure that he wills each person (or thing) some good; nothing would have the good of existence unless God willed it, and love is nothing but willing the good of the other. But, he continues, this does not mean that God wills the same good for everyone and in the same way. Inasmuch, therefore, as he wills some the good of eternal life, he is said to love them more than those to whom he does not will that particular good. I will not even dream of going any further into an analysis of the issue of predestination, which is arguably the most difficult in all of theology, but I will dwell a bit further on this counterintuitive principle that God loves some more than others. What makes Aquinas's treatment odd is that many of us think of love much more subjectively than objectively; that is, we consider the quality of the lover's love rather than what that love produces. John Calvin, in the context of his discussion of predestination, makes the observation that God showers his love everywhere, but unequally: some people are more intelligent, more beautiful, more courageous than others; some plants are more fecund than others; some animals have greater strength and attractiveness than others; and so on. He insists, furthermore, that the God of the Bible is a choosing or electing God, which necessarily means that some are not chosen or elected: Israel and not the other nations, Jacob and not Esau, Abraham and not Lot, Jedediah and not Absalom.[13] In the ninth chapter of Romans the apostle Paul specifies that God the potter made some vessels for display and others for destruction, and who are we to question the wisdom or justice of God?

But lest this analysis conduce toward a voluntarism that renders God's judgments truly arbitrary, one must remember that on the biblical reading God's elections are not so much for the sake of the elect but for the sake of those to whom the elected one has been sent. I do not know a single exception to the

13. John Calvin, *Institutes of Christian Religion*, trans. Henry Beveridge (Grand Rapids: Eerdmans, 1989), 206–9.

principle that any biblical figure who receives the grace of an encounter with God is, concomitantly, sent on mission. This is true of Noah, Abraham, Moses, Joshua, Gideon, Samuel, Isaiah, Jeremiah, Peter, and Paul. Certainly God elects, but his election affords to a human being the deep privilege of participating in the process by which God is saving the whole of humanity. In other words, predestination and the love of predilection are not tantamount to God's "playing favorites" but rather functions of his desire that his lowly human creatures cooperate with him in the act of salvation. Thus in the case of Jedediah—the son of David who, prior to any moral or spiritual attainment of his own, found himself specially loved by God—the divine love of predilection was the condition for the possibility of building a temple that would gather Israel to unified prayer. In a certain sense, Solomon received a special privilege from Yahweh, but he was not, strictly speaking, loved for his own sake. Election always leads to mission.

Another profile of the doctrine of grace becomes especially visible in the Matthean genealogy, which I considered briefly above. The second group of fourteen generations preceding the arrival of Jesus commences as follows: "And David was the father of Solomon by the wife of Uriah" (Matt. 1:6). It is no accident that the evangelist mentions Bathsheba, at least indirectly. One would imagine that a conventional biographer, eager to present his subject in the most flattering light, would choose to overlook the somewhat sordid parentage of Jesus's distant ancestor. But Matthew goes out of his way to draw attention to Bathsheba, and his purpose is to show that God's grace can triumph over any human attempt to thwart it—if I can press the matter a bit, that God can even use human folly and sin in the accomplishment of his goal. Sin is real, but the divine love has the last word.

This psychologically intense and theologically rich chapter ends with a last look at the Ammonite war. David's military chief, Joab, has finally conquered the Ammonite capital of Rabbah, during the seige of which Uriah the Hittite was killed. The general then sends an ambiguous message to his king: "I have fought against Rabbah; moreover, I have taken the water city. Now, then, gather the rest of the people together, and encamp against the city, and take it; or I myself will take the city, and it will be called by my name" (2 Sam. 12:27–28). On the one hand, Joab seems in all humility to be ceding the actual capture of the city to the king. On the other hand, there is no mistaking the fact that Joab is clearly stating that he has done the lion's share of the military work and that if David procrastinates, Joab will go ahead and claim the city in his own name. Is he also not-so-subtly reminding David that in the heat of the battle the king was lounging on the roof of his palace and causing no little mischief for Israel? This oscillation between deference and defiance, which is prominent in Joab, will continue even more clearly in the rest of 2 Samuel, resulting finally in the death of Joab at the hand of Solomon (narrated in 1 Kings).

Following the advice of his general, David joins the battle, takes Rabbah, personally removes the crown from the head of the hapless king Milcom, and brings much treasure out of the city. This is one of the last glimpses given of the David of old, the boldly confident warrior who effortlessly accomplished his ends, and it is a reiteration of the imperial theme highlighted throughout the text. David's kingship over Israel is meant to grow into a kingship over the world, though the means by which this imperial growth occurs does not become plain until we hear the stories of the church's expansion in the Acts of the Apostles.

2 SAMUEL 13

As the twelfth chapter comes to an end, all seems to be well with Israel; the Bathsheba crisis has been brought to a just resolution, and David continues to expand his authority. But in the opening verses of the thirteenth chapter, Nathan's prediction that the sword will never depart from the "house" of David is coming true. Sin can be denied, forgotten, even atoned for, but its consequences remain. David's new Eden, deeply compromised by adultery and murder, will continue to devolve through rape, violence, and political rebellion, and what becomes painfully apparent is that this devolution occurs, as it did in the original Eden, because of bad kingship.

Though the central narrative of the thirteenth chapter concerns one of David's daughters, David's third oldest son, Absalom, is mentioned first: "Some time passed. David's son Absalom had a beautiful sister whose name was Tamar" (2 Sam. 13:1). Perhaps the author is foreshadowing the disaster that Absalom will bring, the most deleterious consequence of David's sin. We are told that Tamar is beautiful; later we will hear of Absalom's extraordinary physical attractiveness. David, of course, had been described as ruddy and handsome, and Bathsheba was of great beauty; even Saul was chosen king because of his impressive appearance. Beauty causes an awful lot of mayhem in this cycle of stories, and it is easy enough to see why. At the heart of the moral life is not so much rectitude of choice but something more primordial upon which choice will depend: the capacity to contemplate the other as other. In order to operate as an authentic moral agent, one must see others as the subjects of rights and desires as basic as one's own. Only through the conditioning of that contemplative or disinterested gaze will a moral agent be capable of responding to the second form of the Kantian categorical imperative:

never treat another human being as a means but only as an end. The sinful or fallen gaze is continually on the lookout for values that can be appropriated for the use of the ego. That look is pornographic rather than properly aesthetic, for it is ordered to the appropriation of value rather than the love of value.

In a moral world composed entirely of fallen subjectivities, one of the greatest obstacles to the attainment of the contemplative gaze is physical beauty in another human being, for that beauty makes the person in question, almost inevitably, an object of sexual desire. Of course, sexual desire is not wicked in itself, and it can indeed be situated in the context of loving contemplation; nevertheless, it exercises a power so extraordinary that it easily enough compromises the detachment from ego necessary for a truly moral decision. This is why sexual attractiveness in a fallen world is both wonderful and deeply dangerous—a dynamic on vivid display in the story of the rape of the beautiful Tamar.

Amnon, Tamar's half brother (the son of David by another wife), develops a lustful attraction for the girl. That this was lust and not authentic love is signaled by the fact that Amnon "was so tormented that he made himself ill because of his sister Tamar" (2 Sam. 13:2). The physical illness is doubtless a correlate to the obsessive and self-absorbed manner in which Amnon is attracted to her. Since Tamar is a virgin and since there were strict laws against sexually aggressing virgins, Amnon is driven mad by his pent-up sexual desire. Were he in love with the girl, he would have desired her good above his own and hence would have subordinated his sexual attraction to that end. How often sin finds those who will aid and abet it: "But Amnon had a friend whose name was Jonadab . . . and Jonadab was a very crafty man" (2 Sam. 12:3). A sinner who suspects that another person is tempted to sin will come swiftly to that person's aid, wanting, indirectly and probably unconsciously, to justify his or her own errant desire. Robert Alter offers "very wise" in place of "very crafty," and the New American Bible gives us "clever," terms that hearken back to the craftiness of the serpent in the garden, who, like Jonadab, gave extraordinarily bad advice to a ruler tasked with protection (Alter 1999: 266). Indeed, the very manner in which Jonadab addresses Amnon ("O son of the king") highlights the governing role that this prince of Israel ought to play. But instead of protecting his own kin, Amnon listens to wicked counsel and conspires to attack the one he is charged with sheltering.

The plan that the crafty counselor lays out is bizarre. Amnon is to play sick and to protest to his father that he will accept nourishment only from the hand of his half sister. Why this would strike anyone as a reasonable request is puzzling, but David falls for it: "David sent home to Tamar, saying, 'Go to your brother

Amnon's house and prepare food for him'" (2 Sam. 13:7). Here the reemergence of a theme of bad fathering can be seen, which is present more subtly in the earlier sections of 2 Samuel and will emerge ever more clearly in the post-Bathsheba sections. Though he himself was a sexual manipulator, David does not seem even to suspect that Amnon might be playing a dangerous game, and this naivete makes David himself complicit in his son's crime. What is apparent, of course, is the sad correspondance between childish, manipulative David and childish, manipulative Amnon, heir to his throne. Recalling Amnon's status as heir also explains more fully the texture of his attraction to Tamar. Her beauty was obviously a factor, but so too was her status as full sister to the impressive Absalom, Amnon's half brother and doubtless a rival claimant to the succession. By raping Tamar, Amnon baldly aggresses his half brother and assertes his dominance over Absalom, and the vehemence of Absalom's reaction to Amnon's act provides a good deal of support for this reading.

As the sad tale unfolds, another striking parallel with David's sin emerges. At the beginning of the Bathsheba story, David lies on his bed and then arranges for a woman to be brought to him. So too Amnon lies on his bed and, with the indirect assistance of David himself, arranges for a woman to be brought to him for the satisfaction of his lust. Robert Alter observes, brutally enough, that David thereby "pimps for his own daughter" (Alter 1999: 267). Entering her brother's house, Tamar falls into Amnon's trap, for in that space he can completely manage the situation, and he orders everyone but his sister out of the place. She prepares some cakes for her brother, and when she presents them to him, he grabs her and makes his intentions plain: "Come, lie with me, my sister" (2 Sam. 13:11). There are two fascinating echoes of the story of Joseph here. First, Joseph used the same command, "Send everyone away from me," which Amnon uses to clear the room before his attempt at rape. Of course, Joseph used it as a dramatic preparation for the exquisitely poignant revelation of his identity to his brothers. The "come lie with me" precisely reproduces the words of Potiphar's wife to Joseph, as she more or less attempted to rape the young man. Given the precision of these allusions, it is hard to believe that the author of the Samuel literature was not aware of at least an early strand of the J tradition of the book of Genesis. Was he perhaps using the greatest story of family conflict in Hebrew literature in order to illumine the complex dynamics of David's family (Alter 1999: 267)?

Tamar could not be simpler and more direct in her response: "No, my brother, do not force me; for such a thing is not done in Israel; do not do anything so vile!" (2 Sam. 13:12). The triple denial completely precludes the possibility of interpreting this encounter as anything but nonconsensual. Moreover, Tamar reminds Amnon not only of the wickedness of the act itself but also of the unbearable burden that the rape will permanently lay upon her: "As for me, where could I carry my shame?" (2 Sam. 13:13). While this act is certainly the height of injustice, Tamar's violation would forever mark her as unworthy of marriage, a pariah. She would be affected far more negatively by Amnon's lust than Bathsheba was by David's. In a last desperate attempt to avoid being raped, Tamar suggests to Amnon the possibility that their father would give the girl to her brother in marriage. Though this sort of incestuous marriage was highly unlikely in an Israelite setting, the situation might have been somewhat different in a royal family, an obvious precedent being the marriage of Abraham and his half sister Sarah. But none of these pleading arguments avail, and Amnon has his way with Tamar. The very bluntness and staccato rhythm of the author's description conveys the awful truth of what it means to be raped: "But he would not listen to her; and being stronger than she, he forced her and lay with her" (2 Sam. 13:14). In these words are echoes of other accounts of sexual violation in the Bible, including the rape of Dinah in Genesis 34, which led to murderous fraticidal violence, as well as the rape of the Ephraimite woman in Gibeah in Judges 19 and the attempted sexual assault of the three angelic visitors in Sodom in Genesis 19. In all of these examples one of the ugliest faces of sin surfaces: the objectification of the other for the sake of one's personal pleasure or advantage.

Having raped his half sister, Amnon is immediately "seized with a very great loathing for her; indeed, his loathing was even greater than the lust he had felt for her" (2 Sam. 13:15). The psychological insight of the author here is astounding, writing two and a half millenia before Freud. Those in the post-Freudian world readily recognize the volatile emotional swing of an unbalanced person as well as the almost inevitable projection of one's anxieties and guilt onto another whom one has violated. Also apparent here is the common strategy, often on display in cases of sexual crime, of blaming the victim. Filled with these irrational and deeply dysfunctional emotions, Amnon orders Tamar out of the room as abruptly as he had invited her to lie with him just a few minutes before. Sensing immediately the acute danger that she is in, Tamar begs, "No, my brother, for this wrong in sending me away is greater than the other that you did to me" (2 Sam. 13:16). The girl would have had at least some moral cover had Amnon agreed to marry her, but now that this is out of the question, Tamar is utterly exposed to ridicule and permanent social exile. With unutterable cruelty, Amnon orders that Tamar be sent away and the door bolted after her, an apt symbolic expression of her exclusion from marriage and the life of the community. In yet another reference to the Joseph story, the author comments on Tamar's distinctive dress: "Now she was wearing a long robe with sleeves; for this is how the virgin daughters of the king were clothed in earlier times" (2 Sam. 13:18). Indeed, Joseph and Tamar are the only two Old Testament figures who are described as wearing this sort of garment, which Robert Alter translates as "ornamental tunic" and the King James Bible translates as "coat of many colors"—certainly a sign of favor and special affection. Perhaps, given what had just been done to her, Tamar's robe was bloodstained, as was Joseph's after his brothers dipped it in an animal's blood in order to deceive their father (Alter 1999: 270). In one of the most pathetic scenes in the entire Bible, Tamar then places ashes on her head, tears her beautiful garment, rests her hand on her head in mourning, and returns home, crying as she goes. She is utterly violated, humiliated, and dominated, much like Joseph sold by his own brothers into slavery.

I would like to dwell a bit further on the Joseph parallel, drawing special attention to the theme of bad fatherhood. The Jacob who clothed his son in a special garment, lavished him with privileges, and then blithely sent him out to rendezvous with his brothers was, to say the very least, naive. Any father even vaguely attentive to the relational dynamics among his children would have known that this sort of treatment of a youngest son would be bound to awaken jealousy. So also David must have been grossly negligent not to have remarked upon the deep psychological dysfunction and dangerous narcissism of his eldest son. And he must have been inattentive to the extreme not to have noticed Amnon's unhealthy attraction to his half sister as well as Amnon's taunting attitude toward Absalom. The eye that was all too capable of taking in the beauty of Bathsheba apparently was blind to these rather obvious states of affairs. Just as Eli permitted Hophni and Phinehas to go about their corrupt business unimpeded, so David permitted Amnon to grow into a twisted prince of Israel. In this both Eli and David resemble the first human father, who not only allowed the serpent sway in the garden but also overlooked the tension between Cain and Abel that culminated in the primordial murder. Shakespeare possessed an extraordinary sensitivity to the havoc that follows from inordinate ambition; both Macbeth and Richard III are obvious cases in point. But fewer remark upon his equally keen awareness of the dangers that follow upon the failure to exercise power. The tragedy of both *King Lear* and *Titus Andronicus* flows from the title characters' refusal, at a propitious moment, to assume real leadership.

At this point in the narrative Absalom makes a curious entry. In language surprisingly courtly and delicate, he asks Tamar, "Has Amnon your brother been with you?" (2 Sam. 13:20). Even on the supposition that Absalom comes on the scene just after the rape when the girl is dissheveled and tear-stained, it is still remarkable that he intuits immediately that Amnon is the perpetrator. Is he more perceptive than David, more attuned to the dark dynamics of the family? Is he, perhaps, looking expectantly for an opportunity to move against his older rival? He then makes a strange remark: "Be quiet for now, my sister; he is your brother; do not take this to heart" (2 Sam. 13:20). The use of "brother" and "sister" so frequently throughout this narrative signals, of course, the incestuous nature of the rape, but it seems here to indicate that the close family connection between Amnon and Tamar somehow lessens the seriousness of the crime. However, given the action that Absalom eventually takes, this cannot be the right interpretation. More likely he is insinuating that if the rapist were any other man, Absalom would take immediate action. But since the perpetrator is his own brother and heir to the throne, he will have to bide his time and make a more careful plan. With that, Tamar disappears into Absalom's home and from the story. Much drama flows from her rape, but she participates in none of it.

Those readers hoping that David will rouse himself to action are given encouragement by the observation, "When King David heard of all these things, he became very angry"; however, their hopes are immediately dashed: "But he would not punish his son Amnon, because he loved him, for he was his firstborn" (2 Sam. 13:21). Surely the king's anger would result in some defense of his violated daughter, and some punishment would be meted out to his obnoxious and violent son. Certainly, the David who dispatched Goliath, slew his tens of thousands, took the foreskins of two hundred Philistines, conquered the Ammonites, and mercilessly killed the Amalekite bringing news of Saul's death would muster some pointed response to an act of brutality within his own household. But it was not to be: "He would not punish his son Amnon, because he loved him, for he was his firstborn." When Yahweh was displeased with David's sin, he acted, sending Nathan to impose judgment and punishment. But the one after Yahweh's own heart does not, in this instance, follow suit. Sadly, he mimics Jacob, who did nothing in response to the rape of Dinah, thus setting the stage for the bloody vengeance carried out by her incensed brothers Simeon and Levi. Significantly, at the close of that episode, Jacob found himself at the mercy of his sons much as David will find himself, at least for a time, at the mercy of his son Absalom.

Into the vacuum created by David's inactivity and bad fatherhood will step someone grossly unqualified to exercise prudent leadership: the vain, ambitious, and hotheaded Absalom. This same dynamic can be seen in *Titus Andronicus* when General Andronicus's refusal to lead creates the vacancy immediately filled by Saturninus, one of the most vicious and bloodthirsty of Shakespeare's villains, and in *King Lear* when Lear's abdication allows for his wicked daughters to hold sway. Absalom plots his revenge in the course of two years, doubtless calculating the political and personal costs of avenging his sister's rape. He decides to act at a sheepshearing, something like a harvest festival or carnival in the cultural context of that time and place, an occasion for much drinking, celebrating, and carousing. Absalom first goes to his father and invites the king to share in the festivities, but in line with his increasingly sedentary habits, David refuses to come. It seems clear that Absalom is counting on this reluctance, for he then presses to have the king allow all of his sons, especially Amnon, attend the celebration. He is playing a subtle game with his father, for if he had immediately petitioned the king to persuade Amnon to come, Absalom's violent intentions might have become rather obvious, since his animosity toward his half brother could scarcely have been a secret. Incredibly, David, who heretofore has been exquisitely sensitive to the political intrigue of his opponents, grants permission that all of his sons, the heirs to his throne, could gather in one place under the aegis of a man bearing a murderous grudge against his eldest son. Had he grown that naive? One of the saddest ironies of this story is that David is being set up as an accomplice to the murder of his son, just as Amnon had previously set him up to be an accomplice to Tamar's rape. The crafty king who attempted to manipulate his way out of responsibility for adultery and murder has now himself become a pathetic object of manipulation.

At the shearing festival Absalom gives the cold-blooded order to his henchmen: "Watch when Amnon's heart is merry with wine, and when I say to you, 'Strike Amnon,' then kill him" (2 Sam. 13:28). In the immediate wake of the murder, all of David's sons, surely fearing a general slaughter of Absalom's rivals, quickly mount their mules, the typical royal means of transport at the time, and scurry away. The murder of one brother by another, of course, hearkens back to the primordial murder of Abel by Cain, and the scattering of the heirs is an apt symbol of the disruptive and centrifugal quality of sin. The tribes came together around David at Hebron and Jerusalem, but here David's own sons scatter to the winds. It is not hard to see that Absalom's murder of Amnon serves a double purpose, both avenging the rape of Tamar and clearing the ground for his own claim to the throne. Which of his brothers could possibly have missed the seriousness of his purpose or harbored any illusions about his ruthlessness?

While the brothers flee, a wild rumor made its way to the palace that Absalom has killed not only Amnon but all of the remaining sons of David. Upon hearing this, David falls into a fit of mourning reminscent of his agony following the death of Saul and the onset of the illness of Bathsheba's firstborn: "The king rose, tore his garments, and lay on the ground; and all his servants who were standing by tore their garments" (2 Sam. 13:31). The general slaughter of all of his male descendants would have been the worst nightmare for a tribal potentate of that period, but especially for a king who was the recipient of an extravagant promise that the line of his progeny would last forever. Soon, however, David is reassured that only Amnon was killed. But those who know the further sweep of the narrative realize that this false rumor is actually a kind of premonition, for three of David's sons—Amnon, Absalom, and Adonijah—do indeed meet violent ends. When the surviving sons of the king return, they and their father break into copious tears, literally in the Hebrew, "weeping a very great weeping." Certainly, they were crying for joy and sheer relief, but doubtless they were also weeping for a family so obviously torn and dysfunctional, a family riven by both rape and murder.

Fearing for his life, Absalom flees to the court of his maternal grandfather in Geshur, north and east of the Jordan and therefore outside of David's immediate jurisdiction. As it turns out, he has no real ground for fear since David chooses not to pursue him, only to "mourn for him day after day" (2 Sam. 13:37). This reaction is comparable to the fierce anger David exhibited after Amnon's rape of Tamar, for it results in no concrete action. We are told that the heart of the king is just not in it. Similar to the beginning of the Bathsheba narrative, David does not go out on campaign precisely when such a sallying forth is called for.

2 SAMUEL 14

The fourteenth chapter of 2 Samuel begins with a mention of Joab, nephew and frequent foil for the king. Joab emerges in this section of the text as the great defender and promoter of Absalom, which, given the peculiar way that their relationship ends, is ironic to say the very least. Why at this stage did Joab support Absalom? Because he loved the young man? Because he wanted him to be king? Because he wanted David and his son reconciled? It is never made clear. Perhaps the most convincing explanation is that the savvy military man senses that Absalom's continuing banishment might provide the groundwork for an eventual rebellion. What the text tells us is simply that Joab intuits that "the king's mind was on Absalom" (2 Sam. 14:1).

The rough-hewn military man demonstrates that he has a calculating side as he concocts a clever plan, not unlike Nathan's a few chapters earlier, to persuade the king to do what Joab wants. The scheme involves a "wise woman" from Tekoa, a town some ten miles north of Jerusalem. It is fascinating to note how the whole David narrative, which centers around powerful military males, nevetheless hinges at certain crucial points on the intervention of strong, intelligent women. Think of Michal's quick thinking in smuggling David out of her room just in advance of Saul's thugs, the subtle tactics employed by Abigail, and later of the role played by a wise woman in the settling of Sheba's rebellion. Joab instructs the woman of Tekoa to present herself as a petitioner of the king, mourning for a lost son, and then coaches her as to what to say. Though she presumably follows the outlines of Joab's script, it is clear that the woman, wise indeed, is nimbly improvising, responding to the king's remarks and moving with the rhythm of the conversation.

She commences with the stock phrase used by any supplicant to the sovereign: "Help, O king!" (2 Sam. 14:4). Then she unfolds a tale of woe, presenting herself as the widowed mother of two sons, one of whom killed the other in a fierce family quarrel (the overtones of the Cain and Abel story surely are not accidental). The entire clan, she goes on, descended upon her, demanding that she give up the killer that he might be executed in accord with the law promulgated in the Torah: "If someone . . . strikes another with the hand, and death ensues, then the one who struck the blow shall be put to death" (Num. 35:20–21). But such an eventuality will leave her, she pleads, utterly devastated emotionally and bereft financially. Though fictional, it is a completely plausible tale, as believable in today's context as in David's time. When the king's immediate response is somewhat ambiguous—"Go to your house, and I will give orders concerning you"—the woman presses him to act: "Please, may the king keep the LORD your God in mind, so that the avenger of blood may kill no more, and my son not be destroyed" (2 Sam. 14:11). At which point David makes the definitive pronouncement: "As the LORD lives, not one hair of your son shall fall to the ground" (2 Sam. 14:11). Just as David's word to Nathan effectively put himself under judgment, so this word to the wise woman effectively saves Absalom, for David could not fail to notice the exact parallel with his son's situation. (Robert Alter makes the intriguing connection between the single hair of the fictional son that David will not allow to fall to the ground and the abundant hair of his real son, by which Absalom will eventually be suspended [Alter 1999: 277].) Once David has taken the rhetorical bait, the woman springs the trap: "For in giving this decision the king convicts himself, inasmuch as the king does not bring his banished one home again" (2 Sam. 14:13). In making this accusation, she knows that she is on dangerous ground, especially given David's history regarding those who bring him bad news, and perhaps this is why she does not directly name Absalom.

No fool, and well acquainted with palace intrigue, especially after the Nathan episode, David immediately sniffs out the prime mover behind this little farce: "Do not withhold from me anything I ask you. . . . Is the hand of Joab with you in all this?" (2 Sam. 14:18–19). The king must have known that Joab had been conspiring to bring Absalom back, and that if he kept his son in exile, an alliance between an angry Absalom and a frustrated Joab might prove disasterous. Robert Polzin even speculates that this is the message that Joab, working through several layers of indirection, in fact wanted the king to receive (Polzin 1993: 142). The Tekoan woman's response, "As surely as you live, my lord the king, one cannot turn right or left from anything that my lord the king has said" (2 Sam. 14:19), has an interesting double valence; on the one hand, it means that David has correctly uncovered the involvement of Joab, and on the other hand, it implies that there is no escaping the applicability of David's judgment in her fictional case to the case of Absalom. Flattering the king rather blatantly, the Tekoan says, "My lord has wisdom like the wisdom of the angel of God to know all things that are on the earth" (2 Sam. 14:20). The irony of this remark could scarcely be lost on the attentive reader of this section of 2 Samuel, for David, who had indeed displayed great cunning and insight earlier in his life, now exhibits a dangerous ham-handedness in regard to both psychological and political matters. Hardly "knowing all things that are on the earth," David is now someone whom others manage to maneuver around and conspire against. When he foolishly assumed a godlike point of view at the outset of the Bathsheba incident, he fell into Adam's sin and invited a similar set of calamitous consequences.

After Joab traps David through the ministrations of the woman from Tekoa, the king is more or less constrained to allow the return of Absalom. So Joab travels to Geshur, the land of Absalom's maternal grandfather, to retrieve the young man. Once more Joab seems to go beyond the call of duty in regard to this murderous and ambitious offspring of David, perhaps indicating his eagerness to use David's son against the king. But when he arrives in Jerusalem, Absalom is told that he can stay at his own house but cannot come into the presence of the king. Is this David's regret at having given in to Joab? Is it the result of David's lingering anger over the murder of Amnon? Is it a rather pathetic "approach and avoidance" strategy, reflective of David's incapacity to finally make up his mind? Judging from Absalom's eventual rebellion, it appears to have been, in any case, a failed strategem.

We then are told of Absalom's beauty: "Now in all of Israel there was no one to be praised so much for his beauty as Absalom; from the sole of his foot to the crown of his head there was no blemish in him" (2 Sam. 14:25). I have already noted the prominence of the category of beauty in this cycle of stories, but no one, David included, is given a more rapturous, even star-struck, description than Absalom. With almost fetishistic fascination, the author describes Absalom's most impressive physical characteristic: "When he cut the hair of his head (for at the end of every year he used to cut it; when it was heavy on him, he cut it), he weighed the hair on his head, two hundred shekels by the king's weight" (2 Sam. 14:26). Here, one sees a sort of soap-opera preoccupation with "pretty people," but something more is under consideration as well: the tragic tendency to be captivated by the surface, by glittering appearances, when God, as we are told in

1 Samuel, sees not the surface but the heart. Study after study reveals that beautiful people are given the benefit of many doubts, have an easier time finding jobs than plain-looking people, and generally are viewed as more likeable and successful than their homelier counterparts. But how far all of that falls from any proper standard of justice! Still another problem with physical attractiveness is how easily it can draw the attractive person into a narcissistic attitude. Two hundred shekels is an extraordinary weight for hair, no matter how luxuriant, but more important, what sort of person was Absalom that he weighed his own hair? The author of our text, who rarely misses an opportunity for irony, tells us that the object of Absalom's narcissistic preoccupation, once tangled in an oak, will become the occasion for his demise. So it goes with inordinate self-love. Robert Pinsky comments, "Absalom's flaw is less the overindulgence of privilege than his delusion that good looks and good fortune could make him the equivalent of David."[1]

A further difficulty with great physical beauty is that it can easily enough stir up emotionality in others. There is probably no greater literary display of this phenomenon than Herman Melville's novella *Billy Budd, Sailor*. Billy's youthful beauty is so striking that his shipmates are initially captivated, but in time it awakens in some of them a resentment so profound that they conspire to kill the young man. It would be hard to miss a similar dynamic in the story of the beautiful Absalom, who after a lifetime of being admired and petted finds himself gleefully stabbed by a gang of soldiers. I do not think it the least bit accidental that Isaiah depicts the suffering servant, who will bring salvation to Israel, as physically unimpressive: "He had no form or majesty that we should look at him, nothing in his appearance that we should desire him" (Isa. 53:2). Jesus's physical appearance is nowhere even gestured toward in the Gospels.

We are told that Absalom has by this time become something of a paterfamilias, giving rise to three sons and a daughter. (This report is utterly at odds with a later text, 2 Sam. 18:18, which clearly states that Absalom had no son. These irreconcilable accounts are the result, no doubt, of different traditions that the editor carelessly conflated.) What is of particular interest is that the author identifies by name not the sons but instead the daughter, who bears the name of her violated aunt. This is most likely an oblique way of indicating that the line of Absalom will not bear the promise.

The budding patriarch and former exile lived, we are told, two years in Jerusalem but never came into the presence of his father. Absalom might be forgiven for

1. Robert Pinsky, *The Life of David* (New York: Schocken, 2005), 133.

wondering why David bothered to bring him back from Geshur in the first place. Was it simply to placate Joab, or was it to assuage, to some degree, his own guilty conscience? At any rate, the paternal cold shoulder is still another example of the vacillating indecision that has plagued the king since the Bathsheba incident, and it practically guarantees that Absalom's impatience and sense of inferiority will grow. At the very least, one would expect that the wise king would keep an eye on a hotheaded potential rival, honoring the dictum that a leader should keep his friends close but his enemies closer. But David, as has become his pattern, does precisely the wrong thing. Frustrated, Absalom sends for Joab, his erstwhile partner, and pleads with him to intervene on his behalf with David, but Joab ignores him. As Robert Alter observes, there is throughout this chapter "a precarious game of power going on" between Joab and Absalom, each one warily sizing up, assessing, cajoling, and using the other for political advantage (Alter 1999: 281).

Angered by Joab's nonresponse, Absalom dramatically takes matters into his own hands, ordering his servants to set fire to Joab's barley field. This scene calls to mind Samson's burning of the Philistines' cornfields described in the fifteenth chapter of the book of Judges. There are in fact a number of references to the Samson narrative in the Absalom story, not the least important of which is the attention given to the hair of both figures. But the burning of his own cousin's field, a remarkably aggressive act within the agrarian culture of the time, certainly signals Absalom's volatility of character and a deep psychological instability. Judging by the behavior patterns of Amnon and Absalom, one sees yet another example that David was far less than an exemplary parent and far less than a responsible king, for these two sons were heirs to the throne of Israel. Once again an echo of the story of Eli and his two dysfunctional sons can be heard. Yet Absalom gets what he wants. When Joab storms over to protest, his cousin tells him more or less that this is the only way to get his attention. Then the young man lays out the situation as he assesses it: "Now let me go into the king's presence; if there is guilt in me, let him kill me!" (2 Sam. 14:32). Absalom is playing a dangerous game here, and he knows it, but he has reached a limit. If the king never receives him, then he is, politically speaking, in a permanent limbo, unable to realize his ambitions. Therefore he has to press the matter to resolution. It is another tragic consequence of David's diffident parenting and kingly leadership that it has to come to this. A good father would have found a way to adequately punish Absalom, mentor him, and finally prepare him for leadership. Instead the young man is allowed to wallow in his self-reproach, anger, and ambition, and this results in more narcissism and violence.

Despite his obvious annoyance with the young heir, Joab once more cooperates with him and sets up an appointment with the king. But what a strange audience it is. Absalom comes into the presence of his father, bows down with his face to the ground, and does the king homage. Was this simply a gesture of respect for David's authority, or was it perhaps also an acknowledgment of guilt for the killing of Amnon? The author does not tell us. He only describes David's highly ambiguous reaction: "And the king kissed Absalom" (2 Sam. 14:33). No words are exchanged, no confession made or forgiveness offered, no counsel or advice either sought or given. The king simply kisses his son. Was this a sign of greeting, a gesture of pardon, or was it even, in the manner of Michael Corleone in *The Godfather*, the "kiss of death"? We do not know, and apparently neither did Absalom. This is perhaps the clearest and most disastrous instance of David's bad fathering, for it allowed a deeply problematic person to go unconstrained throughout the king's new Eden.

2 SAMUEL 15

The ambiguous kiss and the lack of paternal direction and discipline from David pave the way for the awful rebellion of Absalom, which is narrated in the course of the next several chapters. David had been told that the sword would never leave his house. That prediction came tragically true in the Amnon-Tamar-Absalom incident, but it would reach its sad climax in the attempt by David's own son to supplant Yahweh's chosen. Like Bathsheba, Absalom essentially plays the role of the serpent in the garden—a source of evil that the gardener fails adequately to contain. The machinations of this particular serpent will lead to the expulsion of the new Adam from his paradise.

The Absalom who spent two years in exile and who, upon his return, laid low, now bursts forth publicly with extraordinary panache: "After this Absalom got himself a chariot and horses, and fifty men to run ahead of him" (2 Sam. 15:1). The obvious comparison is to a wealthy and ambitious politician today, driving the fastest and most fashionable car and surrounding himself with an impressive posse and bodyguards. Robert Alter refers to Absalom's "vehicular pomp and circumstance," which in the context of his time carried with it "a claim to royal status" (Alter 1999: 283). All of this rather obvious self-promotion, taking place in Jerusalem under the nose of the king, goes unchecked.

Next we are told of a ploy familiar among ambitious and self-serving politicians from any culture and any era. The prince rose early and positioned himself by the "gate road" so as to meet anyone coming into the city. He headed off those who were bringing a suit or request before the king and assured them that their cause, whatever it turned out to be, was right and good, and that if Absalom himself were king, he would surely rule in their favor. Unscrupulous, cynical, and absolutely indifferent to truth or justice though he was, Absalom successfully "stole the hearts of the people of Israel" (2 Sam. 15:6). Doubtless, the prince's striking physical beauty played a role in this charm offensive as well.

This is a most convincing portrait of a demogogue, someone who leads the people but who does so disastrously, precisely in the measure that he disregards the moral context in which decent and productive leadership takes place. A contrast to Absalom's maneuvering by the gate is the scene in *A Man for All Seasons*, in which Thomas More makes his way through a crowd of petitioners, promising only that he will read the cases and give their relatives the same judgment he would give his own daughter, "a fair one, quickly."[1] That More was unsuccessful in "stealing the hearts" of the nation becomes painfully obvious as the story unfolds, but he was, in point of fact, acting as an authentic benefactor of the people. Ambrose makes much the same point in his commentary on this passage: "It is certain that nothing feigned or false can bear the form of true virtue; no it cannot last." In regard to Absalom himself, Ambrose remarks, "So he turned the hearts of all to himself. For flattery of this sort quickly finds its way to touch the very depths of the heart."[2] Sadly, however, this flattering manner of touching the heart is, as the word itself suggests, all *flatus*—puffery, hot air. Thus it might win people over, but only in the short term. Robert Alter suggests, plausibly enough, that many of those arriving in Jerusalem might have been unhappy with the new centralized bureaucracy associated with David's governance: more taxes, more military conscription, more control (Alter 1999: 283). Therefore, they would be particularly susceptible to Absalom's overtures, especially if they were rubes from the country unaccustomed to the ways of the capital city.

Earlier I mentioned that Thomas Aquinas speculates that there are four classic substitutes for God: wealth, pleasure, honor, and power. All four are good in themselves, but they become deeply problematic when proposed as supreme or unconditioned goods. God must be loved first and absolutely, and then the other four can be loved in relation and subordination to that primary love. Loving God, a person will know what to do with wealth, pleasure, honor, and power and will know precisely how to love them. As Augustine puts it, *Ama et fac quod vis* ("Love, and do what you want").[3] Absalom can be seen as an archetype of the man who

1. Robert Bolt, *A Man for All Seasons*, directed by Fred Zinnemann (Hollywood, CA: Columbia Pictures, 1966).

2. Ambrose, "Duties of the Clergy 2.22.112–14," in *Joshua, Judges, Ruth, 1–2 Samuel*, ed. John R. Franke, Ancient Christian Commentary on Scripture: Old Testament 4 (Downers Grove, IL: InterVarsity, 2005), 371.

3. Augustine, *Love One Another, My Friends: Saint Augustine's Homilies on the First Letter of John*, trans. John Leinenweber (San Francisco: Harper & Row, 1989), 73.

has made honor and power his ultimate values and who thereby has fallen into shadows. Honor, Aquinas argues, is a flag or indication of virtue, and in that sense it is altogether good. But when it is sought as the supreme good, it devolves in short order into an addicting obsession of the ego. Power must also be good in itself, for God is described as all-powerful; but when it becomes a substitute for God, it too becomes the object of an attachment. The remainder of the story of Absalom is simply the narrative demonstration of what this dissolution of soul, born of attachment, looks like.

Absalom's capacity for manipulation apparently knew no limits. We are told that when people came forward to pay him homage, he would take them by the hand and then kiss them. The affectionless kiss calls to mind the odd kiss that David gave his son upon the latter's return from Geshur. The implicit insincerity of David's embrace is magnified in the obviously deceitful kisses of his son. Furthermore, the Hebrew verb that lies behind the expression "take them" is the same one used to describe Amnon's "taking" of Tamar. Is the author not-so-subtly suggesting that in Absalom's currying of favor a somewhat less aggressive form of rape is going on (Alter 1999: 284)? Through this entire process, David's son steals the hearts of the people, taking them rather than winning or persuading them. The authentic love that eventually obtained between David and the tribes of Judah and Israel is nowhere apparent here. What is apparent instead is essentially a game of buying and selling, an exchange born of mutual self-interest. How typical of the biblical narrators that Absalom's character is sketched in a few swift strokes. From the twin stories of the murder of Amnon and the wooing of political support, all one needs to know about this man is revealed: his moral status, his fears, and his ambition.

Then it is insinuated that four years pass, during which, presumably, Absalom continues with his ruthless maneuvering and refrains from any contact with David. Only after these years of consolidating support does the son endeavor to move against his father: "At the end of four years Absalom said to the king, 'Please let me go to Hebron and pay the vow that I have made to the LORD'" (2 Sam. 15:7). The request to go to Hebron is, of course, symbolically fraught, since David first became king of Judah at Hebron and later, at that same place, was declared king of all Israel. Could the old king have possibly been so naive or inattentive not to see that his highly ambitious son, organizing a religious ritual in Hebron, was up to something seditious? Did he fail to notice how curious it was that Absalom did not invite his own father? Absalom certainly was aware of the powerful political symbolism of Hebron and also desirous of being far enough away from the capital in order to launch his rebellion relatively unhindered. Though he masks it in false piety, using the name of Yahweh twice in his request, Absalom insinuates the motive for his move when he makes reference to the city to which he had been forced to flee in the wake of the murder of Amnon: "For your servant made a vow while I lived at Geshur in Aram: If the LORD will indeed bring me back to Jerusalem, then I will worship the LORD in Hebron" (2 Sam. 15:8). The only reason that he is in Geshur is that David, at a decisive moment, refused to act; and the only reason, presumably, that he wanted to return to the capital was to supplant the man who had failed so thoroughly to govern properly.

In a supreme irony, David's last words to his son as he sends him to the place where the young man will foment revolution are "Go in peace." The irony is especially thick given that the name "Absalom" means "my father is my peace." Since the young man is going to Hebron with the king's own blessing, no one would suspect his motives or cast in his direction a specially watchful eye. This is precisely why Absalom is able to muster supporters throughout the country, calling in the IOUs that he had accumulated during his years as a glad-hander in Jerusalem. He sends out the word that, at the propitious moment, they should gather behind his leadership: "As soon as you hear the sound of the trumpet, then shout: 'Absalom has become king at Hebron!'" (2 Sam. 15:10). Two hundred men come from Jerusalem with the rebel, though we are told that they know nothing of his intentions. Doubtless, they became swept up in the excitement and confusion of the moment and backed the popular hero when the word went out. A fascinating detail: we hear that while Absalom is performing the sacrifice, he sends for "Ahithophel the Gilonite," who is none other than the grandfather of Bathsheba and a man surely still nursing a grudge against the adulterous king (Hertzberg 1964: 337). That the grandfather of a woman whom David wronged would play a decisive role in a rebellion that almost supplants the king is still another vivid indication that the sword never left David's house.

A messenger then comes to the king informing him that "the hearts of the Israelites have gone after Absalom" (2 Sam. 15:13). If it is understood that David is the one after the heart of Yahweh, then the fleeing of the "hearts" of the people toward the rebel is a sign of deep spiritual dysfunction within Israel. The nation that was meant to be gathered around the true king is organizing itself around a rival power, and this would lead only to disaster. One might appreciate this as a political expression of what happens internally when a person's heart commences to wander after something other than God. In his commentary on Exodus, Origen construes the ancient Israelites as evocative of all of the positive powers within the human being: mind, will, imagination, creativity, and so on. Accordingly, he reads the enslavement of Israel by Egypt as an allegory for the enslavement of those inner powers under the spiritual tyranny of pride, wealth, or hatred.[4] The same could be said in regard to Absalom's tragic sway over the hearts of those who previously had been loyal to David.

Upon hearing the news of the rebellion, David shows uncharacteristic energy, springing immediately into action and issuing the order, "Get up! Let us flee, or there will be no escape for us from Absalom. Hurry, or he will soon overtake us, and bring disaster down upon us, and attack the city with the edge of the sword" (2 Sam. 15:14). Though firm, this is an order to retreat, and for those who have been following the exploits of David throughout the Samuel literature, there is something more than a little pathetic about this kingly command. The wily David, who had always managed to anticipate Saul's moves and outmaneuver his pursuer, now seems like an animal that had been caught sleeping, even as his predators close in around him. As I have shown, David's refusal to take decisive, if risky, action in regard to Tamar, Amnon, and Absalom led to his present difficulties. Even granting the king's middle-aged torpor, it does seem a bit surprising that Absalom could so quickly and thoroughly have gotten the upper hand, so that David's only recourse is to run. Some have suggested that Absalom, during his long years of political maneuvering, managed to co-opt the militia of Jerusalem, or at least its top leadership (Hertzberg 1964: 349). In any case, David and his entourage are forced to move out.

In the remainder of the David-Absalom narrative, two sides rather neatly line up: those who, despite the enormous dangers, remain loyal to the king, and those who side with the upstart prince. Christian readers might notice a parallel to the new David, who said, "Whoever is not with me is against me, and whoever does not gather with me scatters" (Matt. 12:30). Life is filled with ambiguities, and sometimes a certain psychological "pluralism" is permissable, even welcome; but in regard to one's ultimate concern and final allegiance, one has to be clear, unified, and unambiguous. Sometimes, despite strong counterarguments and very grave dangers, a definitive choice has to be made.

David quits his capital city, but he leaves behind his ten concubines to "look after the house." This might be construed as a hopeful gesture, an indication that the king expects to return. But what is most important is that it sets up the fulfillment of one of the direst aspects of Nathan's prophecy. The king's departure is portrayed

4. Origen, "Homilies on Numbers 27.2," in *Exodus, Leviticus, Numbers, Deuteronomy*, ed. Joseph T. Lienhard and Thomas C. Oden, Ancient Christian Commentary on Scripture: Old Testament 3 (Downers Grove, IL: InterVarsity, 2001), 3.

as a sad yet stately march, even a sort of liturgical procession, during which David pauses to greet or respond to figures, most of whom carry some sort of symbolic valence (Polzin 1993: 155). Since all of the momentum of David's story to this point has been toward Jerusalem and the consolidation of the nation around the right praise of God, there is a terrible sadness about this kingly retreat, this loss of the center. The mood of desolation is only heightened when we learn that the king and his entourage leave on foot, signaling not only the rapidity of their escape but also the loss of royal dignity. Before quitting the city, David and his courtiers stop at the last house and permit a parade of retainers and supporters to pass before them, including "all the six hundred Gittites who had followed him from Gath" (2 Sam. 15:18). These were Philistines, who functioned as a kind of bodyguard for David and had joined him during his curious sojourn among the Philistines during the war with Saul (Alter 1999: 286). There is irony, of course, in the fact that David's closest military protectors are not Israelites, but this is also a sign that David's reign is meant to include the many peoples beyond the twelve tribes.

Robert Alter points out that the phrase "crossing over" is used repeatedly in this episode (Alter 1999: 286). David and his entourage cross over from Jerusalem to the Kidron Valley, from the valley to the Mount of Olives, and finally from the mount to the far side of the Jordan River. The church fathers love to play with the christological anticipations on evidence here. The night before he died and just after a last meal with his disciples, which included a man who would betray him and another who would deny him, Jesus left the Holy City, went down into the Kidron Valley, and then climbed the western slope of the Mount of Olives, crossing over from Jerusalem to the garden of Gethsemane. The new David, fleeing as it were from those in rebellion against him, quit Jerusalem and undertook a kind of liturgical procession to a place of intense prayer. Cyril of Jerusalem's christological allegorizing is typical: "Again, after Absalom's rebellion, when David was in flight, with many possible routes before him, he chose to make his escape by the Mount of Olives as good as invoking in his own mind the Deliverer who should from there ascend into the heavens."[5] There were, of course, very good strategic reasons why David and his men took the eastern route: had they moved south, they would have directly encountered the main force of Absalom's army coming up from Hebron; had they ventured north, they would have come into potentially hostile Israelite land; and had they sallied west, they would have come face to face with the Philistines (Hertzberg 1964: 341).

5. Cyril of Jerusalem, "Catechetical Lectures 2.12, 20," in Franke, *Joshua, Judges, Ruth, 1–2 Samuel*, 372.

We then hear a brief conversation between David and Ittai the Gittite. With extraordinary magnanimity, David wonders aloud why this foreigner should put his own life in danger by accompanying the fleeing king. Why not remain in Jerusalem and offer his services to Absalom, to whom David refers already as "the king"? Throughout the Bathsheba and post-Bathsheba period, David was at his worst—calculating, self-absorbed, manipulative, murderous, inactive—but now, curiously, during this time of crisis and retreat, David is at his best once again. To Ittai, David offers what can only be called "steadfast kindness" (*ḥesed*), the compassionate willing of the good of the other that is the very nature of the God of Israel. When it is massively in his self-interest to take with him as many retainers as possible, especially those trained in the art of war, David graciously looks to Ittai's advantage. This is the same *ḥesed* that the younger David demonstrated to Saul when sparing the king's life. As is often the case, compassion awakens compassion, and Ittai responds to David: "As the LORD lives, and as my lord the king lives, wherever my lord the king may be, whether for death or for life, there also your servant will be" (2 Sam. 15:21). This is one of the most beautiful and theologically evocative exchanges in the Samuel literature. The author of these texts knew all about political machination, ruthless self-interest, calculating duplicity, abuse of power, and the rest, but there is none of that here. Here are two men, each in a good deal of danger, expressing concern for one another. There is an echo here of the story of Naomi and her daughter-in-law, David's great-grandmother Ruth. When Ruth's husband died, Naomi urged her daughter-in-law to return to her Moabite relatives, but Ruth resisted the order: "Do not press me to leave you or to turn back from following you! Where you go, I will go; where you lodge, I will lodge; your people shall be my people, and your God my God" (Ruth 1:16).

In the wake of this brief but moving conversation, Ittai and his entourage cross over from Jerusalem to the Mount of Olives, and David follows them, moving through the Kidron Valley. This might be read as a mournful procession away from the Holy City, the reversal of David's exuberant dance into Jerusalem as he accompanied the ark. This interpretation is confirmed by David's next encounter. Up to the king come Abiathar, Zadok, and all of the Levites, "carrying the ark of the covenant of God" (2 Sam. 15:24). After the entire entourage has passed, David tells the priests to bring the ark back into the city. At first blush, one might think that David had the disaster of Eli and his sons in mind and wanted simply to protect the ark from capture. But if attention is given to his explanation, deeper spiritual truths open up. It was an Israelite custom to carry the ark into battle for protection. Prior to its installation in Jerusalem it was much more mobile, a symbol of Yahweh's willingness to travel with his itinerant people. But at this moment of supreme danger, David does not want to use the ark for his own protection. Instead, he demonstrates a remarkable detachment: "If I find favor in the eyes of the LORD, he will bring me back and let me see both it and the place where it stays. But if he says, 'I take no pleasure in you,' here I am, let him do to me what seems good to him" (2 Sam. 15:25–26). Better than anyone else, David understood that the ark's ultimate purpose was to unite the nation (and eventually the world) in right praise. Israel, therefore, existed for the ark, and not the ark for Israel. At a relatively primitive level of religious consciousness, one might see God as an advantageous friend to have, as a supernaturally powerful source of succor and support. But along with the maturing of faith comes the realization that one exists for God and that one's life must be ordered to God's purpose, not vice versa. Manipulation of God, "putting the Lord to the test," is always a sign of a fallen consciousness. In insisting that the ark remain where he originally placed it, David demonstrates both the *apatheia* of which the Greek fathers speak and the *indiferencia* that is so central to the reflections of Ignatius of Loyola.[6]

However, it must be said that the author never lets the reader forget that David remains canny and wily. Indeed, these two priests bring the ark back into the city, but their return also means that David will have two loyalists and their sons, who can spy out the situation once Absalom comes into power: "Look, go back to the city in peace, you and Abiathar, with your two sons. . . . See, I will wait at the fords of the wilderness until word comes from you to inform me" (2 Sam. 15:27–28). It is difficult for anyone in our hypertechnological age to imagine how very challenging it was to wage war in the ancient world. Inadequate reconnaissance, impossibly slow communication, little to no ability to coordinate efforts once a battle was joined—all contributed to an intensely thick "fog of war." Therefore, to have a number of spies capable of overhearing the council of advisors surrounding a rival commander was of incalculable value to David, who was cut off from supply lines and essentially waging a guerrilla war.

With the ark on its way back to Jerusalem, David and his entourage continue their sad trek up the Mount of Olives. The king weeps as he goes, keeping his head covered and his feet bare—all signs of profound mourning (Alter 1999: 288). Could this be read as a penitential exercise, David carrying still the weight of his sin against Uriah? In the film *The Mission*, Rodrigo Mendoza is a ruthless slave trader who commits fratricide. For several months following his brother's

6. Ignatius of Loyola, *The Spiritual Exercises of Saint Ignatius of Loyola*, trans. W. H. Longridge (London: A. R. Mowbray, 1930), 301.

murder, he sits in prison in the very depths of depression, refusing to eat, longing to die. He then is visited by Father Gabriel, a Jesuit priest of enormous compassion and spiritual purpose who convinces the prisoner that there is a way out of his misery. The priest then compels the mercenary to haul a large net filled with helmets, muskets, and swords—the accoutrements of his former way of life—over large tracts of territory, up and down hills and across rivers, coming finally to a Jesuit mission at the top of a waterfall. Only at the end of this excruciating exercise when a member of the tribe that he had oppressed cuts loose the net does Mendoza's character find redemption and release. In a similar manner, David is on a mournful and purgative march. The author includes the lovely details that, as David passed by, "the whole country wept aloud" (2 Sam. 15:23) and "all the people who were with him covered their heads and went up, weeping as they went" (2 Sam. 15:30). In our post-Cartesian, post-Kantian Western culture so marked by subjectivism and individualism, it is hard to grasp this sort of collective solidarity whereby David sums up and gives expression to the entire people. In point of fact, this collective sensibility is still on lively display today in cultures relatively untouched by the Western Enlightenment. The kind of synergy on display here—David recapitulating the people, and the people finding themselves in David—is the condition for the possibility of the Christian claim that universal salvation is truly affected through the actions of one great representative figure.

As he climbs the Mount of Olives, David is told about Ahithophel's desertion to Absalom, and the king utters the heartfelt and pointed prayer that whatever counsel Bathsheba's grandfather gives to Absalom will "turn to foolishness." It is a prayer that the providential God of Israel will promptly answer, for just after offering it, David encounters Hushai the Archite, whose coat is torn and whose head is covered in dirt—signs of his solidarity in sorrow with the king. Seizing immediately on the opportunity, David asks Hushai to go into Jerusalem and to offer himself as a counselor to Absalom and counterweight to Ahithophel. This is still another example of the synergistic, concomitant causality so often on display in this literature. David's move is perfectly explicable on pragmatic political grounds, but it is also the means by which God answers the king's prayer and works the divine purpose out. Retreating from his capitol in mourning, David nevertheless summons extraordinary energy and maps out a plan involving a complex spy network. To Hushai he gives detailed instructions: "Say to Absalom, 'I will be your servant, O king; as I have been your father's servant in time past, so now I will be your servant,' then you will defeat for me the counsel of Ahithophel" (2 Sam. 15:34). He specifies that Zadok and Abiathar the priests will also be undercover with him along with their sons, and that through the sons, Hushai should report what he hears to David. These are not the machinations of someone who has given up or who harbors little hope of success.

The chapter ends with the dramatic report that "Hushai, David's friend, came into the city, just as Absalom was entering Jerusalem" (2 Sam. 15:37). The moment the disease is injected into the body politic, an antibody is injected. Just as David leaves, David's proxy enters; as David's betrayer comes in, Absalom's betrayer comes in. In his discussion of the relationship between particular contingent causes and the universal unconditioned causality of God, Thomas Aquinas employs the image of a king who sends two emissaries on apparently unrelated business precisely so that the two might meet.[7] For the emissaries, their encounter is purely haphazard, a lucky (or unlucky) coincidence, but it is in point of fact the result of a higher, though hidden, intentionality. By his permissive will, God arranged for Absalom to extricate David from Jerusalem, and by his active will, God arranged for Hushai to meet Absalom precisely for the purpose of undermining the rebel king.

7. Thomas Aquinas, *Summa theologiae: Latin Text and English Translation, Introductions, Notes, Appendices, and Glossaries*, ed. Thomas Gilby et al., 61 vols. (New York: McGraw-Hill, 1964–81), 5:95.

2 SAMUEL 16

As this chapter opens, David continues his stately march away from Jerusalem over the top of the Mount of Olives. Robert Polzin remarks that two of David's greatest humiliations in this chapter will happen on heights: Shimei's mockery on the mount and Absalom's taking of David's concubines on the roof of the palace (Polzin 1993: 160). Robert Alter observes that the Hebrew term for "top" or "summit" is *rōʾš*, which can also bear the connotation of "head," and there is indeed much talk of heads in this section. For example, we see Hushai with the earth on his head, Abishai prepared to lop off the head of Shimei, David going forth with his head covered, and Absalom ending up suspended from his hair (Alter 1999: 290). Is an oblique comment being offered here on the dangers associated with headship, with assuming a godlike vision and control?

As the king's march of retreat unfolds, more stylized encounters take place. First, he meets with Ziba, the servant of Mephibosheth, the son of Jonathan, whom David had taken into his household. The slave is carrying a veritable bounty for the king and his retinue, who had been forced to leave the capital hurriedly and under considerable duress. He presents saddled donkeys carrying "two hundred loaves of bread, one hundred bunches of raisins, one hundred of summer fruits, and one skin of wine" (2 Sam. 16:1). This appears to be simply a generous offer from the young man to whom David had shown such extraordinary generosity, but things are in fact a good deal more complicated. When pressed as to the health of his master, the slave replies that Mephibosheth has remained in the city, reveling in David's expulsion and savoring the arrival of Absalom, which represents, however obliquely, the revenge of the house of Saul. It appears as though David takes this explanation at face value, for he promptly promises Ziba all of the land that the king had originally given to Mephibosheth. Yet suspicions crowd in here. Why would Mephibosheth think that David's son, having expelled his father, would show favor to the house of Saul? And why would a man to whom David had shown such bounty, and who had heretofore exhibited preciously little interest in politics, suddenly turn on his benefactor? What becomes clear just a few chapters later is that this little speech by Mephibosheth's slave amounts to Ziba's rather pathetic attempt to ingratiate himself with the vulnerable king and to denigrate any potential rivals. As any student of politics or psychology knows, moments of instability or weakness invite those who had been out of power to move in.

The complex relationship between David and the family of Saul is once more on display in the next encounter, one of the most memorably described in the Samuel literature: the meeting of the king with Shimei, a disgruntled Saulide from the town of Bahurim on the eastern slope of the Mount of Olives. As David approaches, Shimei commences to curse him and throw stones and dirt at him. Given David's typical reaction even to those who simply bring him unwanted news, Shimei must know that he is playing a very dangerous game. Is he confident that David's depressed mood and political weakness will prevent the king from reacting, or is he simply giving vent to a frustration deep enough to make him heedless of the consequences of his actions? The precise content of Shimei's curse is worth dwelling upon: "Out! Out! Murderer! Scoundrel! The LORD has avenged on all of you the blood of the house of Saul. . . . See disaster has overtaken you; for you are a man of blood" (2 Sam. 16:7–8). Those who have been following the story narrated in the books of Samuel know that David was, in fact, not responsible for any of the blood of the house of Saul. Even when given the opportunity on more than one occasion, he assiduously avoided killing Saul, and time and again he protected and made excuses for various Saulides. However, given the violent deaths of Saul, Jonathan, Ishbosheth, and Abner, many, especially members of the house of Saul, must have strongly suspected that David, clandestinely or otherwise, was implicated in these deaths, which in every case advanced his own career. At the same time, we who followed the story of Bathsheba and Uriah know that David is indeed a murderer and something of a scoundrel, and that the blood of Uriah and those who died with him at Rabbah of the Ammonites does cry out against him. And as we saw, the Chronicler recounts that God himself, having refrained from giving David the privilege of constructing the temple, offers as an explanation that the king had shed too much blood. Therefore, though he might not have all of the details right, Shimei is speaking a good amount of God's truth in the presence of the king. If one presses the matter a bit in the manner of the postmodern interpreter eager to pull the hanging "threads" of a narrative, it could be said that the Shimei curse invites one to reconsider the perhaps overly tidy story being told. Is Shimei in fact a kind of Derridean voice compelling the reader to deconstruct the tale and to consider the possibility that David is a figure even darker and more ambiguous than the Bathsheba story suggests?

Unable to contain himself any longer, Abishai, nephew to David and brother to Joab (one of the always hotheaded sons of Zeruiah), speaks up: "Why should this dead dog curse my lord the king?" (2 Sam. 16:9). When Mephibosheth wanted to signal his unworthiness to receive the gracious largesse of the king, he referred to himself as a "dead dog," and indeed the epithet designated, for biblical Jews, the lowest of the low. Abishai wants to bring to light the greatest possible contrast in juxtaposing "dead dog" and "my lord the king." Moreover, he wants to bring Shimei, with one swing of his sword, into close conformity to the metaphor: "Let me go over and take off his head" (2 Sam. 16:9). This was the same Abishai who had to be restrained when he indicated his willingness to put Saul to death with one thrust of his spear. But David, who never hesitates to kill those who he felt needed to be killed, now refuses to order the death of his tormentor, insisting instead that Shimei could well be an agent of Yahweh. No one on the scene, including David, doubts that Shimei is something of a lowlife, "a reptile of the royal house of Saul," as Alexander Whyte calls him.[1] What is remarkable is that the king recognizes that even this vile man is an ingredient in God's purposes and could function as a secondary instrument of divine agency. Here again is the issue of the concomitance and noncompetetiveness between God's causality and finite causality, but the Shimei incident allows another profile of this relationship to emerge. Sometimes God permits even moral evil for the sake of a greater good, or more precisely, he can use wickedness to accomplish his ends. In this case, David discerns that the divine purpose is a cleansing and purifying one. If one of his own sons is in open rebellion against him, he must have permitted (after the manner of Adam's bad kingship) a great dysfunction to emerge in his kingdom, and the cursing of the Saulide is but his just deserts. He also reads the situation in rather karmic terms, hoping that the unjust suffering that he presently endures might be requited later through a divine favor: "It may be that the LORD will look on my distress, and the LORD will repay me with good for this cursing of me today" (2 Sam. 16:12).

During the Reformation period this issue of the relation between God's providence and moral evil became particularly pointed. So insistent were they upon

1. Alexander Whyte, *Bible Characters* (Grand Rapids: Zondervan, 1952), 245.

the absolute sovereignty of God, that Luther (at least in *The Bondage of the Will*) and Calvin argue that moral wickedness itself is actively affected by God in the hearts of evil people. Their preferred test case is the "hardening of the heart" of Pharaoh described in the book of Exodus, though Luther also draws attention to Shimei. The author of Exodus does not imply that God's offer of grace was refused by a stubborn human being but rather that God actively and for his own purposes made Pharaoh stubborn, and David at least seems to insinuate the same thing about his persecutor. Some of the disciples of the great Reformers go so far as to suggest that God actively brought about the original sin of Adam and Eve, since nothing, good or bad, finally escapes the active sovereignty of God. A key text in support of this position can be found in Deutero-Isaiah: "I am the LORD, and there is no other. I form light and create darkness, I make weal and create woe; I the LORD do all these things" (Isa. 45:6–7). Luther explains God's hardening of Pharaoh's heart as follows: "God presents from without to his villainous heart that which by nature he hates; at the same time, he continues by omnipotent action to move within him the evil will which he finds there."[2] So God "galls" Pharaoh by presenting the divine word to him, and God also made possible the very will that finds the divine word galling. With those who might object to God's active engagement in evil, Luther shows no patience, referring them simply to the inscrutability of God's hidden will. And Calvin, considering the possibility that God merely "permits" but does not actively work evil, responds that such a construal of divine providence renders God a weak competitive cause among many and not the sovereign Lord of all creation.[3]

In his *Symbolism*, from the early nineteenth century, Johann Adam Mohler offers the classic Catholic response to this sort of speculation. To say, Mohler maintains, that God actively effects evil in the wills of wicked people simply makes God complicit in evil and hence compromises the divine goodness.[4] At the very best, such theorizing turns God into a capricious and deeply ambiguous character, hardly the moral and ontological rock on whom the vacillating sinner can rely. Instead, God allows for moral corruption under the rubric of permitting the greater good of freedom, and he can also use foreseen wickedness in his overall

2. Martin Luther, *The Bondage of the Will*, trans. J. I. Packer and O. R. Johnston (Grand Rapids: Revell, 1996), 271.

3. John Calvin, *Institutes of Christian Religion*, trans. Henry Beveridge (Grand Rapids: Eerdmans, 1989), 198–200.

4. Johann Adam Mohler, *Symbolism: Exposition of the Doctrinal Differences between Catholics and Protestants as Evidenced by Their Symbolical Writings*, trans. James Burton Robertson (New York: Crossroad, 1997), 37.

providential design. The sovereignty of God does indeed preclude God's being moved or determined by his creatures in such a way that he is "frustrated" by sin or compelled to "adjust" to it. But God can use moral turpitude just as he uses various types of physical evil in order to bring about his purposes. In this sense only, God "creates both weal and woe," as Isaiah says. Since evil, strictly speaking, is a type of nonbeing, it would be metaphysically incoherent to speak straightforwardly of God "creating" it; moreover, it would be morally incoherent to maintain that God could ever fall away from the ethical ideal. Therefore, the most satisfying explanation of the "creation" of woe and the hardening of Pharaoh's heart is that God sovereignly permits evil and creatively uses it for an ultimately good end. Both human freedom and chance make possible a sort of surd not directly willed by God or even at odds with his fundamental intention. But even this surd can be redeemed by the One who is sovereign over both history and nature. Here is how Augustine handles the problem of reconciling divine sovereignty and sinful freedom in the case of Shimei: "Now what prudent reader will fail to understand in what way the Lord bade this profane man to curse David? It was not by a command that he bade him, in which case his obedience would be praiseworthy; but he inclined the man's will, which had become debased by his own perverseness, to commit this sin by his own just and secret judgment."[5]

Christians cannot help but hear an echo of Christ in the narrative of Shimei and the king. As Jesus walked away from Jerusalem the night before he died, following the same path as the retreating David, he entered into a dreadful period during which he would be massively abused by a whole series of Shimeis: his own fearful and denying disciples, the temple guard, the corrupt Sanhedrin, Herod, Pilate, the soldiers of the Roman garrison, and the mocking bystanders on Calvary. Having taken upon himself the sins of the world, Jesus became on object of contempt and derision, and, like his ancient prototype, he did nothing to prevent his persecutors from attacking him. In point of fact, he accepted it as the will of his father. In Galatians, Paul interprets the cross of Jesus as the locus of both curse and blessing: "Christ redeemed us from the curse of the law by becoming a curse for us . . . in order that in Christ Jesus the blessing of Abraham might come to the Gentiles" (Gal. 3:13–14). The curse imposed by God the Father on the suffering Jesus, through the mediation of an army of Shimeis, became the condition for the possibility of a benediction for the human race.

5. Augustine, "On Grace and Free Will 41.20," in *Joshua, Judges, Ruth, 1–2 Samuel*, ed. John R. Franke, Ancient Christian Commentary on Scripture: Old Testament 4 (Downers Grove, IL: InterVarsity, 2005), 375.

On a somewhat more mundane level, one might see in David's attitude toward the cursing Shimei a valuable lesson in leadership. One of the surest ways for a leader to lose authority is an unwillingness to accept legitimate criticism. The king or president or bishop who is surrounded only by sycophants rapidly falls victim to egotism and managerial incompetence. It is said that Lyndon Johnson, during his presidential years, had a full-time staffer whose job was to report to the president precisely what his critics were saying. One might well argue that the David who submitted to Shimei's abuse was a far more reliable king than the David who strode arrogantly on his palace roof and casually manipulated his courtiers.

As David hits bottom, his rebellious son enters Jerusalem. This is, doubtless, the nadir of David's life, the lowest point in this remarkably up-and-down drama. One might read David here as evocative of compromised and threatened Israel and Absalom as a personification of all of those dark powers that would invade Jerusalem in the centuries to come: Assyria, Babylon, Greece, and Rome. Jerusalem was meant to be the new Eden, the center of a liturgical empire, and God's anointed was meant to be its ruler; but less than savory forces—the first coming from within David's own household—would, throughout Israelite history, consistently undermine it (Beale 2011: 58–63). One might also interpret this icon of David's exit and Absalom's entry in a more personal and spiritual manner. When the worship of God is no longer central to one's life, inevitably some other form of worship obtains; some Absalom enters to replace the exiled David.

As Absalom enters the city, he is accompanied by Ahithophel, the grandfather of Bathsheba—a man noted for his wise counsel. Wickedness can be practically undermined by folly, but when it is accompanied by wisdom and perceptiveness, it is dangerous indeed. The combination of Absalom and Ahithophel—a rebellious spirit and a canny intelligence—produces a formidable obstacle to David and his purposes. What follows in the narrative is the complex battle between Absalom's advisors. Hushai, David's plant, presents himself to Absalom with what appears to be disarming loyalty and good cheer: "Long live the king; long live the king!" (2 Sam. 16:16). But it does not require an insightful reading to note that Hushai does not specify to which king he is referring. The irony becomes even thicker when Absalom (playfully or scornfully?) challenges Hushai: "Is this your loyalty to your friend? Why did you not go with your friend?" (2 Sam. 16:17). The undercover spy responds cagily and with studied ambiguity: "The one whom the LORD and this people and all the Israelites have chosen, his will I be, and with him I will remain" (2 Sam. 16:18). Once again, it is not the least bit clear whether Hushai is referencing David or Absalom here; plausible deniability is preserved whether his words are interpreted as indicating loyalty to the father or the son. Due to his vanity and superficiality, Absalom remains oblivious to the duplicity of Hushai's language, and he takes the former Davidide counselor into his confidence.

But first he turns to Ahithophel for advice, and Bathsheba's grandfather offers a brutal counsel that certainly is born of his deep resentment at the way his granddaughter had been treated by the cavalier and manipulative king: "Go into your father's concubines, the ones he has left to look after the house; and all Israel will hear that you have made yourself odious to your father, and the hands of all who are with you will be strengthened" (2 Sam. 16:21). The sexual possession of the women of one's opponent was, at that time, a particularly clear sign of dominance and contempt. And, as Ahithophel shrewdly notes, it is also in this case an unmistakably plain indication that no reconciliation between the rebel and his father is possible. It is a public burning of bridges and boats and hence a move that constrains the people to make a choice. Absalom follows Ahithophel's recommendation, erecting a tent on the roof of the royal palace for the coupling of Absalom and his new harem. We recall that Nathan, in his devastating speech to David in the twelfth chapter, predicted to the king that his wives would be given to another who would "lie with your wives in the sight of this very sun" (2 Sam. 12:11) so that David would be ashamed before all of Israel. And so, according to that strangely biblical law of karma, it happens. Also, who could miss the cruel irony that David's humiliation takes place on the very palace roof from which he had first spied Bathsheba, inaugurating his finally self-destructive machinations (Alter 1999: 295)? If the account is literally true, one can only marvel at Absalom's sexual prowess—having intercourse with ten women in the course of an afternoon! Whether the story is accurate in its details, its purpose is to show Absalom's brutally aggressive assertion of dominance over and usurpation of his father.

The sixteenth chapter ends with another affirmation of Ahithophel's shrewdness and wisdom: "Now in those days the counsel that Ahithophel gave was as if one consulted an oracle of God; so all the counsel of Ahithophel was esteemed, both by David and by Absalom" (2 Sam. 16:23). This reputation helps to explain why David was so chagrined to hear that Bathsheba's grandfather had gone over to Absalom, and it is certainly born out in the advice that Ahithophel gave to the rebel son, a recommendation that was, from a pragmatic standpoint, clever indeed. As we will see in the following chapter, Absalom's undoing will be the direct result of his failure to heed the counsel of this ancient Israelite version of

Bismarck or Kissinger. At the same time, one may fairly speculate whether the author indulges in a bit of ironic commentary, characterizing the rather sordid recommendation to go publicly into the concubines of David as a quasi-divine oracle! Who speaks for God and how one knows it are nagging questions throughout the Samuel literature.

2 SAMUEL 17

Oracle or not, as the seventeenth chapter gets under way, Ahithophel continues to give energetic and provocative advice. Having recommended that Absalom humiliate his father by taking sexual possession of David's concubines, he now advises that Absalom cut to the chase and eliminate his rival to the throne. He asks the upstart king of Israel for permission to take twelve thousand men and attack David and his troops, who are depressed, undernourished, and disorganized after their hasty retreat from Jerusalem. Ahithophel puts one in mind of Lincoln after the battles of Antietam and Gettysburg, desperately pleading with his generals to press the advantage and destroy the enemy army before it can escape and regroup. From a strategic standpoint, it would be hard to argue with his recommendation. But as he presses his case, one senses that something stranger and far less than rational is afoot: "I will come upon him while he is weary and discouraged, and throw him into a panic; and all the people who are with him will flee. I will strike down only the king, and I will bring all the people back to you as a bride comes home to her husband" (2 Sam. 17:2–3). The grandfather of Bathsheba wants not simply to supplant David politically but to personally strike down the man who violated his granddaughter and murdered her husband. Tellingly, he wants the rest of David's troops to return as a bride to a husband, precisely what Bathsheba was never able to do vis-à-vis Uriah (Hertzberg 1964: 350). Moreover, the image of an army fleeing so as to leave only one man vulnerable certainly calls to mind the strategy that Joab employed to arrange for the death of Bathsheba's husband. Once more the biblical author is insisting that sin begets sin, resentment gives rise to answering resentment, and violence unmistakably awakens in its victim a mimetic violence.

Ahithophel's counsel is so wise, so obviously right, that it "pleased Absalom and all the elders of Israel" (2 Sam. 17:4). But then the usurper makes the fateful mistake of seeking further advice, this time from Hushai, David's man on the inside. Doubtless, the author means to convey something of Absalom's immaturity and inexperience, his excessively cautious tendency toward consensus building when a decisive move is called for. It proves to be his undoing. Hushai commences his intervention with a nod toward Ahithophel that is both flattering and challenging. Though he acknowledges Ahithophel is usually quite correct, this time the great counselor is mistaken. Hushai then proceeds to rehearse the legend of King David, a portrait quite out of step with the David whom we have come to know in the last several chapters. Though he saw the rag-tag band that wended its way out of Jerusalem, Hushai refers to David's men as fierce fighters and opines that they are even now cannily hiding themselves in pits, ready to pounce when Absalom's army comes upon them. Furthermore, he continues, David himself is "expert in war" and will easily outmaneuver the inexperienced forces that Absalom has gathered around himself. In an image that calls to mind the young David's valiant defense of his flock, Hushai compares the king and his men to an enraged bear robbed of her cubs. Therefore, Hushai concludes, it is best to wait, allowing "all of Israel . . . from Dan to Beer-sheba" to rally to Absalom and only then, when he is at full strength, to attack his father's army. Whereas Ahithophel proposed himself as the leader of the posse in pursuit of David, Hushai cleverly appeals to Absalom's vanity and proposes that the usurper himself lead the battle. Whereas Ahithophel recommended something like delicate surgery—removing the one offending person and sparing his army—Hushai advocates the annihilation of David's entire company. The game he is playing is subtle indeed, for, despite the bravado, Hushai is actually advocating something like General McClellan's approach at the outset of the Civil War—endlessly training his army, ever convinced of the insufficient number of his troops, always reluctant to act. Hushai is stalling for time, giving his exiled master the opportunity to organize his defense.

Stunningly, Absalom and his elders, who only a moment before had enthusiastically supported the grandfather of Bathsheba, now turn completely around: "The counsel of Hushai the Archite is better than the counsel of Ahithophel" (2 Sam. 17:14). Was this reversal the result of Absalom's vanity and insecurity, and was the acquiescence of his coterie of aides the result of their sycophancy? Probably. But as is his wont, the author suggests an ultimate cause, an agency that works precisely through the actions of secondary agents: "For the LORD had ordained to defeat the good counsel of Ahithophel, so that the LORD might bring ruin on Absalom" (2 Sam. 17:14). There is no need to return to the details of my discussion of this issue above. Suffice it to say that God's "ordaining" here has nothing to do with God actively sinning but rather with God's capacity to work with and through even moral weakness and intellectual stupidity in order to realize his providential designs. The ironies are thick in this account, for the advice of the clear-eyed advisor is ignored while the cockeyed recommendations of the schemer are taken for wisdom; and God makes the latter conducive to his purpose. Things are never entirely neat, either in the earthly courts of kings or in the heavenly court of Yahweh.

Though the decision seems to have been made definitively, Hushai is unaware of it, or perhaps simply unsure that Absalom would follow it. He counsels his allies Zadok and Abiathar to tell David quickly to cross over the Jordan and establish himself there, lest he and his men be "swallowed up." What follows is a fascinating vignette that carries overtones of the story of Rahab the prostitute and the Israelite spies recounted in the book of Joshua. Zadok and Abiathar convey Hushai's message to Jonathan and Ahimaaz, two Davidide loyalists, who in turn endeavor to convey it to the king. But on their way, they are spied out by a boy who reports their activity to Absalom. The spies then hide themselves in a well in Bahurim, whose mouth is subsequently covered over by a woman, presumably a supporter of David. When the soldiers of Absalom come to the house and inquire after the two men, the woman blithely lies, "They have crossed over the brook of water" (2 Sam. 17:20). This seemingly incidental narrative is meant to show, first, how terribly divided the nation was at the time of the Absalom rebellion: supporters of both king and usurper were thick upon the ground and often engaged in a complex chess game of move, countermove, and deception (Alter 1999: 300). Consider the fact that Bahurim, where David's men were successfully hidden, was the hometown of Shimei, perhaps the king's bitterest opponent. Second, it also demonstrates, precisely through the parallel to the Rahab incident, that the loyalists to David were the true Israelites and the partisans of Absalom were the enemies of Yahweh. As always, the division within Israel itself is sadder and more debilitating than any war between Israel and its foreign opponents.

Upon emerging from the well, Jonathan and Ahimaaz make their way directly to David and tell him that Ahithophel's advice had been followed, and thus the king should move quickly. A fair amount of the "fog of war" emerges in this incident, since all of the major players, from Hushai down, seem confused about exactly what Absalom had resolved to do. But the confusion serves David well, since it compels him to move and take advantage of the extra time that Hushai had bought him. The king then ensconces himself and his entourage safely on the eastern side of the Jordan, where they are able to prepare themselves for the coming battle.

The seventeenth chapter, which is something of a transitional section in the overall narrative of the Absalom rebellion, comes to a close on a chilling note with the story of the suicide of Ahithophel. There is something almost Shakespearean in the telling of this tragic tale. Once he understands that his advice has not been acted upon, Ahithophel rides his donkey (a sophisticated mode of transport) to his hometown, sets his affairs in order, and then hangs himself. It is far too simplistic to suggest that the courtier kills himself simply out of disappointment. Despite his high reputation, it strains credulity to think that his advice had remained unheeded many times before. Always clear-eyed, Ahithophel sees that the following of Hushai's advice will lead inevitably to Absalom's downfall and hence to Ahithophel's own execution for treason. By taking matters into his own hands, he makes sure that his inevitable death will happen on his terms and in a manner most convenient to him and his family. One sign of his practicality: his suicide in his hometown assures that he will be safely buried in his ancestral tomb long before David can desecrate his dead body in the manner of Saul's or Mephibosheth's. Though there is a stoic, Cato-like quality to Ahithophel's suicide, it is important to remember that it is also one more tragedy flowing from David's sin with Bathsheba, which continues to radiate bad karma in every direction.

Following the advice of his spies, David crosses the Jordan, but Absalom is in hot pursuit. In accord with the author's sense of irony, the son (Absalom) has become the father (Saul), and David is once more the hunted prey, running for his life in the open country. We hear that Absalom places Amasa, a cousin to Joab, over his rebel army, thus assuring that cousin will meet cousin in the climactic battle. Once more, the terrible internecine quality of this struggle is on display: Israel tearing itself apart, the unity that David forged at Hebron and subsequently in Jerusalem fatally compromised. When the king arrives at Mahanaim, an Israelite walled city in the Transjordan, he is met with a coterie of Israelite and Ammonite allies, a remnant of the Davidide empire: "Shobi son of Nahash from Rabbah of the Ammonites, and Machir son of Ammiel from Lo-debar, and Barzillai the Gileadite from Rogelim" (2 Sam. 17:27). These friends bring to him and his army an array of much needed supplies and victuals: "beds, basins, and earthen vessels, wheat, barley, meal, parched grain, beans and lentils, honey and curds, sheep, and cheese from the herd" (2 Sam. 17:28–29). It is hard to miss the parallel between this list of goods and the similar lists of precious metals and weapons acquired for the decoration of the temple. David is, even in his weakened condition, still a great gathering force (Alter 1999: 302).

2 SAMUEL 18

This pivotal chapter, which deals with the final military struggle between the forces of David and the army of Absalom, concludes with what is arguably the most humanly moving scene in the entire Old Testament, the weeping of the king for his rebellious son: "Absalom, my son, my son." One could argue that David's adultery with Bathsheba bears its bitterest fruit in this pathetic and heartbreaking episode.

As the chapter opens, we see David energetic and on the move. There is no hint of the listlessness and inactivity that contributed to the king's moral lapse. He is the commander of old, sizing up the situation and organizing his troops accordingly into three main groups, the first of which he places under the command of Joab, the second under Joab's brother Abishai, and the third under Ittai, his Gittite ally. The author means to show that the deceptive strategy of Hushai has borne fruit, since David has been given a chance to regroup and prepare his army for battle. The king wants to lead the battle in person (this is the newly energetic David), but his troops wisely oppose him, given that his death is the principal goal of Absalom and his army. They sagely comment, "You shall not go out. For if we flee, they will not care about us. If half of us die, they will not care about us. But you are worth ten thousand of us" (2 Sam. 18:3). The king acquiesces ("Whatever seems best to you I will do"), which is not cowardice but simply common sense. Thus David stays behind at the gate of Mahanaim and watches as his army streams out to meet Absalom. Moshe Garsiel notes a fascinating correspondence between David standing at the gate in this episode and Absalom loitering by the gate of Jerusalem at the very commencement of his attempt to seize power from his father (cited in Alter 1999: 312).

As the troops sally forth, David gives a final command to Joab, Abishai, and Ittai: "Deal gently for my sake with the young man Absalom" (2 Sam. 18:5), and the people overhear this father's plea. This might be read as indicative of David's compassion and willingness to forgive his enemies, but one might also construe it as another sign of the king's weakness and unwillingness adequately to discipline his children. In the course of the last several chapters David's bad parenting led to disaster after disaster. One wonders whether Joab and the other commanders sense that, given this history, the following of David's command will lead only to further trouble. A hard moral truth emerges here: the responsible judge usually has to make determinations in abstraction from any sentimental attachments, lest true justice and the common good be compromised. Is the relatively cold-blooded Joab perhaps more clear-sighted in regard to Absalom than David? At the same time, David is a man after the very heart of Yahweh. The God of Israel is indeed a just judge, but his mercy "mocks" his justice. Though he thunders at his children, he tends, finally, to indulge and forgive them. The magnificent Psalm 103 touchingly expresses the fatherly indulgence of the God of Israel: "He will not always accuse, nor will he keep his anger forever. . . . As a father has compassion for his children, so the LORD has compassion for those who fear him. . . . But the steadfast love of the LORD is from everlasting to everlasting" (Ps. 103:9, 13, 17). Therefore, does David's "weakness" for his children, his sentimental failure to exact true justice in their regard, in fact not represent the deeper and higher judgment of God?

The battle is joined in the forest of Ephraim, and the matter is settled rather quickly. Though the biblical narrator, typically enough, provides very little detail concerning the unfolding of the military action, it is fair to surmise that David's well-trained and well-organized troops met Absalom's inexperienced band and put them to rout. Most likely, the three battalions of David attacked the rebel soldiers from three sides and panicked them, their confusion exacerbated by the thickly wooded terrain. Indeed, the author's dry remark that "the forest claimed more victims that day than the sword" (2 Sam. 18:8) is reminiscent of descriptions of the Wilderness Campaign during the American Civil War. From a theological point of view, the author probably is insinuating that nature itself conspired against the numerically superior rebel forces in order to assure a victory by Yahweh's beloved (Baldwin 1988: 288).

Absalom, we are told, happens to encounter some servants of David. Though this sounds a bit odd, the reader must remember that the fog of war had definitely descended on this particular wooded battlefield, and the rebel king probably was as disoriented as his troops. As would have been appropriate for a high-status figure,

Absalom is mounted on a mule, and the animal, perhaps in a panic, scoots under a large oak. Before he can react, Absalom finds himself caught by the hair in the tangle of the tree's branches. The bizarre, almost comical, image of the young man suspended between heaven and earth is, as Robert Alter comments, a wonderfully apt summary of this entire section of 2 Samuel (Alter 1999: 304). Who could miss the irony in the fact that Absalom's hair, which had been the very focus of his narcissistic pride, would become the means of his undoing? On the biblical reading, happiness flows not from self-preoccupation but rather from a forgetting of self and a surrendering to the purposes of God. Also, the royal animal running off and leaving his rider suspended is a particularly apt symbol for the unseating, the dethroning, of Absalom. Like his former counselor Ahithophel, Absalom ends his life strung up, undone by his own errant machinations. Of course, the church fathers cannot overlook the thematic rhyming of this episode with the Gospel accounts of the death of Judas, another betrayer from the inner circle of the king who ends in a bad way. Cassiodorus's comment is typical: "When Absalom was cruelly attacking his father David, the speed of his mule caused him to collide with a thick oak tree, and the branches wound round his neck so that he was suspended high in the air. This was a prefiguration of the Lord's betrayer. Just as Judas ended his life in the knot of a noose, so also David's persecutor breathed his last through the pressure on his throat."[1]

One of the Israelite soldiers who had surprised Absalom now informs Joab that the rebel leader is hanging helplessly from the oak. The nephew of David testily wonders why the man did not finish off Absalom and thereby procure a reward. But the soldier piously protests that even if he had been offered a thousand pieces of silver, he would never have gone against the explicit command of the king. (Remember that the order not to harm Absalom was overheard by "the people," meaning many of the soldiers.) There is an echo here of the many times that David refused to raise his hand against Saul, even when Saul was utterly vulnerable to him, and there is also the humble and uncomplicated obedience of a loyal soldier. The impetuous Joab brushes aside these Uriah-like pieties. Saying, "I will not waste time like this with you," he "took three spears in his hand, and thrust them into the heart of Absalom" (2 Sam. 18:14). There is some ambiguity in the Hebrew at this point. The word *šĕvātîm*, rendered in the New Revised Standard Version as "spears" and in the King James Version as "darts," is translated by Robert Alter

1. Cassiodorus, "Exposition of the Psalms 3.1," in *Joshua, Judges, Ruth, 1–2 Samuel*, ed. John R. Franke, Ancient Christian Commentary on Scripture: Old Testament 4 (Downers Grove, IL: InterVarsity, 2005), 382.

as "sticks." The sense seems to be that Joab did not deliver a definitive and killing blow with a large weapon but rather that he stabs at Absalom with something less lethal, causing blood to flow but not ending the life of the young man. Prompted by this signal, Joab's ten young armor bearers then attack the hapless Absalom and put him to death. It is possible that in his use of less-than-deadly weaponry, Joab was honoring, however imperfectly, his king's command. But more likely, he was lashing out with whatever was at hand, utterly convinced of the folly of David's instruction. Though impetuous, Joab was also, as I have pointed out on a number of occasions, endowed with great practical intelligence. He saw more clearly than David that allowing the rebel leader to live would guarantee almost perpetual civil unrest in Israel. And so he acted.

With Absalom dead, the rebellion is effectively over. Thus Joab calls in the army, and some of his men take down the body of Absalom, throw it into a pit in the forest, and then raise over it a mound of stones. The point is that this was in every detail a shameful burial for an ancient Israelite, especially since a pit covered in stones would in very short order be unrecognizable as a grave. Many accursed figures in biblical history find a similar grave—for example, Achan and the king of Ai. The irony becomes especially thick when one recalls that Absalom constructed a large funerary pillar for himself outside of Jerusalem, a monument that was meant to preserve his memory for centuries.

Ahimaaz, identified as the son of Zadok, then volunteers to bring the report of Absalom's death to David, but Joab intervenes, doubtless out of concern for what David might do to a bearer of bad news: "You are not to carry tidings today; you may carry tidings another day, but today you shall not do so, because the king's son is dead" (2 Sam. 18:20). Joab obviously is fond of Ahimaaz and does not want him to suffer the fate of the Amalekite who thought that he was bringing David the good news of Saul's death, or of the murderers of Ishbosheth, who, with equal enthusiasm, carried the head of Saul's son to David. Instead Joab turns to a non-Israelite, a Cushite, to bring the news. The messenger takes off, but Ahimaaz reasserts himself, insisting that, come what may, he will bring the news to the king. Once again, Joab tries to prevent him, pleading with him, "Why will you run, my son, seeing that you have no reward for the tidings?" (2 Sam. 18:22). Ignoring the older man's wise advice and caught up in the excitement of the moment, the young messenger sets out and soon enough overtakes his Cushite counterpart.

Now our attention shifts to David, waiting impatiently at the gate between the outer and inner walls of the city, suspended, as it were, between staying home and going forth. Robert Polzin notes that David's posture and position are exactly those of Eli as he waited for word from the dreadful battle in which his two sons had been killed and the ark of the covenant taken. Like Eli, David is a negligent father whose failure to discipline an errant son leads to disaster, both personal and political. We hear that the lookout went up on the parapet of the outer gate and saw one man running. David concludes that this must be good news, presumably because a lone runner would be a courier, whereas a number of runners might be stragglers from a defeated army. When the second runner, the Cushite, is spotted, David is once more encouraged, and when the first figure is identified as Ahimaaz, the king excitedly responds, "He is a good man, and comes with good tidings" (2 Sam. 18:27). One is struck, first, by the irrationality of this. Why could the first two figures not be couriers sent from a desperate and defeated Joab? And why in the world would the moral character of a courier determine the content of the message he bears? This is not the thinking of the knowing, clever David of old but rather the projections and wishful thinking of an increasingly panicked father. The reader might also notice the topography of the scene. David's troubles began when he placed himself in a godlike position on the roof of his palace and proceeded to manipulate things for his own pleasure. Now he is on the ground, looking up to his servants who have mounted the heights. The bad karma of the Bathsheba incident simply keeps on coming.

Upon arriving and presenting himself to David, Ahimaaz utters the simple word *šālôm*. Usually translated as "all is well," the word has incomparably rich overtones in Hebrew, signaling the very peace that God wants his people to have. It is also the last two syllables of Absalom's name, *ʾabšālôm*, an irony that David picks up on when he wonders, "Is it is well [*šālôm*] with the young man Absalom [*ʾabšālôm*]?" (2 Sam. 18:29). Ahimaaz delivers the good news, "Blessed be the LORD your God, who has delivered up the men who raised their hand against my lord the king" (2 Sam. 18:28), but David is interested only in his son. Overwhelmed to be in the presence of David and doubtless unnerved by the king's inquiry about Absalom's well-being, Ahimaaz delivers gibberish: "When Joab sent your servant, I saw a great tumult, but I do not know what it was" (2 Sam. 18:29). It is hard even to guess to what the flustered courier is referring to or how it bears on Absalom. With exasperation, David turns to the Cushite and asks the same question concerning the *šālôm* of *ʾabšālôm*. A bit steadier on his feet than his counterpart, this messenger replies obliquely but clearly enough, "May the enemies of my lord the king, and all who rise up to do you harm, be like that young man" (2 Sam. 18:32). Upon hearing the news that he fears the most, David withdraws to a chamber over the gate and gives himself over to intense grief: "O Absalom, my son, my son Absalom! Would that I had died instead of you. O Absalom, my son, my son!" (2 Sam. 18:33).

As I noted at the outset of this chapter, this is one of the most humanly affecting scenes in the entire Bible. Any parent who has experienced the uniquely wrenching pain of losing a child can identify with David's agony. But the matter becomes more complicated and more spiritually interesting when one bears in mind that Absalom was a child in open rebellion against his father, a child who had, in the grossest way possible, publicly embarrassed his father and indeed was aggressively attempting to kill him. That David could say, in regard to *that* son, "Would that I had died instead of you," shows the depth of his paternal love. Here again David is the man after the heart of Yahweh, the God who relentlessly loves even those who repudiate him. John Chrysostom recognizes in the attitude of David toward Absalom the model of a good pastor who grieves over the suffering of his errant flock and indeed desires to take their suffering upon himself.[2] The sheer bewilderment that attends this intense grief is evidenced in the simplicity and repetitiveness of David's speech. The king who composed an achingly eloquent elegy on the deaths of Saul and Jonathan is now reduced to moaning the name of his son over and over again. There is a kind of declension in the manner in which David responds to the deaths of those close to him. The poetic elegy to Saul and Jonathan is succeeded by the far briefer and less lyrical elegy to Abner. That song is succeeded by the "somber words" spoken upon the death of his infant son with Bathsheba, which finally gives way to mere sobbing and groaning at the death of Absalom (Alter 1999: 311).

2. John Chrysostom, "Homilies on Romans 29," in Franke, *Joshua, Judges, Ruth, 1–2 Samuel*, 385.

2 SAMUEL 19

As the nineteenth chapter commences, Joab is told of David's reaction to the death of Absalom. The tough but wily commander must have experienced more than a little trepidation, for he had been directly and explicitly told not to harm the young man. Joab is playing a dangerous game, trusting that his actions will not excite the royal wrath against him, and he proves to be right. But it will be his own chutzpah that will guarantee his safety. When word spreads throughout the army, the troops slink back to the city "as soldiers steal in who are ashamed when they flee in battle" (2 Sam. 19:3). Were they simply ashamed at their own complicity in the death of Absalom, or were they perhaps wary of an impending war between David and his sometimes obedient commander? The simplest and best explanation is that they were sympathizing with the mourning of their king. When David was declared king in Hebron, the Israelites considered themselves bone of David's bone and flesh of his flesh. There was, indeed, a kind of mystical body of David—a kind of elemental solidarity that could obtain between a people and its king that may be opaque to our consciousness but was altogether real in ancient Israel.

In his chamber above the gate David continues to mourn, still pathetically repeating the name of his dead son. Certainly aware of the risky gambit he is about to undertake, Joab moves into the king's space and directly challenges him: "Today you have covered with shame the faces of all your officers who have saved your life today, and the lives of your sons and your daughters and the lives of your wives and your concubines, for love of those who hate you and for hatred of those who love you" (2 Sam. 19:5–6). It is a bold and extremely clever speech, for it counters David's emotion with cold reason. Joab knows that preserving the life of Absalom, though psychologically satisfying to David, would be disastrous for the nation, because it would pave the way for permanent unrest and civil war. Moreover, he knows that David's indulgence of his emotions is striking a mortal blow to the morale of the army upon which his political survival will depend. He argues that the king, in fact, is mooning over an enemy who raped his women and tried to usurp his throne, even while he insults those who risked their lives for him. From a "reader response" point of view, Joab's intervention is fascinating, since it undermines the reader's own temptation to give in to sentimentalism. It slaps both David and the reader in the face. What matters finally for the biblical authors is fidelity to the mission, and Joab has, piously or not, intuited what is needed for the furtherance of David's mission. Emotionalism is fine in its place, but if it gets in the way of the hard work that must be done, it has to cede. Certainly in our romantic age when emotions are encouraged, regularly stirred up, and valorized, it is bracing to hear Joab's summons back to the good and the just, those values that must be embraced even when it is emotionally unsatisfying to do so. Many centuries later, the new David would say, "Whoever comes to me and does not hate father and mother, wife and children, brothers and sisters, yes, and even life itself, cannot be my disciple" (Luke 14:26). As the incarnation of the very Logos of God, Jesus embodies the absolute demand of justice, which must have primacy over even those persons to whom one feels the strongest emotional attachment.

The disgruntled commander concludes his speech to the king with what can only be characterized as a threat: "So go out at once and speak kindly to your servants; for I swear by the LORD if you do not go, not a man will stay with you this night; and this will be worse for you than any disaster that has come upon you from your youth until now" (2 Sam. 19:7). Not to put too fine a point on it, he implies, unless you stop this moaning for Absalom and show your appreciation for the troops who have risked their lives to save your throne, you will fall from power. There is special significance in the fact that Joab, who has witnessed so much of David's career up close, could say that such a loss would be greater than any that the king had previously suffered. In fact, is Joab perhaps hinting here that he himself would turn the army against David? The king is able to meet Joab's demand halfway. Whereas the commander ordered the king to "go out and speak kindly to your servants"—that is, to take an active role in reconciling himself to them—David simply presents himself passively at the gate and allows the troops to come to him. This constitutes a sort of compromise between the lounging David at the beginning of the Bathsheba incident and the energetic warrior David of the early years. Jan Fokkelman rightly suggests that the gap between Joab's demand

and David's act "calls up the image of a man beaten to a pulp, who can barely stand, and does only the minimum requested or expected of him" (quoted in Alter 1999: 313). The same Joab who once sent Uriah the Hittite to his death at David's orders now orders the king about.

What ensues is a fascinating little summary of a political argument that must have been raging throughout Israel in the wake of the great battle. We are told that "all the people" ruminate as follows: "The king delivered us from the hand of our enemies, and saved us from the hand of the Philistines; and now he has fled out of the land because of Absalom. But Absalom, whom we anointed over us, is dead in battle. Now therefore why do you say nothing about bringing the king back?" (2 Sam. 19:9–10). What strikes the reader is the dispassionate quality of this review. There seems little real affection for either Absalom or David, just a clear-eyed assessment of the political situation and the tentative conclusion that the old king should be welcomed back. Is this a foreshadowing of the endless civil wars that will plague Israel in the coming centuries and an indication of the people's realism in the sizing up of kings and their ambitions?

During this period of political deliberation David turns to the priests Zadok and Abiathar, asking them to speak to the elders of Judah, David's own tribe, and to encourage them to get behind the king. David attempts a subtle shaming of the Judahites: "Why should you be the last to bring the king back to his house? The talk of all Israel has come to the king. You are my kin, you are my bone and my flesh" (2 Sam. 19:11–12). There again is that evocative phrase first used by the elders of Israel when they submitted themselves to David at Hebron. If they are "bone of my bone and flesh of my flesh," David insinuates, how much more so the children of Judah. The outreach to Judah intensifies with the king's stunning proposal to replace Joab as commander of the army with Amasa, another of his nephews, who held that position under the rebellious Absalom. David knows that it is imperative that he draw back the Judahites, who had largely gone over to Absalom, and so he makes this extraordinary "team of rivals" gesture, taking as his chief military officer the leader of the rebellion and dismissing Joab, who has been with him from the beginning. To be sure, this decision is designed to win Judahite support, but it also represents a severe chastisement of Joab, the killer of the king's son (Alter 1999: 314). At the awful moment when he sat over the gate and mourned for Absalom, David had given in to the demands of Joab, but here he recovers his keen judgment and sense of purpose quickly enough. Whatever the combination of motives behind the king's decision, it clearly works, for Amasa himself "swayed the hearts of all the people of Judah as one, and they sent word to the king, 'Return, both you and all your servants'" (2 Sam. 19:14).

At this point, we witness a fascinating reversal of David's flight from Jerusalem, a playing backward of his quasi-liturgical procession away from the capital. There is a sort of chiastic structure to this procession, since the king will meet many of the same figures he had met on his flight away from Absalom. David's departure, of course, was a disaster for Israel, for the entire raison d'être of David's kingship was to provide for the scattered tribes a common focal point. His return, therefore, is a boon for the nation and an anticipation of Jesus's journey up to Jerusalem at the climax of his life and ministry. It is also a historical analogy to Ezekiel's great prophetic vision of Yahweh returning to his temple after a lengthy absence.

The first significant figure whom David encounters as he approaches the Jordan is the last one he met on his way out, Shimei, the Saulide who had so thoroughly abused the king just days before. Now Shimei comes with a thousand members of the tribe of Benjamin, Saul's tribe, not to battle David but to welcome him. Throwing himself at the feet of the returning king, Shimei delivers a rather pathetic speech, admitting his guilt and begging for forgiveness: "May my lord not hold me guilty or remember how your servant did wrong on the day my lord the king left Jerusalem. . . . For your servant knows that I have sinned" (2 Sam. 19:19–20). I suppose one could read this as honest contrition (at least Shimei does not pretend that his words had been misunderstood or his actions misconstrued) or as shameless political calculation (blowing with the ever-shifting winds of fortune). But what matters more is David's reaction. Flush with victory and returning triumphantly to his capital, he could easily enough and with complete moral justification have repaid Shimei for his brutality and his at least implicit treachery. Abishai, true to character, urges that Shimei be put immediately to death. Instead, David upbraids his nephew for his preemptory judgment and takes the path of mercy: "What have I to do with you, you sons of Zeruiah, that you should today become an adversary to me? Shall anyone be put to death in Israel this day?" (2 Sam. 19:22). With that, David assures Shimei that he will not be put to death, and he backs it up with an oath. In this moment, it is particularly clear that David is a man after the heart of Yahweh. If Shimei is Israel in constant rebellion against its divine king, David is Yahweh himself, responding to that rebellion with forgiveness and the guarantee of life. As is so often the case in regard to the house of Saul, David exhibits a stunning enemy love, which lifts his manner of kingship far above that of the potentates around him and anticipates the manner in which his crucified and risen descendant would manifest his power: "Father, forgive them, for they do not know what they are doing" (Luke 23:34).

After this, Mephibosheth comes to meet the king. On his outward journey, David had conversed with Mephibosheth's servant, who reported that his master had joined Absalom's rebellion. But now the grandson of Saul and the son of Jonathan comes unshaven and in tatters, signs of mourning meant to indicate that he had never been disloyal to David. When the king asks why Mephibosheth did not join him on his flight from Jerusalem, the bedraggled man explains that Ziba, his servant, had gone ahead while Mephibosheth, due to his lameness, was slowly trying to saddle his mule. When Ziba met the king, he betrayed his master, hoping thereby to inherit Mephibosheth's property, and David had acquiesced to Ziba's demand, leaving the son of Jonathan bereft. Mephibosheth throws himself on the mercy of the returning king and signals, with exquisite subtlety, that he both blames David for the deaths of the Saulides and hopes for his clemency: "For all my father's house were doomed to death before my lord the king; but you set your servant among those who eat at your table. What further right have I, then, to appeal to the king?" (2 Sam. 19:28). The negative insinuation is not lost on David, for the king cuts off his courtier abruptly and announces the preemptory judgment that Mephibosheth and Ziba should divide the land equally between them. At first blush, this might appear to be a fair, even Solomonic determination, but on closer inspection it indicates, if anything, David's instability. If Mephibosheth is right in saying that Ziba betrayed him, then giving Ziba anything seems unjust; if Ziba is right in stating that Mephibosheth is a traitor, then it appears that the son of Jonathan deserves only capital punishment. Splitting the property is thus the least logical and least satisfying solution possible. Happily, Mephibosheth rescues the situation, telling David, "Let him [Ziba] take it all, since my lord the king has arrived home safely" (2 Sam. 19:30). It would be hard to construe this intervention as anything other than a sincere acknowledgment of joy and gratitude on the part of Mephibosheth and thus as a fairly clear indication that Ziba was lying. Once more the strange love-hate dynamics that obtain in the relationship between David and the Saulides can be seen.

Next, the returning king encounters Barzillai the Gileadite, who had accompanied David on his outward journey and who continues to show unswerving support. One can discern a sort of crescendo in these meetings, moving from lesser to greater loyalty to David: Shimei to Mephibosheth to Barzillai. In gratitude, David promises to "provide" for the aged Barzillai in Jerusalem, but the old man demurs: "How many years have I still to live, that I should go up with the king to

Jerusalem? Today I am eighty years old; can I discern what is pleasant and what is not? Can your servant taste what he eats or what he drinks? Can I still listen to the voice of singing men and singing women?" (2 Sam. 19:34–35). It is a fascinating response. On the one hand, he could simply be implying that he would be a burden to David; on the other hand, he is offering what could be construed as a subtle critique of the frivolous life being led at the court of the king. Perhaps the old man, who has seen the entire arc of David's career, is commenting on the corruption that contributed to the king's decline. In any case, Barzillai asks leave to return to his hometown so that he can be buried with his ancestors, but as a parting gift, he presents his servant (or son, in some translations) Chimham to David. Obviously moved, David kisses Barzillai and continues on his journey. Robert Alter suggests that in contrast to the cold kiss David gave to Absalom upon his son's return and the calculating kisses Absalom gave to the courtiers at the gate, this embrace at last seems sincere (Alter 1999: 318). In this crescendoing series of encounters, the author means to show the still deeply divided state of Israel in the wake of the Absalom rebellion. Some are like Barzillai (steadfastly loyal, though a touch critical), others like Shimei (calculating and vacillating), and still others like Mephibosheth (ambiguous and more than a little frightened).

David then crosses back across the Jordan, recapitulating the moves of Joshua and the Israelites as they entered the promised land centuries before. The king had been in a kind of exile and had indeed undertaken a sort of exodus. His first stop upon crossing the river was Gilgal, the place where Saul was crowned king and where his kingship was wrested from him. Once more, the author signals the Davidic supplanting of the house of Saul. Then the author says that "all the people of Judah, and also half the people of Israel, brought the king on his way" (2 Sam. 19:40). Here one can see a partial recapitulation of David's gathering of the nation at Hebron, when all of the southern tribes and all of the northern tribes accepted him as king. At this point, managing to garner only half of the north is a sign of the deterioration of David's kingly leadership and a compromising of his magnetic power. Like any worldly political figure, even the greatest, David had, in the course of his long career, managed to offend a variety of his constituents and hence to lose a good deal of his clout. Only the Son of David who was also the Son of God would manage to "draw all people" to himself (John 12:32), and he would do it not through political machinations or military conquest but through the weirdly attractive power of his death on an instrument of torture. In drawing only half of Israel, David shows that he remains an incomplete fulfillment of the promise made to Abraham, Joseph, Judah, and Moses.

In yet another awful foreshadowing of the split to come after the reign of Solomon, the Judahite and Israelite supporters of David immediately fall into quarreling. The northerners come to David and complain, "Why have our kindred the people of Judah stolen you away and brought the king and his household over the Jordan?" And the southerners retort, "Because the king is near of kin to us. Why then are you angry over this matter?" But the Israelites come right back: "We have ten shares in the king, and in David also we have more than you" (2 Sam. 19:41–43). This beautifully stylized exchange between "whole peoples" expresses the fights over relatively trivial matters—tribal identity, favoritism, ego needs, and so on—that divided the nation that David had tried to unite under God's law and for God's purpose. A large part of the apostle Paul's genius is the way in which he extrapolates from this history of conflict within Israel to explain the power of Christ's cross, which managed, he argues, to put to death the enmity that divided not only Jews from one another but also Jews from all of the other tribes of the world. The cross of Jesus was not only the throne from which the definitive Davidic king would reign but also the instrument by which that king would bring about the unity that David could not. The clash of words with which this chapter ends gives way soon enough to a clash of swords as many of the northern tribes, just after the end of one rebellion, join another.

2 SAMUEL 20

Just when it seems that David had finally found some peace, another revolution, in some ways more threatening than that of Absalom, breaks out. It is led by a man whom the author promptly identifies as "a scoundrel," Sheba the son of Bichri, a member of the tribe of Benjamin who was there on the fields of Gilgal as the tribes argued over who had a stake in David. Blowing a ram's horn, Sheba shouts to his fellow northerners, "We have no portion in David, no share in the son of Jesse! Everyone to your tents, O Israel" (2 Sam. 20:1). This stands, of course, in direct contradiction to those Israelites who had just protested that they had ten parts in David versus Judah's one. It is impossible not to notice the deeply corporate sense of identity on display here. Sheba is seeking definitively to undo the "mystical body of David" the tribes had acknowledged at Hebron, and in so doing he functions as a particularly apt symbol of sin, which is nothing other than a refusal to participate in the communion of the mystical body of the Son of David. The same cry—"What share do we have in David? We have no inheritance in the son of Jesse. To your tents, O Israel"—is taken up by the northern rebels under Jeroboam, breaking with Rehoboam's rule. Splintering, splitting, and dividing are, as always, the marks of sin—*Ubi divisio ibi peccatum*, as Origen puts it.[1]

And so the northern tribes split against Judah in the south, setting up the terrible separation that would endure through the post-Solomonic period all the way to the time of Jesus. Isaiah's reference to "heathen Galilee" and Nathaniel's taunt—"Can anything good come out of Nazareth?"—certainly are conditioned at least in part by a typically southern suspicion of the north. At first, David seems

1. Origen, *Homilies 1–14 on Ezekiel*, trans. Thomas P. Scheck (New York: Newman Press, 2010), 117.

to respond rather laconically to the rebellion. Under the protection of the Judahites, he returns to his capital and deals with the concubines whom Absalom had so publicly violated. Essentially, he puts them away, placing them under a sort of house arrest and refusing to have sexual relations with them. "So," we hear, "they were shut up until the day of their death, living as if in widowhood" (2 Sam. 20:3). It is hard to overlook the parallel with Michal, David's first wife, who because of her resentment and infidelity was destined to remain childless for the rest of her life. As always in the Old Testament narratives, sexual union and fertility are key indicators of Yahweh's favor, and hence the shutting down of sex indicates some moral or spiritual failure.

David then turns to his new commander, Amasa, who had replaced Joab as military chief. The king orders him to call the Judahite troops together within the span of three days and prepare themselves to put down the new rebellion. But Amasa delays, and David panics: "Now Sheba son of Bichri will do us more harm than Absalom" (2 Sam. 20:6). Perhaps David's fear in this case is understandable given the ordeal that he had just endured, but it seems out of step with the confidence of the young David, who managed to garner two hundred Philistine foreskins when he was asked for one hundred and who outmaneuvered the militarily superior Saul with such shrewdness. One can see here yet another of the negative consequences of the moral disintegration that commenced with the Bathsheba incident. In any case, David sends Abishai, Joab's brother, in pursuit of Sheba, who David fears will hole himself up in a fortified city and prove to be a nuisance. The attentive reader will at this point perhaps wonder precisely what happened to Joab, the great commander whom David sacked just after the resolution of the Absalom affair. It turns out that even as David is directing Abishai to deal with Sheba, Joab is, with no official sanction from the king, riding out with a substantial army to meet the rebel. Questions crowd the mind at this juncture: What gives Joab the confidence to make this move on his own? Is this another indication of how tenuous David's hold on power is in Israel? Is Abishai in cahoots with his brother? Is Joab simply trying to worm his way back into the king's good graces, or is he attempting his own seizure of power? And do the troops in question realize where the real authority in Israel lies?

At any rate, the armies of Amasa and Joab stumble into one another at "the large stone that is in Gibeon" (2 Sam. 20:8)—the very place where the civil war between the houses of Saul and David originally broke out, with the famous "play" of the sword-bearing champions from either side. In the wake of that deadly game, Abner killed Joab's brother Asahel, who had foolishly pursued the superior warrior. By situating the encounter at Gibeon, the narrator sets up the expectation of violence and internecine struggle (Alter 1999: 323). We are told that Joab wears a soldier's tunic with a belt strapped across it, and on the belt is a sword and sheath. When Amasa approaches the always unpredictable Joab, the latter bends down (to feign homage?) and the sword tumbles out of his belt. Grabbing his counterpart by the beard and making as if to kiss him, Joab blandly asks, "Is it well with you, my brother?" But before Amasa can respond, Joab takes up the fallen sword and thrusts it into Amasa's midsection, killing the unfortunate man instantly. The gesture recalls the lethal moves made by the young gladiators on that spot years before and also Joab's murder of Abner at Hebron. Joab is perhaps the prime example in this narrative of a man who lives by the sword—and who will indeed, according to Jesus's principle, die by it. He represents something like Plato's "spirited" quality, undisciplined by reason or moral demand. Although he has often proven to be a useful weapon in David's arsenal, he is decidedly not someone who should be in a position of political leadership. He functions therefore as a symbol of the lethal violence that would plague Israel for centuries following the time of David. He represents one aspect of the Israelite (and indeed human) character that is wrenched out of its proper relationship to the center and therefore rendered dysfunctional. Moreover, Joab is perhaps the most vivid and literal confirmation of Nathan's brutally accurate prophecy that due to David's infidelity with Bathsheba, the sword would never leave David's house.

One of Joab's men, desperately attempting to suture the king and his former commander together, stands athwart the body of Amasa and shouts, "Whoever favors Joab, and whoever is for David, let him follow Joab" (2 Sam. 20:11). This is a particularly bold move given that a substantial army has just witnessed the murder of its commander. A civil war could easily have broken out on the spot, but this nameless man's quick action seems to ease the tension, for we hear that once the body of Amasa is covered up and put out of the way, his army readily joins the forces of Joab in pursuit of Sheba. One can only marvel at how deftly Joab has solved the problem of his dismissal. Without awakening any significant opposition from David, Joab killed his replacement and effortlessly reclaimed control of the entire army of Israel. Doubtless, it is fair to suppose that none of this would have happened unless the army itself supported Joab, but it would be inadequate to overlook how cleverly Joab manipulated events to achieve his goal. None of this gainsays what I claim about Joab representing the divorce of forceful action from reason. The cleverness that he clearly demonstrates is not tantamount to a reasonable grasp of moral ends and purposes; it is a canniness in service of primal emotion, something like Freud's ego, which is permanently subordinated to the demands of the id.

Meanwhile, Sheba retreats to the far northern reaches of the promised land to Abel of Beth-maacah, a fortified stronghold where he is joined by his clansmen and others. Joab hotly pursues him there and lays siege to the fortifications, setting up a ramp and battering ram. There is something uniquely awful about laying siege to a city, a military technique that endured from ancient times until the industrial age. It meant, for the aggressors, long months (even years) of tedium and back-breaking work; for the aggressed, it meant slow starvation. It was, in a word, deeply in the interest of everyone to bring a swift end to a siege. This helps to explain the prompt intervention of yet another "wise woman" in this Samuel narrative. We remember the quick-thinking Abigail, who saved the day when David and Abigail's husband were about to fall to fighting, as well as the sagacious woman of Tekoa, whom Joab called in to heal the breach between David and Absalom (Alter 1999: 325). Here an unnamed woman cries out from the walls of the besieged city, speaking in hieratic, almost oracular fashion: "Listen! Listen! Tell Joab, 'Come here, I want to speak to you'" (2 Sam. 20:16). Then she and Joab exchange words that can only be likened to a liturgical call and response: "'Are you Joab?' He answered, 'I am.' Then she said to him, 'Listen to the words of your servant.' He answered, 'I am listening'" (2 Sam. 20:17).

The quasi-liturgical language prepares the way for an incantatory speech in which the woman characterizes Abel as a city of major historical importance, a place where people sought wisdom and reconciliation in times of trouble: "I am one of those who are peaceable and faithful in Israel; you seek to destroy a city that is a mother in Israel" (2 Sam. 20:19). The woman announces herself as a Davidide loyalist, someone taking part in neither the Absalom nor Sheba rebellions, and furthermore as the defender of a "motherly" city, a place that nurtures peace. From the heart of this very masculine narrative, which is marked at every turn by terrible acts of violence, she speaks for distinctively feminine values. Joab, the archetypal man of war, shows himself beguiled by this speech, even to the point of profound self-deception: "Far be it from me, far be it, that I should swallow up or destroy! That is not the case!" (2 Sam. 20:20–21). As even the most inattentive reader of this story knows, it is indeed the case. But Joab presses on, arguing that he is interested not in destroying the entire city but only in capturing the man whose rebellion has unsettled the nation. If Sheba is handed over, he says, he will end the siege and withdraw. Without a moment's hesitation and, it seems, without the slightest moral scruple, the woman accepts Joab's terms and arranges for the head of the rebel to be thrown over the wall. It is testament to her status and influence within the town that, at her word, the deed is done: "Then the woman went to all the people with her wise plan, and they cut off the head of Sheba, son of Bichri, and threw it out to Joab" (2 Sam. 20:22). There is little doubt that this move averted a general slaughter, but it does raise the vexing moral question of ends and means. Does the attainment of a positive goal justify the means employed to achieve it? Another way to put the same question: Are there some moral acts that by their very nature are so wicked that they can never be justified through an appeal to the good consequences that they produce? The decapitation of Sheba doubtless "saved lives," but so did the nuclear bombing of Nagasaki. Was either act thereby justified? The mainstream of the Catholic moral tradition, which eschews all forms of consequentialism, certainly replies in the negative. But in the hurly-burly of ancient Israel, such refined distinctions were unmade. Even if they were inchoately made, they were most likely ignored.

Once the head is turned over to Joab, the trumpet sounds and "all went to their homes," a phrase that echoes the "everyone to your tents" at the commencement of the Sheba narrative. But Joab returns not to his native place of Bethlehem but to Jerusalem and the king. The text itself tells us nothing at this point about Joab's motives or fears, but one can confidently guess at the complexity of his situation, both psychological and political. He had been summarily dismissed as head of the army; he subsequently murdered the man whom David had personally chosen to replace him, and then he blithely assumed control of the army once again. Did he fear David's wrath? Was he plotting still another rebellion or coup? Was he attempting a personal reconciliation with his uncle the king? And what was David thinking? Was he terrified of Joab or perhaps angry with him because of his insubordination? The text does not answer these questions directly, but it does tell us laconically enough that in the wake of the Sheba rebellion, "Joab was in command of all the army of Israel" (2 Sam. 20:23). Whether through David's direct order or simply by dint of David's trepidation or indifference, Joab recovers his old job. This ultimate survivor seems to have no interest in supplanting the king or angling for more political influence. An inveterate man of military command and a loyal kinsman of David, he is doubtless delighted to have manipulated affairs so artfully as to be back in the one position that he truly savors.

The twentieth chapter concludes with a terse recitation of David's "cabinet," an enumeration that nicely mirrors that given in the eighth chapter at the beginning of David's kingly administration. It is interesting to note that Adoram, the overseer of David's army of forced laborers, is not mentioned in the earlier accounting but is mentioned here probably in anticipation of the key role that he will play in the construction of the temple under Solomon (Alter 1999: 328). Alongside of the hereditary priests Zadok and Abiathar, Ira the Jairite is mentioned as David's personal priest. In the eighth chapter some of David's sons are described as priests. Does their disappearance from the list of priests in the present chapter represent the growing conviction that the conflation of the political and the religious was not altogether good for Israel? Or does it reflect the fact that David's family situation had simply become too scandalous? One also wonders why Nathan is nowhere mentioned in this accounting of David's bureaucracy and inner circle. He cannot have died, for he will play a key role later in the ascension of Solomon to power. Has David at this point marginalized him because his prophetic rebuke still stung the king's conscience? In any case, one sees in this dry listing of officials a clear indication that David's government has survived both the terrible instability prompted by the Bathsheba affair and two attempts at usurpation. Yahweh's king reigns once again within the garden.

SERIES FIVE

TOWARD THE TEMPLE

2 SAMUEL 21

The four chapters with which 2 Samuel concludes are generally taken to be a sort of appendix or coda to the principal narrative. They are written in a variety of literary styles, all differing from the style of the main story, suggesting that the final redactor of the Samuel literature borrowed from a number of texts or oral traditions. Further, the chronological setting of the stories and poems that make up the final four chapters is unclear and certainly out of step with the preceding narrative. The best guess is that they describe events from the middle years of David's career, when he was still battling with the Saulides. As many scholars point out, this sort of "collaging" of materials drawn from disparate sources was altogether typical in the composition of texts in the ancient world (Alter 1999: 329). The literary structure of these "appendices" is remarkably chiastic: a story of a national disaster that David addresses, a list, then a poem, which is followed by a poem, a list, and a story of a national disaster that David addresses (Alter 1999: 329). Therefore, though they are from disparate sources and chronologically anomalous, they are hardly tacked on indiscriminately.

We hear, first, that there was a famine at some point during David's kingship that lasted three years. David does the right thing, seeking out the will of Yahweh, most likely through inquiring of an oracle, as he often did in the early days of his career. He discovers that the source of the famine is an outrage perpetrated many years before by Saul: the massacre of the Gibeonites—an event not described anywhere else in the Samuel literature. It appears that Saul had promised to protect them but attempted to eradicate them "in his zeal for the people of Israel and Judah" (2 Sam. 21:2). So David approaches the Gibeonites to ask how he might make amends for the outrage perpetrated by his predecessor. In accord with a rather primitive moral sensibility, the Gibeonites tell him that it is a matter not of monetary restitution but rather of an eye for an eye and a tooth for a tooth: "The man who consumed us and planned to destroy us, so that we should have no place in all the territory of Israel—let seven of his sons be handed over to us, and we will impale them before the LORD at Gibeon" (2 Sam. 21:5–6). A clear sacrificial framework is manifest here, a Girardian moral landscape in which the sacrifice of designated victims will restore a lost peace. The number of the victims doubtless has a ritual significance and does not represent a strict correspondence to the number of Gibeonites slain by Saul.

In sharp contrast to the main narratives in which David is scrupulously presented as refusing to cooperate in the murders of anyone in the household of Saul, here the king readily agrees, as though he is following a formal ritual prescription: "I will hand them over" (2 Sam. 21:6). Pointedly, he spares Mephibosheth in accord with the promise he made to the young man's father, Jonathan, but he surrenders two of Saul's sons born to Rizpah and five sons of Merab, one of Saul's daughters. These seven unfortunates are then "impaled on the mountain before the LORD" (2 Sam. 21:9). Some scholars suggest that the impaling implies a sort of crucifixion, but the principal point seems to be that the bodies are left exposed to the elements (McCarter 1984: 443). The clear indication that they are killed in the presence of Yahweh underscores the religious and sacrificial nature of the act: this is not simply an act of vengeance, but an attempt to restore a lost equilibrium in nature. Indeed, the author underscores that "they were put to death in the first days of the harvest, at the beginning of the barley harvest" (2 Sam. 21:9), indicating that they were a kind of blood offering meant to render fecund the dried-up fields. They also "perished together," the same phrase used to describe the simultaneous deaths of the twenty-four gladiators at the beginning of the David-Saul civil war, a mass killing that also has strong ritualistic overtones.

We then hear the story of Rizpah, the mother of five of the slain who is rightly described as a Hebrew Antigone (Alter 1999: 332). Though prevented by the terms of the agreement to take the bodies down, she builds a sort of tent over them. Throughout the long summer, from spring harvest until the rains fell the following fall, she keeps watch, assuring that the birds and animals do not devour the decaying flesh of her sacrificed sons. As in the Greek world, so in the Hebrew moral universe it was considered the height of disrespect to leave a corpse unburied. So Rizpah, keeping this long and emotionally painful watch, performs a deeply beautiful and noble act reminiscent of Tobit's burial of those who had been left exposed to the elements. Respect for the bodies of the dead is enshrined as one of the "corporal works of mercy" urged upon all Catholics. So impressed is David by this heroic act of maternal piety that he ends his acquiescence to the Gibeonite demands and takes down the remains of the Saulides. He then retrieves the bones of both Saul and Jonathan and inters all of the Saulide dead in the family tomb in Benjamite territory, at which point, we are told, "God heeded supplications for the land" (2 Sam. 21:14).

Theologically speaking, a number of questions remain at this point. Did this dreadful transaction—the ritual killing of seven young men in answer to Saul's slaughter of the Gibeonites—in fact satisfy God's anger and contribute thereby to the reestablishment of the order of nature? Does the God of Israel truly respond to or sanction this sort of primitive calculus? I think it fair to say that this text reflects a relatively undeveloped religious consciousness. As I discussed earlier, sacrifice is deeply ingrained in the theo-logic of ancient Israel, for it represents the reordering of a world that has fallen out of right relationship with the giver of all being. Accordingly, the Creator God has no need of sacrifice; however, those who perform the offering are, in the very process, made whole. But the logic of the primitive sacred on display in this story is a kind of strict karmic calculus whereby a blood-for-blood exchange restores balance. Though here and there evident throughout the Old Testament, this manner of thinking is trumped by the principal trajectories and themes of the Bible, including especially the story of the interrupted sacrifice of Isaac as well as the teaching of Jesus, which insists that human morality ought to imitate the divine manner of answering evil with benevolence: "He makes his sun rise on the evil and on the good" (Matt. 5:45). Hans Wilhelm Hertzberg remarks in regard to this enigmatic tale, "With its references to blood vengeance, human sacrifice and rain magic, it points to a world which was banished by the Old Testament itself" (Hertzberg 1964: 385). Nowhere is the canceling of the primitive sacrificial logic clearer than on the cross when Jesus speaks a word of forgiveness to those who are brutally executing him. That the crucifixion is referred to as an act of sacrifice makes clear precisely what kind of offering is acceptable to the God of Israel.

The second story recounted in this chapter concerns David's battle with a Philistine behemoth called not Goliath but Ishbi-benob. We are told that David had grown weary during battle with the Philistines and that Ishbi-benob saw his opportunity to take out the Israelite king. Like Goliath, this Philistine warrior is outfitted with an impressive array of offensive and defensive accoutrements: his "spear weighed three hundred shekels of bronze, and he was fitted out with new weapons" (2 Sam. 21:16). Sensing the frailty of the king, Abishai, Joab's brother, heads off Ishbi-benob and kills him. At this point, David's men inform the king that he will never again go forth with the army. One wonders why this curious and rather unglamorous episode is included in the text. Doubtless, the best explanation is that it represents a key turning point in the career of the warrior king: the beginning of his decline. And perhaps it helps to explain, once put in its proper chronological position, why David, at the time of the Bathsheba incident, was unwilling to go out with his army. One can sense as well the iteration of a theme often underscored in the Samuel literature: the mysterious identification between David and the nation. By intervening against the Philistine giant, Abishai is not merely protecting the person of the king; he is expressing his membership in the mystical body of David and his conviction that David's death in battle would be an unmitigated disaster for the entire people of Israel. All of this is beautifully summed up in the words of the common soldiers in the wake of this incident: "You shall not go out with us to battle any longer, so that you do not quench the lamp of Israel" (2 Sam. 21:17). This is made even more poignant and powerful when one recalls that the soldiers are obliquely referencing the light burning in the sanctuary before the ark of the covenant (Baldwin 1988: 305). A very similar argument was made by the Davidide troops just prior to the great confrontation with Absalom's army.

Augustine offers a fascinating gloss on this minor episode to the effect that sometimes spiritual leaders are obliged to flee danger and persecution in order to benefit their communities.[1] As an example, the great saint cites Athanasius, who in the face of fierce Arian persecution more than once fled from Alexandria. This was not cowardice but rather a frank acknowledgment that his demise could well lead to the snuffing out of the light of the orthodox faith. By fleeing to the west, Athanasius was able to defend and preach the Nicene faith, which otherwise might have been fatally compromised. John Chrysostom specifies that in spiritual warfare, the dark powers energetically go after the leaders of the Christian community, just as the Philistine giant targeted David: "For in wars too, the one who is on the opposite side endeavors before all others to overthrow the general. For this reason all his fellow combatants hasten there. For this reason there is much tumult, every one endeavoring to rescue him; they surround him with their shields, wishing to preserve his person."[2]

The pericope that brings the twenty-first chapter to a close is one of the most puzzling in the Samuel literature, for it directly contradicts one of its most famous

1. Augustine, "Letter 228," in *Joshua, Judges, Ruth, 1–2 Samuel*, ed. John R. Franke, Ancient Christian Commentary on Scripture: Old Testament 4 (Downers Grove, IL: InterVarsity, 2005), 389–90.

2. John Chrysostom, "Homilies on 2 Thessalonians 4," in Franke, *Joshua, Judges, Ruth, 1–2 Samuel*, 390.

stories. The account that in many ways sets the tone for David's early career is the narrative of the young man's slaying of Goliath. But at the end of the twenty-first chapter we are blithely told that Goliath, "the shaft of whose spear was like a weaver's beam" (2 Sam. 21:19), is killed not by David but by "Elhanan son of Jaare-oregim, the Bethlehemite." In both ancient and modern times, attempts have been made to reconcile the two narratives. It is suggested, for example, that "Goliath" is not a proper name but rather a sort of Philistine title of respect. What seems most plausible in point of fact is that the account in the present chapter is the correct one, and that it was later associated with the young David and retold with particular literary flair by the final editor of the Samuel literature. At any rate, this cluster of stories about David's confrontation with various Philistine giants and ogres—including a man with twenty-four fingers and toes—is meant to show the power of Yahweh over and against the darker powers of the earth. Here one might recall the motif of David as new Adam, the king and orderer of the garden of God's good creation, which became marred by sin. In the Gospels the Son of David is presented not simply as a spiritual teacher but as someone who also actively does battle with the ill effects of the fall, including a variety of physical and psychological maladies. This too is part of the process of restoring the lost Eden.

2 SAMUEL 22

The twenty-second chapter of 2 Samuel corresponds basically to Psalm 18, with slight textual variants (Baldwin 1988: 306). Specialists in the Psalms note that the language of this particular poem is archaic, perhaps dating from the tenth century BC or even to David himself. It is by no means unimportant that the Samuel literature begins more or less with the great canticle of Hannah and ends more or less with the great psalm sung by David. Throughout this narrative the spiritual power of speech is on steady display, especially that rare and peculiar form of speech that is called a prayer of praise. Both Hannah and David sing their praise of God, thereby underscoring the central theme of the Samuel literature and indeed of the Bible as a whole: the right ordering of the sinful human race happens through the recovery of right worship.

Both Psalm 18 and 2 Samuel 22 are introduced by a brief description of the context for David's singing of his great hymn. The phraseology in each case is virtually identical: "David spoke to the LORD the words of this song on the day when the LORD delivered him from the hand of Saul" (2 Sam. 22:1). This is meant to be, therefore, the voice of David before his middle-age decline, before the tragedy with Bathsheba and Uriah—the David who was still ready to rely on the help of Yahweh, perhaps just after the battle on Mount Gilboa. He begins: "The LORD is my rock, my fortress, and my deliverer, my God, my rock, in whom I take refuge" (2 Sam. 22:2). William Albright and others note that many of the gods worshiped by ancient Semitic peoples were deities of the mountain, and therefore it should not be surprising that the author of this text reaches for the metaphor of height and strength quite readily (Alter 1999: 337). But one must also keep in mind that the imagined composer of the song was a warrior who had just spent many months fleeing and hiding from a relentless pursuer. Thus the image of God as a "rock in whom I take refuge" was, for him, altogether natural.

But there is a deeper theological dimension to this evocative image. The earliest philosophers of the Western tradition recognized and made fundamental to their intellectual programs that the world of ordinary experience is marked by evanescence. Heraclitus knew that everything changes, and Plato taught that the sensual realm is like flickering shadows cast on a wall. Accordingly, much of philosophy became a quest to find the permanent, ontological *terra firma*. The Logos, the forms, the prime mover, prime matter, and so forth were proposed as candidates for this honor. Something similar can be discerned in the biblical tradition. The scriptural authors knew well that nothing either in nature or in human affairs is ultimately reliable. They were especially sensitive to the shifting and morally compromised quality of the political order. No biblical writer is even vaguely tempted toward the apotheosizing of kings and princes as were the avatars of so many other ancient cultures. They knew that the only firm foundation, both ontologically and ethically, is the Creator God. Hence the psalmist sings, "For God alone my soul waits in silence; from him comes my salvation. He alone is my rock and my salvation, my fortress; I shall never be shaken" (Ps. 62:1–2); Isaiah declares, "Trust in the LORD forever, for in the LORD GOD you have an everlasting rock" (Isa. 26:4); and the author of Deuteronomy asserts, "For I will proclaim the name of the LORD; ascribe greatness to our God! The Rock, his work is perfect, and all his ways are just. A faithful God, without deceit, just and upright is he" (Deut. 32:3–4).

The great theologians of the Christian tradition combine the philosophical and the biblical in their musings on ontological truths. Thus Thomas Aquinas, in his third argument for God's existence in the *Summa theologiae*, demonstrates that a radically contingent world can be explained finally only through recourse to some reality that exists through the power of its own essence, whose very nature is to be. This noncontingent ground of contingency must be, Aquinas shows, purely actualized in its reality, since any potentiality in it would indicate an ordering to something more existentially basic. This *actus purus*, this unconditioned reality, is the permanent ground the ancient philosophers sought and the Creator God the biblical authors recognized as the Rock.[1]

In his analysis combining elements drawn from classical philosophy, the Bible, and post-Freudian psychology, Paul Tillich draws attention to what he calls the

1. Thomas Aquinas, *Summa theologiae: Latin Text and English Translation, Introductions, Notes, Appendices, and Glossaries*, ed. Thomas Gilby et al., 61 vols. (New York: McGraw-Hill, 1964–81), 2:15.

"categories of finitude."[2] These are the qualities that mark all of finite being, and they include time, space, causality, and substance. All four of those features produce what Tillich calls "the shock of non-being," since all of them are characterized by impermanence. When they are concretely experienced, they give rise, accordingly, to a keen sense of anxiety. What alone can calm that existential angst is the power of being, which goes beyond, even as it includes, those four features. From this transcendence of the categories of finitude one can deduce some of the classical names of God. In the measure that he goes beyond time, God is rightly called "eternal"; in the measure that he transcends space, he is rightly called "omnipresent"; inasmuch as he supersedes causality, he is rightly termed "self-sufficient"; and inasmuch as he pushes past substance, he is rightly termed "infinite." Tillich's overall point is that only the properly unconditioned ground of being can function as the comfort upon which a human being can rely: "Only in God is my soul at rest."[3] Both Aquinas and Tillich bring to more precise philosophical expression what "David" implicitly acknowledges when he speaks of Yahweh as his rock and refuge.

The poet speaks of God not only as rock of refuge but also as shield and horn. That last image, used quite frequently throughout the Bible, is meant to call to mind the dangerous horn of a charging ram or bull. God is not only the ontological and moral foundation but also a personal power actively on the offensive against all those forces that stand opposed to him. C. S. Lewis remarks that much of the liberal theology of the nineteenth and twentieth centuries presents a God who functions as a grand but essentially passive background to life.[4] Schleiermacher's theology of God is a particularly good illustration of Lewis's point. Even Tillich's presentation that I sketched above might be construed in this direction. But the biblical God is more than a principle of being or a passive ground upon which the activity of the universe is predicated; he is an actor, a director, and a warrior with purposive intent. David's God is working his providential purpose out, though his manner and time frame often seem confounding. Very early on in this commentary I drew attention to the Amalekites as symbolic of all of Yahweh's enemies. There are indeed powers that oppose themselves to God's creative intentions for the world that he has made. To be sure, their being depends on God, and their activities are, for God's own reasons, permitted by God; nevertheless they stand athwart Yahweh, who comes after them like a raging bull with its horns pointed

2. Paul Tillich, *Systematic Theology*, 2 vols. (London: Nisbet, 1953–57), 1:91.
3. Ibid., 1:264.
4. C. S. Lewis, *Mere Christianity* (New York: Simon & Schuster, 1943), 141.

menacingly forward. One is reminded here of Jesus's edgy remark that the gates of hell shall not prevail against the church, a saying that is often oddly understood in a "defensive" way, as though Jesus were suggesting that the church will always manage to withstand the onslaughts of hell. But of course the remark should be read in a properly "offensive" way, for it suggests that hell, envisioned as an enemy city protected by strong gates, will inevitably give way to the aggressive attack of the church.

Next, the author poetically expresses what it felt like to be pursued by the relentless Saul: "For the waves of death encompassed me, the torrents of perdition assailed me; the cords of Sheol entangled me, the snares of death confronted me" (2 Sam. 22:5–6). Ancient Israelites were terrified of the sea. When they were compelled to travel on it, they hugged the shore. As I pointed out earlier, the *tōhû wābōhû* (Gen. 1:2), the "watery chaos," is the privileged symbol for the formless negativity from which God brings created order. Thus it is altogether predictable that David would reach for metaphors of waves and torrents when speaking of a mortal threat. Moreover, he speaks of the tangles of Sheol, the pit to which the dead are consigned, reaching out to drag him down. A relatively superficial reading of the narrative line of the Samuel books might give the impression that the young David was a cocky, Errol Flynn–like hero, effortlessly escaping the traps that his enemies set for him, but this poem gives a far more psychologically realistic account of what it must have been like to be pursued by an implacable opponent for years.

At this moment of supreme distress the author performs the supremely simple act of calling out to God for help. At the beginning of *The Divine Comedy*, Dante finds himself alone and lost, having wandered from the straight path. He sees a mountain bathed in light and recognizes it as the lodestar of his quest, but when he attempts to climb, he is blocked by three ravenous beasts. At this point, in utter despair, he cries out for divine help.[5] What follows is the account of how God came to guide the lost poet. At certain key moments in his journey, Dante, whether in hell, purgatory, or heaven, gets stuck, and all he can do is, in a beggarly spirit, ask. While cooperation with grace is certainly necessary, at the heart of the spiritual life, as the Bible lays it out, is an openness to receive the unmerited help of God, to cry out like a child to one's father. There are indeed a variety of forms of prayer, but at bottom, all prayer is a kind of asking, a begging for mercy and grace. What David does here so simply and beautifully is what he forgot to do at

5. Dante Alighieri, *The Divine Comedy: Inferno*, trans. Henry Wadsworth Longfellow (New York: Barnes & Noble, 2008), 3–8.

the time of the Bathsheba incident. Then, instead of asking, he assumed a godlike attitude and commanded.

As in *The Divine Comedy*, so in the story of David, Yahweh responds to an honestly expressed *cri de coeur*. We are told that God heard the cry of David from his "temple" in heaven. David had brought the ark of the covenant into Jerusalem and provided a tabernacle for it; eventually, this arrangement was replaced by the great temple of Solomon, and from that temple arose the prayers and cries of the people Israel. There was in the imagination of ancient Israel a correspondence between that temple on Mount Zion and the temple that God inhabited in heaven, the former functioning as an icon of the latter (Beale 2011: 626–32). Therefore, it is evocative that David's plea, symbolically anticipatory of every authentic prayer that would be offered from the Jerusalem temple, arrived precisely at this heavenly house of Yahweh.

The author then characterizes the divine arrival as the advent of a powerful and destructive storm: "The earth reeled and rocked; the foundations of the heavens trembled and quaked. . . . He bowed the heavens, and came down; thick darkness was under his feet" (2 Sam. 22:8–10). Yahweh himself is described in frankly, even crudely, anthropomorphic terms borrowed from more primitive Ugaritic sources: "Smoke went up from his nostrils, and devouring fire from his mouth" (2 Sam. 22:9; Alter 1999: 338). One would do well to call to mind here what was clarified earlier in regard to the punishment of Uzzah: God's anger is metaphorical of his passion to set things right. Furthermore, it is helpful to remember that this vivid poetry is not finally at odds with the theology of God's noncompetitive transcendence, which has been stressed throughout this commentary. What is intended here is not, as one reads in much of classical mythology, that the world must give way in order for the divine to appear but rather that God's power to change, rearrange, and save is irresistible.

The fire-breathing Yahweh is then presented as bestriding a peculiar mount: "He rode on a cherub, and flew; he was seen upon the wings of the wind" (2 Sam. 22:11). In the ancient Near Eastern religious imagination the cherub was a fierce, winged creature, probably in the form of a lion with a human head, infinitely dissimilar to the bare-bottomed baby pictured in pious art. The Yahweh who commands such a beast is indeed the "sky God," the lord of the winds. Once again, one must not literalize this language but rather see to its theological depths. The sky is that which both transcends and encompasses the whole of the earth and hence is a particularly apt metaphor for the Creator God who cannot be construed as a being in the world but who must be understood as pressing upon and involving himself in every aspect of the world. More storm imagery follows: "The LORD thundered from heaven; the Most High uttered his voice. He sent out arrows, and scattered them—lightning, and routed them" (2 Sam. 22:14–15). One is meant to sense here something of the sublimity (what Kant calls the *Erhabenheit*) of God. The Creator God is, of course, close to creation, and he exhibits tender mercy toward human beings, but he is decidedly not a reality that can be categorized or domesticated. God in fact so floods our receptive powers that he remains permanently incomprehensible, even threatening. Paul Tillich speaks in this context of the "Lordliness" of God, specifying that the term carries the double meaning of command and sublimity. On the one hand, God the Lord is the one to be obeyed (and how prominent this theme is in the biblical revelation); on the other hand, God the Lord is the numinous one in whose presence one experiences awe.

The striking theological poetry continues: "Then the channels of the sea were seen, the foundations of the world were laid bare" (2 Sam. 22:16). Not a being among many, the Creator God is the unconditioned ground of the world's existence. This is why his authority and power reach all the way down to the fundaments of both the sea and the dry land. If he were a god of the sea alone, the land would stand against him; if he were a god of the land alone, the sea would stand against him; if he were a being, either on land or in the sea, the foundations of neither land nor sea would be available to him. This resembles the theology implicit in Deutero-Isaiah. The theological poet behind that text upbraids his reader: "You have forgotten the LORD, your Maker, who stretched out the heavens and laid the foundations of the earth" (Isa. 51:13).

With this description of the Yahweh of the storm, the first part of the psalm/poem concludes. The second half unfolds as the account of how this mighty and overwhelming God dealt with "David" throughout his life and career. Biblical authors are never interested in presenting a pure theology of the divine attributes; they are invariably interested in how the Creator God calls, chastises, saves, and redeems human beings. So the God of the storm lifted David up out of the waters: "He delivered me from my strong enemy, from those who hated me; for they were too mighty for me" (2 Sam. 22:18). This, once again, is a reference to the primacy of grace: when we are utterly incapable of saving ourselves, either from the attacks of our military enemies or from the assaults of sin, we can only open ourselves to the inrushing of God's unmerited love. Why did Yahweh rescue David? "He brought me out into a broad place; he delivered me, because he delighted in me" (2 Sam. 22:20). It was not David's virtues that attracted the divine love and brought about salvation; Yahweh loved David and hence resolved to save him. To forget or overlook this primacy is to set the entire spiritual life off-kilter.

However, this is only part of the spiritual economy. There is no question that the Bible consistently emphasizes the priority of God's unconditional and undeserved grace, but there is equally no question that the Bible consistently couples that unconditional love with a decidedly conditional form of love. Nowhere is this on clearer display than in the book of Deuteronomy, in the course of which one finds dozens of examples: "Do what is good and right in the sight of the LORD, so that it may go well with you, and so that you may go in and occupy the good land that the LORD swore to your ancestors to give you" (Deut. 6:18). The unmistakably clear implication is that God will reward Israel precisely for its fidelity to the divine commands. How might one reconcile these seemingly contradictory affirmations? The Catholic tradition consistently maintains that access to the divine life is utterly a matter of divine grace accepted in faith. But a sinner, once invited into God's household, is invited next to live fully according to the rules and demands of the place. The sinner is encouraged, in short, to stop being a sinner and truly become a saint. This can happen only through a cooperation with grace, a real living out of the moral life. In short, unconditional love is followed by conditional love, precisely so that love can be fully appropriated.

One sees this principle strictly applied through the second half of the present chapter. "David," who has just acknowledged his utter dependence upon unmerited divine love, says, "The LORD rewarded me according to my righteousness; according to the cleanness of my hands he recompensed me. For I have kept the ways of the LORD, and have not wickedly departed from my God. . . . I was blameless before him, and I kept myself from guilt" (2 Sam. 22:21–24). Even more pointedly, "With the loyal you show yourself loyal; with the blameless you show yourself blameless; with the pure you show yourself pure, and with the crooked you show yourself perverse" (2 Sam. 22:26–27). In other words, David's success, both spiritually and politically, cannot simply be ascribed to the divine mercy tout court; it is also a function of his active cooperation with God's demands. Indeed, could not the whole of 2 Samuel be read as an exemplification of this great Deuteronomistic principle of conditional divine love?

At this point care must be taken, for one can easily enough fall into a sort of psychologizing misunderstanding. Within the framework of the fallen world, conditional love is frequently a function of manipulation, psychological neediness, insecurity, or downright cruelty. The notion of God's conditional love must obviously be purified of all this. The divine conditional love is like that of a parent who sets high standards for a beloved child or a professor who rewards a gifted student for fine work and punishes an even more gifted student for shoddy work. The unconditional source of existence has no need of anything and hence in no way benefits from manipulative games or the acting out of competitive fantasies. The play of unconditional and conditional love on the part of God is part of God's overall desire that his rational creatures come fully to life. It is a function of his wish that sinners be drawn at last into real friendship with him, for friendship can never simply be a matter of receiving "unconditional positive regard" from one's friend. The tension between the two modes of love is beautifully resolved in the following verses. "David" sings his own praise in a certain sense, reminding the reader how he was able to "crush a troop" and "leap over a wall," but he immediately clarifies that this was "by my God." What he is describing is how his own moral and military excellence unfolded only in the context of a prior redeeming and enabling love. Other examples of this noncompetitive causality follow: "He [God] made my feet like the feet of deer, and set me secure on the heights. He trains my hands for war, so that my arms can bend a bow of bronze. . . . You have made me stride freely. . . . I pursued my enemies and destroyed them" (2 Sam. 22:34–36). It was really David who acted and fought and strode in accordance with God's commands, but it was the grace of God that made such cooperation possible.

What makes this peculiar relationship between God and his creatures possible? As I have argued throughout this book, it is the metaphysical uniqueness of God, his strangeness, if you will. And the author of this great poem, very much in the spirit of the author of Deutero-Isaiah, acknowledges it: "For who is God, but the LORD? And who is a rock, except our God?" (2 Sam. 22:32). Yahweh is not simply greater than other gods; he is incomparable to them. If Yahweh were one local god among many, he would not be able to relate to finite things except in an interruptive or bullying manner. Since he is qualitatively different from any creature or any possible god, the true God can love unconditionally and can preside over a conditional love that is utterly free of manipulation or self-involvement.

As David continues to reflect on his career, which unfolded under the protection and direction of God, he avers to the surprising truth that he became king not simply over Israel but over foreign peoples as well: "You delivered me from strife with the peoples; you kept me as the head of the nations; people whom I had not known served me" (2 Sam. 22:44). As I have shown, this is an affirmation of Israel's destiny to be the bearer of the true God to the nations as well as a rather striking anticipation of the work of the risen Christ, the Son of David and the Lord of the world. When the resurrected Christ, on the verge of the ascension, tells his disciples to be his witnesses to the ends of the world, he is not commanding them simply to be the bearers of news concerning an extraordinary event; he is instructing them to let the nations know that they have a new king.[6] The apostle Paul's *Iēsous Kyrios* is not merely a spiritual theme; it is a subversive political and cultural claim. At the conclusion of the Acts of the Apostles, Paul is in Rome, the center of the empire, announcing Jesus without constraint and spreading the gospel throughout the Roman world. All of this is the surprising fulfillment of David's becoming, in however limited a sense, the lord of many nations.

The psalm prayer ends on an exultant note of praise and thanksgiving, clearly indicating that this composition is in the genre of the *tôdāh*, a song of gratitude to God: "For this I will extol you, O LORD, among the nations, and sing praises to your name" (2 Sam. 22:50; Alter 1999: 344). Here the narrator moves with assurance and joy into the stance of Adam prior to the fall, which is to say the attitude of *adoratio*. Whenever Israel gives highest honor to Yahweh, it is set right. The very last lines are a confident reiteration of the great Nathan promise in the seventh chapter of 2 Samuel. Yahweh, we hear, will show "steadfast love" to David and his family forever. The prophecy cannot be taken in a completely literal sense, since it was known to be false by the end of the sixth century—that is, by the time this text was definitively redacted. Therefore its presence here is an indication of a hope against hope that Yahweh would make the impossible possible.

6. N. T. Wright, *Jesus and the Victory of God*, Christian Origins and the Question of God 2 (Minneapolis: Fortress, 1996), 660.

2 SAMUEL 23

The moving victory psalm in the preceding chapter is followed in the present one by a second text that scholars characterize as archaic; some even date it to David's own time. The editor provides the intriguing superscript to the effect that these are the king's "last words," a somewhat anomalous remark given that David speaks quite a bit in the twenty-fourth chapter. Perhaps it is meant to suggest that these are David's final poetic or theologically motivated utterances. In any case, there is a strong connection to the "last words" of Moses in Deuteronomy and of Jacob in Genesis, a patriarchal handing on of final wisdom and direction (Hertzberg 1964: 399).

The prophetic status of the speaker is designated through the lofty phrase "the oracle of David, son of Jesse," which Kyle McCarter compares to "the utterance of Balaam son of Beor" in the book of Numbers (McCarter 1984: 479). His kingly status is signaled through "the anointed of the God of Jacob, the favorite of the Strong One of Israel" (2 Sam. 23:1). The last phrase, *nĕʿîm zĕmirôt yiśrāʾēl* in the Hebrew, can be rendered in a number of ways. One possibility is "the favorite of the songs of Israel," designating the uncontestable truth that David is one of the most celebrated figures in Israelite literature. Another is the undeniably beautiful King James Version rendering, "the sweet singer of Israel." Robert Alter maintains that the New Revised Standard Version, which I have reproduced above, is in fact no more obvious than the King James Version (Alter 1999: 345–46). One might bring all three together and understand David as the darling of Yahweh who becomes, as such, both the hero of the nation and the leader of the nation's liturgy.

As the "last words" begin, we hear David claiming a prophetic identity: "The spirit of the LORD speaks through me, his word is upon my tongue" (2 Sam. 23:2).

Nowhere in the narratives of the Samuel literature is it claimed that David, unlike Saul when he moved among the prophets, ever fell into a prophetic trance, though certainly he feigned madness at one point. The divine speaking in question here, then, is congruent with the overall theology of noncompetitive transcendence presented throughout this commentary. While retaining fully his own faculties of mind, imagination, and speech, David nevertheless becomes a conveyer of God's truth, the divine agency in no way compromising the integrity of David's human agency. At any rate, this clear assertion of David's prophetic quality makes him one of the most striking examples of an Old Testament figure who exercises the triple office of priest, prophet, and king. His kingship is on obvious display throughout the narratives; his priesthood becomes apparent in his ecstatic dance before the ark; and his prophecy emerges in his theologically inspired singing. This makes him, along with Moses, the most thorough anticipation of Jesus, who of course brings all three offices to their fulfillment.[1]

The prophetic message itself now follows: "One who rules over people justly, ruling in the fear of God, is like the light of morning, like the sun rising on a cloudless morning, gleaming from the rain on the grassy land" (2 Sam. 23:3–4). The trope of sun for king is a fairly common one throughout the ancient Near East—Hammurabi comes readily to mind—and the morning dew probably refers to the fruitfulness that comes from the meeting of just leadership and an obedient people. To be sure, the classical philosophical tradition placed great emphasis on the indispensability of upright rule. One needs only to think of Plato's philosopher-king or Aristotle's just monarch who reigns for the sake of the common good. But what is most interesting in this context is how the line functions as a summary of the entire Davidic narrative, which has been a sustained meditation on kingship. From the time of Adam, the human race has required good leadership. Without rightly ordered kingship, the garden devolves into a desert, and human beings become the victims of threatening powers. David's emergence as a righteous king, ruling in accord with divine purposes, was the condition for the possibility of Israel's flourishing as a prosperous empire. And his devolution into unrighteous leadership led by a short road to disaster both political and religious. When law, governance, and power become simply the means for the king's aggrandizement or tools by which he can manipulate the people, the nation falls into deep dysfunction. If Plato's criterion for measuring right rule is the realm of the forms and Aristotle's the intuition of virtue, the Bible's criterion is none other than the lordship of God.

1. John Henry Newman, "The Three Offices of Christ," in *Sermons Bearing on Subjects of the Day* (London: Longmans, Green, 1891), 52.

Next, the singer makes another reference to the Nathan prophecy: "Is not my house like this with God? For he has made with me an everlasting covenant, ordered in all things and secure" (2 Sam. 23:5). The tragedy, of course, is that the well-ordered kingdom began to fall apart in David's own lifetime and definitively splintered during the reign of his son. The only house that fulfills the expectation expressed here is the house of Christ's body, which proves across time that the God of Israel is eternally faithful to his promises. The wicked are then compared to unsavory and dangerous plants that make their way into the garden: "But the godless are like thorns that are thrown away; for they cannot be picked up with the hand; to touch them one uses an iron bar or the shaft of a spear. And they are entirely consumed in fire on the spot" (2 Sam. 23:6–7). How unlike the verdant green, glistening with dew under the warming influence of the sun. And how telling that the wicked, according to this trope, can be dealt with only through the mediation of metal, the connection through the warmth of flesh having been lost. The whole tragedy of Israel's wars (and all those of the human race) is contained in that image (Alter 1999: 348).

The final words of David's last poem are appropriate enough in the measure that they celebrate a warrior king's act of extricating evil from the nation. The killer of the Amalekites and Philistines, the suppressor of the Absalom and Sheba rebellions, is a new Adam figure resisting the wiles of the snake and preventing it from gaining influence in the garden. David at his best did what Saul could not do: put the ban on Israel's enemies, burning *das Nichtige* in the bonfire. At his worst, as we have seen over and over again, he toyed with evil—appropriating it, tolerating it, using it for his own purposes. Once again, it was only Christ, the definitive Son of David, who battled evil all the way down, dealing with the *tōhû wābōhû* thoroughly and finally. One cannot help but think, however, of the deeply ambiguous feelings that the avenging king must have had when his own son was one of these thorns, which had to be "entirely consumed in fire on the spot."

The twenty-third chapter concludes with a listing of many of David's confreres and comrades in arms and a recounting of some of their more spectacular exploits. Since the literary style of this section is somewhat crabbed and since it features very little narrative elaboration, many scholars speculate that it goes back quite far, perhaps even to the time of David (Alter 1999: 348). Among the many heroes, three are singled out for special treatment: Josheb-basshebeth, who killed eight hundred Philistines in one encounter; Eleazar son of Dodo, who stood his ground against a formidable Philistine contingent when his fellow Israelites had withdrawn; and Shammah son of Agee, who similarly withstood a Philistine raid in a field of lentils when the Israelite army had fled. One cannot help but wonder whether there is more than a hint of irony in the redactor's choice of these last two worthies for special mention, since they had been put precisely in the position of Uriah the Hittite. As always in the Samuel literature, the theological emphasis is clear; after the recounting of the mighty deeds of these men, the author adds, "The LORD brought about a great victory that day" (2 Sam. 23:10). Forgetting the transcendent cause is, on the biblical reading, invariably a source of mischief.

What follows is a brief narrative that the church fathers found fascinating. It has to do with a curious incident when David was engaged in the Philistine wars. It appears that David and his men were encamped not far from Bethlehem, which was occupied by the enemy. Perhaps recalling the sweetness of the water from his hometown cistern, David muses aloud, "O that someone would give me water to drink from the well of Bethlehem that is by the gate!" (2 Sam. 23:15). Overhearing this kingly wish, three of David's men (somewhat in the spirit of the courtiers of Henry II) set out at considerable risk to fetch the water. When they bring the coveted prize to their leader, David pours it on the ground as an offering to Yahweh and says, "The LORD forbid that I should do this. Can I drink the blood of the men who went at the risk of their lives?" (2 Sam. 23:17). It is easy enough to understand why this story, which combines risk with moral heroism, is preserved in the Israelite literary tradition. How can one not notice the sharp contrast between this noble David and the king who actively arranged for the murder of an Israelite soldier in order to cover up a terrible sin? The David of the Bethlehem episode gives in, however obliquely and by means of a stated velleity, to the temptation to abuse his power while the king of the Bathsheba incident shamelessly abuses his power through carefully considered machinations over an extended period of time.

Gregory the Great remarks on the same contrast following the chronology implied in the text: "The water he poured out was changed into a sacrifice to the Lord, because he slaughtered his sin of eager desire by the penance of self-censure. The man who had once been unafraid to lust after another man's wife was later terrified at having desired water. Since he remembered he had committed something forbidden, he was strict with himself and refrained even from what was allowed."[2] Gregory's "eager desire" is concupiscence, or errant and self-interested desire. What the sixth-century pope finds so impressive is that David was able

2. Gregory the Great, "Forty Gospel Homilies 34," in *Joshua, Judges, Ruth, 1–2 Samuel*, ed. John R. Franke, Ancient Christian Commentary on Scripture: Old Testament 4 (Downers Grove, IL: InterVarsity, 2005), 394.

to counter evil at an incipient stage of its development by means of self-sacrifice. Ambrose sees in this story the battle between desire and reason: "This incident is evidence that uncontrolled desire indeed comes before reason but that reason resists irrational desire. David suffered what is human—an irrational longing—but it is praiseworthy that he cheated the irrational desire in a rational manner with the remedy that was at hand."[3] The reason in question here seems to be moral reason, the faculty by which one firmly grasps the values that are in play in a given ethical situation and the prudential moves that are called for in order to actuate them. What stands against ethical reasoning is a self-interested passion that moves the actor away from love and justice. The curious incident under consideration shows also that right moral reasoning is tied closely to right worship, since David counteracts his concupiscence precisely through an act of praising God. Once the true center is found, the ethical tends to fall naturally into place. Augustine places this episode in relation to a variety of other biblical stories in which people are tempted from the true good by sensual pleasure: Esau, who repudiates his blessing for a mess of pottage; the Israelites in the desert who grumble against Moses because of their wretched food; and even the Lord Jesus, who feels the temptation to turn stones into bread. Augustine's commonsensical application is, "Having been placed among these temptations, then, I struggle daily against undisciplined desire in eating and drinking."[4]

The last section of the chapter is more or less a list of David's men, including many of the "thirty," doubtless a sort of privileged bodyguard for the king. Some scholars remark that most of the names are of Judahites from the region of Bethlehem, perhaps many of David's boyhood friends and neighbors. The last person mentioned in this lengthy list is, of all people, Uriah the Hittite. It is doubtless the case that the final redactor of the text inherited this list from an earlier written source whose author surely meant no irony by the inclusion of Uriah's name, especially at the very end of the list. The fact that the editor kept Uriah's name there cannot be an accident. Even as the praises of David and his men are sung, the reader is pointedly reminded that at the very height of his power, this wonderful king betrayed and murdered one of his own most loyal defenders. Here were dozens of men willing to sacrifice their lives for David, and David ends up killing one of them—still another indication (as if another were needed) that David, with all of his virtues, was not the definitive king of Israel. Israel would have to await another.

3. Ambrose, "Jacob and the Happy Life 1.1.3," in Franke, *Joshua, Judges, Ruth, 1–2 Samuel*, 395.
4. Augustine, "Confessions 10.31.46-47," in Franke, *Joshua, Judges, Ruth, 1–2 Samuel*, 394.

2 SAMUEL 24

The book of 2 Samuel concludes with a portentous chapter rife with theological complexity that stands to a large degree outside the literary tradition that precedes it. The central problematic is the king's order of a census and the subsequent divine punishment. Things are murky right from the start, for we hear that the "anger of the Lord was kindled against Israel, and he incited David against them, saying, 'Go, count the people of Israel and Judah'" (2 Sam. 24:1). First of all, what is God angry about? We are not told. Second, why would the taking of a census be reasonably construed as something negative, the consequence of divine anger? And third, why would God "incite" David to do something wicked or unjust? The second question can be answered with some assuredness, in the measure that the taking of a census is seen as a supreme act of domination on the part of a tyrannical king. If he counts the people accurately, he can tax them more efficiently and draft them into military service more expeditiously.

In order to respond to the third question, it might be helpful to consult the parallel passage in 1 Chronicles. The Chronicler ascribes the inciting of David not to Yahweh but to the cosmic accuser: "Satan stood up against Israel, and incited David to count the people of Israel" (1 Chr. 21:1). This might read as paralleling the book of Job, in which God gives permission to Satan to do cruel things to Job precisely as a way of testing the servant of God. In his final prayer, as recounted by the Chronicler, David refers to the census and says, "I know, my God, that you search the heart, and take pleasure in uprightness" (1 Chr. 29:17). The term for "search" in this context, *bhn*, is a synonym of *nsh*, the word typically used to name God's "testing" of his covenant people (Hahn 2012: 87). God tests his partners in order to see whether they are truly living up to the demands of the covenant he made with them. The Bible does not see this as cruel or arbitrary but rather as an ingredient in God's providential and parental care for Israel.

So incited—either by God directly or by Satan acting at God's prompting—David orders the census "from Dan to Beer-sheba," which is to say, from top to bottom of Israel. It is hard to miss the imperialistic quality of this administrative move. Indeed, when Luke wants to signal how aggressive and domineering Roman government is, he says that "a decree went out from Emperor Augustus that all the world should be registered" (Luke 2:1). No first-century Jew reading that phrase would have missed the oblique reference to David's censured census. When Joab hears the command of the king, he responds with disbelief ("Why does my lord the king want to do this?") and a subtle theological commentary: "May the Lord your God increase the number of the people a hundredfold, while the eyes of my lord the king can still see it!" (2 Sam. 24:3). This seems to be a reference to God's promise to Abraham that he would increase the patriarch's descendants past counting: "Look toward heaven and count the stars, if you are able to count them. . . . So shall your descendants be" (Gen. 15:5). Thus the real problem is revealed. As always, trust in the Lord is the key to joy and success for Israel. Trouble comes, invariably, when the nation and its rulers try to seize control, fend for themselves, and make their own arrangements and plans. The David furiously and meticulously counting his people is like the David who pulled every string in order to get Bathsheba into his bed and Uriah into his grave. Another reference is important in this context, namely, the story of Gideon (Judg. 6–7). We recall that Gideon was raised up by Yahweh to fight for Israel against the Midianites and the Amalekites. When twenty-two thousand Israelite troops gathered around their leader, the Lord was displeased, for people would say that the mighty Israelite army had carried the day. Therefore he dispersed much of the host and then compelled Gideon to whittle his "army" down to three hundred men. With that tiny band, Israel won the battle. As always, the covenant people are asked to trust and not to count. Doesn't all of this point back, finally, to the beginning of the book of Genesis and the story of the fall? Adam and Eve reach for the fruit of the tree of the knowledge of good and evil, seeking thereby control over God and the things of God. Having established himself as the new Adam in the garden of a rightly ordered Israel, David is in danger here of following his distant forebear into willfull rebellion.

David easily enough overcomes the resistance of Joab and orders his commander to carry out the census. And so Joab and his officers set out on a remarkably thorough journey through the land of Israel. Their first stop, Aroer, is fifteen miles east of the Dead Sea. They then move north through the Transjordan to Gilead and Kadesh, and from there they proceed west through the northern reaches of the promised land, reaching Dan, the fabled northernmost point. From Dan they journey to Sidon and Tyre by the sea and finally make their way to the Negeb and Beer-sheba in the extreme south. In a word, they make an ellipse around the whole of Israel. At the conclusion of this exercise, they return to Jerusalem. We are told that the proceedings took nine months and twenty days. Can it be an accident that this census-taking, which results in so much death for Israel, lasted precisely as long as a typical pregnancy (Alter 1999: 354)? Joab dutifully reports the results of his work to the king: "In Israel there were eight hundred thousand soldiers able to draw the sword, and those of Judah were five hundred thousand" (2 Sam. 24:9). There is in the disproportion of those numbers a foreshadowing of the successful rebellion of north against south that would happen within a generation of this counting. But in particular, one can see the astonishing numbers of fighting men that the nine-month work revealed. According to his promise, God has indeed been generous to Israel. The problem was that David could not relax and allow God to take care of his chosen people. He had to survey the whole country just as he had surveyed the whole of his capital city from the rooftop of his palace.

Though he should have been deeply reassured by his great military strength, we are told that David is troubled in heart. The relevant Hebrew term here is *nakah*, which carries the connotation of attack or assault; the New Revised Standard Version gives "stricken to the heart." Though he sinned often, David was a man quick to repent. Though he could be wicked, he had a tender conscience, for indeed he was someone after the heart of the Lord. To his enormous credit, he now turns to the Lord in contrition: "I have sinned greatly in what I have done. But now, O Lord, I pray you, take away the guilt of your servant; for I have done very foolishly" (2 Sam. 24:10). David has thereby placed himself in the right spiritual attitude, and therefore whatever follows, no matter how immediately or superficially painful it is, will be for the good. Ambrose comments: "Thus by his humility he became more acceptable to God, for it is not strange that people sin, but it is reprehensible if they do not acknowledge that they have erred and humble themselves before God."[1]

The next day the word of the Lord comes to David through Gad, who is identified as the king's "seer." Gad in fact is mentioned in passing earlier in the Samuel

1. Ambrose, "Letter 3," in *Joshua, Judges, Ruth, 1–2 Samuel*, ed. John R. Franke, Ancient Christian Commentary on Scripture: Old Testament 4 (Downers Grove, IL: InterVarsity, 2005), 397.

literature as someone who advised David during the struggle with Saul (1 Sam. 22:5). The seer says that Yahweh will punish David but that he will allow the king himself to choose among three possible punishments: three years of famine upon the whole land; being pursued by his enemies for three months; or three days of pestilence. The decreasing amount of time in each case is directly proportionate to the intensity of the punishment; therefore it is impossible to determine, prima facie, which punishment is preferable. David does not actively choose any of the three; he only eliminates the second, explaining that he would rather suffer at the hand of a merciful God than at the hands of treacherous human beings. I would be remiss not to point out that this is the only time in the scriptures that a human person is given the opportunity to choose the sort of punishment he will receive. Normally, this is left to the sovereign decision of God himself. One can only conclude that this privilege was given uniquely to David as yet another sign of God's favor to the man after his own heart. There is an acute psychological perceptiveness behind the king's reasoning. Human beings are all too willing to be the agents of punishment for the sins of others, for they are always operating out of need and self-interest. This helps to explain why acts of vengeance and retribution are so particularly cruel. David intuits that God punishes not out of self-interest but simply out of a desire to benefit those he disciplines.

So Yahweh chooses to punish Israel by means of the three-day pestilence, and seventy thousand people died throughout the country, "from Dan to Beer-sheba," the entire area that Joab's men had canvassed. The laconic description of the pestilence barely gestures toward the reality of the situation. The deaths of so many in such a short period of time indicates a disease more virulently contagious than the black death at the height of its fury. The recent census delivered the number of 130,000 fighting men, and the deaths from the contagion amount to just past half that number. In his darkly ironic way, the author carefully counts the number of the dead to mock the arrogant counting that David made with the help of Joab. Though it lasted but a short time, its impact on the entire nation must have been horrific. Once more, the keen sense of karma that is present in so many of the biblical authors can be seen: sin has consequences, and the more serious the sin, the more brutal the effects. In addition, one can see that the God of Israel is a punishing God who actively disciplines his people. Earlier in this commentary, I explored some of the standard theological accounts of God's involvement with evil, but this story is found lacking. No matter how satisfying the theological framework for explanation might be, it seems difficult indeed to justify the deaths of tens of thousands at the hand of God for a sin that they did not commit. We who stand on the far side of the Holocaust feel the pressure of this problem with particular sensitivity.

Some of the greatest spirits of the tradition have certainly wrestled with the dilemma. Jerome comments on the episode under consideration by placing it within a much wider biblical context:

> Deign to remain ignorant of why God has brought certain events to pass, such as why thousands died for David's sin: allow God to exercise his rightful power over creation. . . . Bring a yet graver charge against God and ask him why, when Esau and Jacob were still in the womb, he said, "Jacob I have loved, but Esau I have hated." Accuse him of injustice because, when Achan the son of Carmi stole part of the spoil of Jericho, he butchered so many thousands for the fault of one. Ask him why for the sin of the sons of Eli the people were well-nigh annihilated. . . . Why should Christ's coming have been delayed to the last times? Why should he not have come before so vast a number had perished?[2]

In this passage, the problem is not exclusively "numbers" (how could God have permitted the deaths of so many?) but rather stark unfairness. How could God simply say, "I love Jacob and hate Esau"? As discussed earlier, the only "answer" to this difficulty is the one given to Job, namely, that all of God's moves, including his punishments, have to be seen against a cosmic horizon. God's ultimate purpose has to be good (otherwise he becomes capricious), but the working out of that purpose remains stubbornly opaque. It is helpful to keep in mind Flannery O'Connor's beautifully bland remark to the effect that one shouldn't assume physical death is the worst of fates. What God effects or permits in this world—including the deaths of tens of thousands—is part of a design, the contours of which cannot be seen, even in principle. To say otherwise is to say that God should not be God.

The climax of the census-pestilence narrative occurs when "the angel stretched out his hand toward Jerusalem to destroy it" (2 Sam. 24:16). There is an unmistakable reference here to the destructive angel at Passover, but now the celestial agent of the Lord is threatening to wipe out not the oppressors of the Jews but thousands of Israelites gathered in the capital of the newly constituted nation. It appears as though God, in his fury at David, is about to act in a self-defeating way. To be sure, the editor of this text, writing in the postexilic period, was an Israelite wrestling mightily with this very issue, since he knew that Yahweh had in fact used the instrument of the Babylonian invaders to wipe out David's city

2. Jerome, "Letter 133.9," in Franke, *Joshua, Judges, Ruth, 1–2 Samuel*, 398.

and Solomon's temple. When Yahweh sees the destroyer threatening Jerusalem, he "relented concerning the evil, and said to the angel who was bringing destruction among the people, 'It is enough; now stay your hand'" (2 Sam. 24:16). This must not be read as God's repentance or the changing of the divine mind. As indicated earlier, the Creator of all things, the unconditioned ground of existence, cannot pass in and out of emotional states or rearrange his plans in light of conditioned events. As Thomas Aquinas explains, this sort of language, typical of scripture, signals more one's impression of or reaction to what God has eternally deigned to do. Certainly from the human perspective, the sudden end to the pestilence must have seemed the result of an abrupt shift in God's attitude, but this would be a superficial extrapolation from one's ordinary experience.

When David sees the angel closing in on his beloved Jerusalem, he gives voice to one of the most affecting and beautiful of his prayers: "I alone have sinned, and I alone have done wickedly; but these sheep, what have they done? Let your hand, I pray, be against me and against my father's house" (2 Sam. 24:17). On the one hand, the entire episode is predicated on the premodern sensibility of deep solidarity between leader and people that I spoke of earlier. Since the people of Israel are bone of David's bone and flesh of his flesh, their suffering for his sin is not altogether incomprehensible. On the other hand, David rather clearly acknowledges the limits of that conceptuality, for he knows that mutual implication ought not involve collective guilt tout court. The last part of David's prayer is of enormous significance, for it anticipates both the sacrificial attitude that will be sung in Isaiah's passages concerning the suffering servant and the sacrificial death of the Son of David himself: the king asks that the hand of the Lord be upon him; the suffering servant bears the sins of the multitude; and Jesus will take upon himself the suffering of the people, enduring their punishment for them. This sacrificial mutuality is the biblical foundation for what Charles Williams calls "the coinherence of the mystical body of Christ."[3] Though it runs counter to individualistic assumptions, pain and guilt can through love be transferred from one person to another.

The text specifies that David sees the angel "by the threshing floor of Araunah the Jebusite" (2 Sam. 24:16). As we recall, David had conquered the city (Jebus) some years before, and so the presence of a Jebusite within the walls of Jerusalem proves that David most likely did not instigate a wholesale massacre of the native population, as was fairly customary at the time. Araunah is not a semitic name, and

3. Charles Williams, *The Descent of the Dove: A Short History of the Holy Spirit in the Church* (New York: Pellegrini & Cudahy, 1939), 10.

most scholars seem to think it is Hittite or Hurrian in origin. The presence of this man in Jerusalem and his prominence in this episode indicate once again the "international" theme in the Samuel literature, that is to say, the nation-transcending significance of David's kingship. A threshing floor is mentioned thirty-six times in the scriptures, perhaps most famously in the Gospels of Matthew and Luke in connection with a saying of John the Baptist. Describing the mission of the coming Messiah, John says, "His winnowing fork is in his hand, and he will clear his threshing floor and will gather his wheat into the granary" (Matt. 3:12). The threshing floor was a flattened surface on which stalks of harvested grain were arranged and crushed in order to separate the edible portion of the plant from the husky chaff. To complete the process, one took a winnowing fan or shovel and tossed the mixture of wheat and chaff into the air so that the lighter elements were blown away. Accordingly, as in the statement of the Baptist, threshing floors were used symbolically to designate the act of divine judgment—the separation of good from bad, just from unjust. This usage, for example, can be found in Daniel's interpretation of Belteshazzar's dream: "Then the iron, the clay, the bronze, the silver, and the gold were all broken in pieces and became like the chaff of the summer threshing floors; and the wind carried them away" (Dan. 2:35). It can also be found in Jeremiah's prophecy of judgment against Babylon: "Daughter Babylon is like a threshing floor at the time when it is trodden; yet a little while and the time of her harvest will come" (Jer. 51:33). Earlier in our story, Uzzah is struck down for touching the ark, and we are told that the offense took place "on the threshing floor of Nacon" (2 Sam. 6:6). What emerges therefore on the threshing floor of Araunah is a place of judgment, separation, and decision—a place where evil is separated from the good and blown away in the wind. This is exactly what happened through the millions of animal sacrifices that were made on that site for the next thousand years. As the animals were killed and burnt up, the sacrificer imagined his sins being purged and carried off in the wind; that threshing floor became the place of separation and cleansing par excellence.

Gad the seer tells David, "Go up and erect an altar to the Lord on the threshing floor of Araunah the Jebusite" (2 Sam. 24:18). So the king himself approaches the Jebusite, who protests, even as he prostrates himself, "Why has my lord the king come to his servant?" (2 Sam. 24:21). The custom of the time was that the king never lowered himself to come to one of his subjects. Rather, if he wanted to see one of his inferiors, the king sent for him. What Araunah reacts to, accordingly, is an extraordinary act of humility on the part of the king. It is as though David intuitively grasps that what he is arranging for here—namely, the building of the great temple—requires him to set aside any pretentions to self-importance. He frankly tells Araunah that he would like to buy his threshing floor in order to build an altar to the Lord. How different this is from Jezebel's violent acquisition of Naboth's vineyard, recounted in the first book of Kings (1 Kgs. 21), and indeed from David's own aggressive taking of Uriah's wife earlier in our narrative. The temple will be the place where kings and the most ordinary Israelites will present themselves equally before the Lord.

David then specifies that the altar he wants to erect is for the purpose of preventing the contagion from coming upon Jerusalem. A sacrifice of atonement and reparation would be offered on the site; divinity and humanity, which had fallen out of joint, would be reconciled there. This makes the threshing floor of Araunah akin to so many other sacred spots in the history of Israel: the garden of Eden; the rock where Jacob slept and dreamt of the angels ascending and descending; Mount Sinai, where the law was given; the tabernacle in the desert; Shiloh, where Eli and Samuel ministered; Mount Moriah, where the binding of Isaac happened; and so on. All were places of alignment between God and his people and hence, as I explained earlier, places of adoration. The connections between the Jebusite threshing floor and Mount Moriah are especially emphasized in the Chronicler's telling of this story. In his version, the angel of destruction stands between heaven and earth, his sword unsheathed and raised threateningly above Jerusalem, just as Abraham's knife is raised menacingly over Isaac. By divine order, both the killer angel and the sacrificing patriarch are stopped. Further, both stories end with a reference to the temple, one explicit and the other implicit. On the Chronicler's reading, David recognizes the threshing floor as the site of the house of God, and the Genesis account of the Akeda concludes with the observation, "So Abraham called that place 'The Lord will provide,' as it is said to this day, 'On the mount of the Lord it shall be provided'" (Gen. 22:14). This densely textured association is made absolutely explicit in 2 Chronicles, where we hear that "Solomon began to build the house of the Lord in Jerusalem on Mount Moriah, where the Lord had appeared to his father David, at the place that David had designated, on the threshing floor of Ornan the Jebusite" (2 Chr. 3:1). Therefore it can be safely asserted that for the Chronicler, and implicitly for the author of the Samuel literature, the setting up of the Jerusalem temple was the fulfillment of the promise made to Abraham, namely, that God would bless all nations through Isaac and his seed forever. David is, as we have often seen, a new Adam figure, but he is also a new Abraham, a priestly and kingly father of many nations (Hahn 2012: 5–6).

Still another Abrahamic overtone is the very manner in which David makes the financial arrangements for the sale of the site. Araunah, perhaps overwhelmed by the directness of the king's address, offers the land as well as the oxen and threshing sledges for the burnt offering as a free gift. But David protests, "No, but I will buy them from you for a price; I will not offer burnt offerings to the Lord my God that cost me nothing" (2 Sam. 24:24). This echoes very precisely the Genesis account of Abraham's purchase of a burial ground for his wife, Sarah (Alter 1999: 358). The grieving patriarch, we are told, approaches some Hittites at Hebron and offers to pay for a grave. Impressed by Abraham's dignity and stature, the Hittites make a gracious counterproposal: "Hear us, my lord; you are a mighty prince among us. Bury your dead in the choicest of our burial places; none of us will withhold from you any burial ground for burying your dead" (Gen. 23:6). But Abraham refuses the kind offer, determined to own the grave outright: "For the full price let him give it to me in your presence as a possession for a burying place" (Gen. 23:9). Accordingly, the burial ground at Hebron, which would eventually receive the bodies of Abraham, Isaac, Jacob, and their wives, became the only section of the promised land that was gained through purchase and not through military conquest (Hahn 2012: 94). Furthermore, it was acquired with the peaceful, even gracious cooperation of non-Israelites. Both the burial caves at Hebron and the threshing floor of Araunah symbolize, therefore, the great truth that through the Jews salvation will come to all the nations. Nowhere would this be clearer than in regard to the temple that David's son would build on the site of the threshing floor of Araunah:

> And the foreigners who joined themselves to the Lord, to minister to him, to love the name of the Lord, and to be his servants, all who keep the sabbath, and do not profane it, and hold fast my covenant—these will I bring to my holy mountain, and make them joyful in my house of prayer; their burnt offerings and their sacrifices will be accepted on my altar; for my house shall be called a house of prayer for all peoples. (Isa. 56:6–7)

A thousand years after the purchase of the threshing floor of the Jebusite, the one called the Son of David entered the temple, saw the money changers doing their unsavory work, and pronounced a prophetic curse on the place, referencing the Isaiah quote just mentioned: "It is written, 'My house shall be called a house of prayer'; but you are making it a den of robbers" (Matt. 21:13). In John's version of this episode, Jesus specifies that he will tear down the corrupt temple and rebuild it in three days, referring to the temple of his body. As we have seen, the very person of Jesus is the place where divinity and humanity meet and hence where right praise is offered. And to that place everyone—Jew and Gentile—is invited. That is why a sign written in Hebrew, Latin, and Greek was fixed to the cross of Jesus and why upon the death of Jesus the curtain in the temple was torn in two from top to bottom, giving everyone access to the Holy of Holies. The reconciliation of Jew and Gentile, prefigured in both Abraham and David, comes to fulfillment in the One about whom Paul says, "There is no longer Jew or Greek, there is no longer slave or free, there is no longer male and female; for all of you are one in Christ Jesus" (Gal. 3:28).

The whole of the Samuel literature, which commenced with the story of an Israelite woman begging for a child in the temple at Shiloh, ends with the buying of the land on which the great temple of Jerusalem would be constructed, a place from which would go forth the begging prayers of Israel for a millennium. What began with the story of a confused, leaderless, and demoralized Israel concludes with the narrative of David—priest, prophet, and king—ready to make sacrifice to save the capital city of a united Israel. That the great story does not definitively conclude with this Davidic achievement is clear to anyone who has eyes to see. Just after the building of the temple, Israel would fall into civil war, and the tribes that David had united would splinter into warring factions. The temple itself would become a place marked by corruption, both religious and political. The chaos that threatened the nation at the time of Eli and Samuel would seem like nothing compared to the chaos that would come upon Israel at the time of the Babylonian captivity. And so the people of God continued to dream and hope that a definitive David would arrive, that the temple would finally be cleansed and purified, that the enemies of the nation would be defeated, and that a king, a Son of David, would come to reign as Lord of the nations.

BIBLIOGRAPHY

Alter, Robert. *The David Story: A Translation with Commentary of 1 and 2 Samuel.* New York: W. W. Norton, 1999.

Baldwin, Joyce G. *1 and 2 Samuel: An Introduction and Commentary.* Tyndale Old Testament Commentaries. Nottingham: Inter-Varsity, 1988.

Beale, G. K. *A New Testament Biblical Theology: The Unfolding of the Old Testament in the New.* Grand Rapids: Baker Academic, 2011.

Hahn, Scott W. *The Kingdom of God as Liturgical Empire: A Theological Commentary on 1–2 Chronicles.* Grand Rapids: Baker Academic, 2012.

Hertzberg, Hans Wilhelm. *I & II Samuel: A Commentary.* Translated by J. S. Bowden. Old Testament Library. Philadelphia: Westminster, 1964.

McCarter, P. Kyle, Jr. *II Samuel: A New Translation, with Introduction, Commentary, and Notes.* Anchor Bible 9. Garden City, NY: Doubleday, 1984.

Murphy, Francesca Aran. *1 Samuel.* Grand Rapids: Brazos, 2010.

Polzin, Robert. *David and the Deuteronomist: 2 Samuel.* Indiana Studies in Biblical Literature. Bloomington: Indiana University Press, 1993.

SUBJECT INDEX

SCRIPTURE INDEX